Mometrix
TEST PREPARATION

NES®
Gifted Education Secrets Study Guide

DEAR FUTURE EXAM SUCCESS STORY

First of all, **THANK YOU** for purchasing Mometrix study materials!

Second, congratulations! You are one of the few determined test-takers who are committed to doing whatever it takes to excel on your exam. **You have come to the right place.** We developed these study materials with one goal in mind: to deliver you the information you need in a format that's concise and easy to use.

In addition to optimizing your guide for the content of the test, we've outlined our recommended steps for breaking down the preparation process into small, attainable goals so you can make sure you stay on track.

We've also analyzed the entire test-taking process, identifying the most common pitfalls and showing how you can overcome them and be ready for any curveball the test throws you.

Standardized testing is one of the biggest obstacles on your road to success, which only increases the importance of doing well in the high-pressure, high-stakes environment of test day. Your results on this test could have a significant impact on your future, and this guide provides the information and practical advice to help you achieve your full potential on test day.

Your success is our success

We would love to hear from you! If you would like to share the story of your exam success or if you have any questions or comments in regard to our products, please contact us at **800-673-8175** or **support@mometrix.com**.

Thanks again for your business and we wish you continued success!

Sincerely,
The Mometrix Test Preparation Team

Need more help? Check out our flashcards at:
http://mometrixflashcards.com/NESINC

TABLE OF CONTENTS

INTRODUCTION 1

SECRET KEY #1 – PLAN BIG, STUDY SMALL 2

SECRET KEY #2 – MAKE YOUR STUDYING COUNT 3

SECRET KEY #3 – PRACTICE THE RIGHT WAY 4

SECRET KEY #4 – PACE YOURSELF 6

SECRET KEY #5 – HAVE A PLAN FOR GUESSING 7

TEST-TAKING STRATEGIES 10

LEARNER DEVELOPMENT AND THE LEARNING ENVIRONMENT 15

- CHARACTERISTICS OF GIFTED STUDENTS 15
- APPROACHES TO DEVELOPMENT OF GIFTED STUDENTS 20
- CHALLENGES FACED BY GIFTED STUDENTS 25
- LEARNING ENVIRONMENTS 31
- DEFINING GIFTEDNESS 34
- CHAPTER QUIZ 37

ASSESSMENT, CURRICULUM, AND INSTRUCTION 38

- RESEARCH AND STATISTICS IN GIFTED EDUCATION 38
- MEASURING INTELLIGENCE 42
- MEASURING CREATIVITY 45
- MODELS OF INSTRUCTION 47
- CURRICULUM DEVELOPMENT 49
- DIFFERENTIATED INSTRUCTION 52
- INDIVIDUALIZED EDUCATION PROGRAMS 59
- ASSESSMENT METHODOLOGY 65
- CHAPTER QUIZ 78

PROFESSIONAL AND ETHICAL PRACTICE AND COLLABORATION 79

- CHOOSING A PROGRAM 79
- PROFESSIONALISM 82
- EQUITY IN EDUCATION 84
- LEGAL AND ETHICAL OBLIGATIONS SURROUNDING STUDENT RIGHTS 85
- TEACHER'S ROLE AS AN ADVOCATE 88
- PROFESSIONAL DEVELOPMENT 89
- PARTICIPATING IN THE LOCAL EDUCATIONAL COMMUNITY 93
- FAMILY INVOLVEMENT AND COLLABORATION 94
- CHAPTER QUIZ 101

NES PRACTICE TEST 102

ANSWER KEY AND EXPLANATIONS 140

HOW TO OVERCOME TEST ANXIETY 156

ONLINE RESOURCES 162

Introduction

Thank you for purchasing this resource! You have made the choice to prepare yourself for a test that could have a huge impact on your future, and this guide is designed to help you be fully ready for test day. Obviously, it's important to have a solid understanding of the test material, but you also need to be prepared for the unique environment and stressors of the test, so that you can perform to the best of your abilities.

For this purpose, the first section that appears in this guide is the **Secret Keys**. We've devoted countless hours to meticulously researching what works and what doesn't, and we've boiled down our findings to the five most impactful steps you can take to improve your performance on the test. We start at the beginning with study planning and move through the preparation process, all the way to the testing strategies that will help you get the most out of what you know when you're finally sitting in front of the test.

We recommend that you start preparing for your test as far in advance as possible. However, if you've bought this guide as a last-minute study resource and only have a few days before your test, we recommend that you skip over the first two Secret Keys since they address a long-term study plan.

If you struggle with **test anxiety**, we strongly encourage you to check out our recommendations for how you can overcome it. Test anxiety is a formidable foe, but it can be beaten, and we want to make sure you have the tools you need to defeat it.

Secret Key #1 – Plan Big, Study Small

There's a lot riding on your performance. If you want to ace this test, you're going to need to keep your skills sharp and the material fresh in your mind. You need a plan that lets you review everything you need to know while still fitting in your schedule. We'll break this strategy down into three categories.

Information Organization

Start with the information you already have: the official test outline. From this, you can make a complete list of all the concepts you need to cover before the test. Organize these concepts into groups that can be studied together, and create a list of any related vocabulary you need to learn so you can brush up on any difficult terms. You'll want to keep this vocabulary list handy once you actually start studying since you may need to add to it along the way.

Time Management

Once you have your set of study concepts, decide how to spread them out over the time you have left before the test. Break your study plan into small, clear goals so you have a manageable task for each day and know exactly what you're doing. Then just focus on one small step at a time. When you manage your time this way, you don't need to spend hours at a time studying. Studying a small block of content for a short period each day helps you retain information better and avoid stressing over how much you have left to do. You can relax knowing that you have a plan to cover everything in time. In order for this strategy to be effective though, you have to start studying early and stick to your schedule. Avoid the exhaustion and futility that comes from last-minute cramming!

Study Environment

The environment you study in has a big impact on your learning. Studying in a coffee shop, while probably more enjoyable, is not likely to be as fruitful as studying in a quiet room. It's important to keep distractions to a minimum. You're only planning to study for a short block of time, so make the most of it. Don't pause to check your phone or get up to find a snack. It's also important to **avoid multitasking**. Research has consistently shown that multitasking will make your studying dramatically less effective. Your study area should also be comfortable and well-lit so you don't have the distraction of straining your eyes or sitting on an uncomfortable chair.

The time of day you study is also important. You want to be rested and alert. Don't wait until just before bedtime. Study when you'll be most likely to comprehend and remember. Even better, if you know what time of day your test will be, set that time aside for study. That way your brain will be used to working on that subject at that specific time and you'll have a better chance of recalling information.

Finally, it can be helpful to team up with others who are studying for the same test. Your actual studying should be done in as isolated an environment as possible, but the work of organizing the information and setting up the study plan can be divided up. In between study sessions, you can discuss with your teammates the concepts that you're all studying and quiz each other on the details. Just be sure that your teammates are as serious about the test as you are. If you find that your study time is being replaced with social time, you might need to find a new team.

Secret Key #2 – Make Your Studying Count

You're devoting a lot of time and effort to preparing for this test, so you want to be absolutely certain it will pay off. This means doing more than just reading the content and hoping you can remember it on test day. It's important to make every minute of study count. There are two main areas you can focus on to make your studying count.

Retention

It doesn't matter how much time you study if you can't remember the material. You need to make sure you are retaining the concepts. To check your retention of the information you're learning, try recalling it at later times with minimal prompting. Try carrying around flashcards and glance at one or two from time to time or ask a friend who's also studying for the test to quiz you.

To enhance your retention, look for ways to put the information into practice so that you can apply it rather than simply recalling it. If you're using the information in practical ways, it will be much easier to remember. Similarly, it helps to solidify a concept in your mind if you're not only reading it to yourself but also explaining it to someone else. Ask a friend to let you teach them about a concept you're a little shaky on (or speak aloud to an imaginary audience if necessary). As you try to summarize, define, give examples, and answer your friend's questions, you'll understand the concepts better and they will stay with you longer. Finally, step back for a big picture view and ask yourself how each piece of information fits with the whole subject. When you link the different concepts together and see them working together as a whole, it's easier to remember the individual components.

Finally, practice showing your work on any multi-step problems, even if you're just studying. Writing out each step you take to solve a problem will help solidify the process in your mind, and you'll be more likely to remember it during the test.

Modality

Modality simply refers to the means or method by which you study. Choosing a study modality that fits your own individual learning style is crucial. No two people learn best in exactly the same way, so it's important to know your strengths and use them to your advantage.

For example, if you learn best by visualization, focus on visualizing a concept in your mind and draw an image or a diagram. Try color-coding your notes, illustrating them, or creating symbols that will trigger your mind to recall a learned concept. If you learn best by hearing or discussing information, find a study partner who learns the same way or read aloud to yourself. Think about how to put the information in your own words. Imagine that you are giving a lecture on the topic and record yourself so you can listen to it later.

For any learning style, flashcards can be helpful. Organize the information so you can take advantage of spare moments to review. Underline key words or phrases. Use different colors for different categories. Mnemonic devices (such as creating a short list in which every item starts with the same letter) can also help with retention. Find what works best for you and use it to store the information in your mind most effectively and easily.

Secret Key #3 – Practice the Right Way

Your success on test day depends not only on how many hours you put into preparing, but also on whether you prepared the right way. It's good to check along the way to see if your studying is paying off. One of the most effective ways to do this is by taking practice tests to evaluate your progress. Practice tests are useful because they show exactly where you need to improve. Every time you take a practice test, pay special attention to these three groups of questions:

- The questions you got wrong
- The questions you had to guess on, even if you guessed right
- The questions you found difficult or slow to work through

This will show you exactly what your weak areas are, and where you need to devote more study time. Ask yourself why each of these questions gave you trouble. Was it because you didn't understand the material? Was it because you didn't remember the vocabulary? Do you need more repetitions on this type of question to build speed and confidence? Dig into those questions and figure out how you can strengthen your weak areas as you go back to review the material.

Additionally, many practice tests have a section explaining the answer choices. It can be tempting to read the explanation and think that you now have a good understanding of the concept. However, an explanation likely only covers part of the question's broader context. Even if the explanation makes perfect sense, **go back and investigate** every concept related to the question until you're positive you have a thorough understanding.

As you go along, keep in mind that the practice test is just that: practice. Memorizing these questions and answers will not be very helpful on the actual test because it is unlikely to have any of the same exact questions. If you only know the right answers to the sample questions, you won't be prepared for the real thing. **Study the concepts** until you understand them fully, and then you'll be able to answer any question that shows up on the test.

It's important to wait on the practice tests until you're ready. If you take a test on your first day of study, you may be overwhelmed by the amount of material covered and how much you need to learn. Work up to it gradually.

On test day, you'll need to be prepared for answering questions, managing your time, and using the test-taking strategies you've learned. It's a lot to balance, like a mental marathon that will have a big impact on your future. Like training for a marathon, you'll need to start slowly and work your way up. When test day arrives, you'll be ready.

Start with the strategies you've read in the first two Secret Keys—plan your course and study in the way that works best for you. If you have time, consider using multiple study resources to get different approaches to the same concepts. It can be helpful to see difficult concepts from more than one angle. Then find a good source for practice tests. Many times, the test website will suggest potential study resources or provide sample tests.

Practice Test Strategy

If you're able to find at least three practice tests, we recommend this strategy:

Untimed and Open-Book Practice

Take the first test with no time constraints and with your notes and study guide handy. Take your time and focus on applying the strategies you've learned.

Timed and Open-Book Practice

Take the second practice test open-book as well, but set a timer and practice pacing yourself to finish in time.

Timed and Closed-Book Practice

Take any other practice tests as if it were test day. Set a timer and put away your study materials. Sit at a table or desk in a quiet room, imagine yourself at the testing center, and answer questions as quickly and accurately as possible.

Keep repeating timed and closed-book tests on a regular basis until you run out of practice tests or it's time for the actual test. Your mind will be ready for the schedule and stress of test day, and you'll be able to focus on recalling the material you've learned.

Secret Key #4 – Pace Yourself

Once you're fully prepared for the material on the test, your biggest challenge on test day will be managing your time. Just knowing that the clock is ticking can make you panic even if you have plenty of time left. Work on pacing yourself so you can build confidence against the time constraints of the exam. Pacing is a difficult skill to master, especially in a high-pressure environment, so **practice is vital**.

Set time expectations for your pace based on how much time is available. For example, if a section has 60 questions and the time limit is 30 minutes, you know you have to average 30 seconds or less per question in order to answer them all. Although 30 seconds is the hard limit, set 25 seconds per question as your goal, so you reserve extra time to spend on harder questions. When you budget extra time for the harder questions, you no longer have any reason to stress when those questions take longer to answer.

Don't let this time expectation distract you from working through the test at a calm, steady pace, but keep it in mind so you don't spend too much time on any one question. Recognize that taking extra time on one question you don't understand may keep you from answering two that you do understand later in the test. If your time limit for a question is up and you're still not sure of the answer, mark it and move on, and come back to it later if the time and the test format allow. If the testing format doesn't allow you to return to earlier questions, just make an educated guess; then put it out of your mind and move on.

On the easier questions, be careful not to rush. It may seem wise to hurry through them so you have more time for the challenging ones, but it's not worth missing one if you know the concept and just didn't take the time to read the question fully. Work efficiently but make sure you understand the question and have looked at all of the answer choices, since more than one may seem right at first.

Even if you're paying attention to the time, you may find yourself a little behind at some point. You should speed up to get back on track, but do so wisely. Don't panic; just take a few seconds less on each question until you're caught up. Don't guess without thinking, but do look through the answer choices and eliminate any you know are wrong. If you can get down to two choices, it is often worthwhile to guess from those. Once you've chosen an answer, move on and don't dwell on any that you skipped or had to hurry through. If a question was taking too long, chances are it was one of the harder ones, so you weren't as likely to get it right anyway.

On the other hand, if you find yourself getting ahead of schedule, it may be beneficial to slow down a little. The more quickly you work, the more likely you are to make a careless mistake that will affect your score. You've budgeted time for each question, so don't be afraid to spend that time. Practice an efficient but careful pace to get the most out of the time you have.

Secret Key #5 – Have a Plan for Guessing

When you're taking the test, you may find yourself stuck on a question. Some of the answer choices seem better than others, but you don't see the one answer choice that is obviously correct. What do you do?

The scenario described above is very common, yet most test takers have not effectively prepared for it. Developing and practicing a plan for guessing may be one of the single most effective uses of your time as you get ready for the exam.

In developing your plan for guessing, there are three questions to address:

- When should you start the guessing process?
- How should you narrow down the choices?
- Which answer should you choose?

When to Start the Guessing Process

Unless your plan for guessing is to select C every time (which, despite its merits, is not what we recommend), you need to leave yourself enough time to apply your answer elimination strategies. Since you have a limited amount of time for each question, that means that if you're going to give yourself the best shot at guessing correctly, you have to decide quickly whether or not you will guess.

Of course, the best-case scenario is that you don't have to guess at all, so first, see if you can answer the question based on your knowledge of the subject and basic reasoning skills. Focus on the key words in the question and try to jog your memory of related topics. Give yourself a chance to bring the knowledge to mind, but once you realize that you don't have (or you can't access) the knowledge you need to answer the question, it's time to start the guessing process.

It's almost always better to start the guessing process too early than too late. It only takes a few seconds to remember something and answer the question from knowledge. Carefully eliminating wrong answer choices takes longer. Plus, going through the process of eliminating answer choices can actually help jog your memory.

Summary: Start the guessing process as soon as you decide that you can't answer the question based on your knowledge.

How to Narrow Down the Choices

The next chapter in this book (**Test-Taking Strategies**) includes a wide range of strategies for how to approach questions and how to look for answer choices to eliminate. You will definitely want to read those carefully, practice them, and figure out which ones work best for you. Here though, we're going to address a mindset rather than a particular strategy.

Your odds of guessing an answer correctly depend on how many options you are choosing from.

Number of options left	5	4	3	2	1
Odds of guessing correctly	20%	25%	33%	50%	100%

You can see from this chart just how valuable it is to be able to eliminate incorrect answers and make an educated guess, but there are two things that many test takers do that cause them to miss out on the benefits of guessing:

- Accidentally eliminating the correct answer
- Selecting an answer based on an impression

We'll look at the first one here, and the second one in the next section.

To avoid accidentally eliminating the correct answer, we recommend a thought exercise called **the $5 challenge**. In this challenge, you only eliminate an answer choice from contention if you are willing to bet $5 on it being wrong. Why $5? Five dollars is a small but not insignificant amount of money. It's an amount you could afford to lose but wouldn't want to throw away. And while losing $5 once might not hurt too much, doing it twenty times will set you back $100. In the same way, each small decision you make—eliminating a choice here, guessing on a question there—won't by itself impact your score very much, but when you put them all together, they can make a big difference. By holding each answer choice elimination decision to a higher standard, you can reduce the risk of accidentally eliminating the correct answer.

The $5 challenge can also be applied in a positive sense: If you are willing to bet $5 that an answer choice *is* correct, go ahead and mark it as correct.

Summary: Only eliminate an answer choice if you are willing to bet $5 that it is wrong.

Which Answer to Choose

You're taking the test. You've run into a hard question and decided you'll have to guess. You've eliminated all the answer choices you're willing to bet $5 on. Now you have to pick an answer. Why do we even need to talk about this? Why can't you just pick whichever one you feel like when the time comes?

The answer to these questions is that if you don't come into the test with a plan, you'll rely on your impression to select an answer choice, and if you do that, you risk falling into a trap. The test writers know that everyone who takes their test will be guessing on some of the questions, so they intentionally write wrong answer choices to seem plausible. You still have to pick an answer though, and if the wrong answer choices are designed to look right, how can you ever be sure that you're not falling for their trap? The best solution we've found to this dilemma is to take the decision out of your hands entirely. Here is the process we recommend:

Once you've eliminated any choices that you are confident (willing to bet $5) are wrong, select the first remaining choice as your answer.

Whether you choose to select the first remaining choice, the second, or the last, the important thing is that you use some preselected standard. Using this approach guarantees that you will not be enticed into selecting an answer choice that looks right, because you are not basing your decision on how the answer choices look.

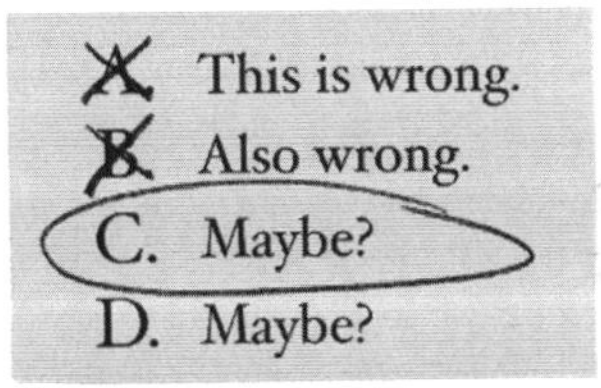

This is not meant to make you question your knowledge. Instead, it is to help you recognize the difference between your knowledge and your impressions. There's a huge difference between thinking an answer is right because of what you know, and thinking an answer is right because it looks or sounds like it should be right.

Summary: To ensure that your selection is appropriately random, make a predetermined selection from among all answer choices you have not eliminated.

Test-Taking Strategies

This section contains a list of test-taking strategies that you may find helpful as you work through the test. By taking what you know and applying logical thought, you can maximize your chances of answering any question correctly!

It is very important to realize that every question is different and every person is different: no single strategy will work on every question, and no single strategy will work for every person. That's why we've included all of them here, so you can try them out and determine which ones work best for different types of questions and which ones work best for you.

Question Strategies

✓ Read Carefully

Read the question and the answer choices carefully. Don't miss the question because you misread the terms. You have plenty of time to read each question thoroughly and make sure you understand what is being asked. Yet a happy medium must be attained, so don't waste too much time. You must read carefully and efficiently.

✓ Contextual Clues

Look for contextual clues. If the question includes a word you are not familiar with, look at the immediate context for some indication of what the word might mean. Contextual clues can often give you all the information you need to decipher the meaning of an unfamiliar word. Even if you can't determine the meaning, you may be able to narrow down the possibilities enough to make a solid guess at the answer to the question.

✓ Prefixes

If you're having trouble with a word in the question or answer choices, try dissecting it. Take advantage of every clue that the word might include. Prefixes can be a huge help. Usually, they allow you to determine a basic meaning. *Pre-* means before, *post-* means after, *pro-* is positive, *de-* is negative. From prefixes, you can get an idea of the general meaning of the word and try to put it into context.

✓ Hedge Words

Watch out for critical hedge words, such as *likely, may, can, often, almost, mostly, usually, generally, rarely,* and *sometimes.* Question writers insert these hedge phrases to cover every possibility. Often an answer choice will be wrong simply because it leaves no room for exception. Be on guard for answer choices that have definitive words such as *exactly* and *always.*

✓ Switchback Words

Stay alert for *switchbacks.* These are the words and phrases frequently used to alert you to shifts in thought. The most common switchback words are *but, although,* and *however.* Others include *nevertheless, on the other hand, even though, while, in spite of, despite,* and *regardless of.* Switchback words are important to catch because they can change the direction of the question or an answer choice.

⊘ Face Value

When in doubt, use common sense. Accept the situation in the problem at face value. Don't read too much into it. These problems will not require you to make wild assumptions. If you have to go beyond creativity and warp time or space in order to have an answer choice fit the question, then you should move on and consider the other answer choices. These are normal problems rooted in reality. The applicable relationship or explanation may not be readily apparent, but it is there for you to figure out. Use your common sense to interpret anything that isn't clear.

Answer Choice Strategies

⊘ Answer Selection

The most thorough way to pick an answer choice is to identify and eliminate wrong answers until only one is left, then confirm it is the correct answer. Sometimes an answer choice may immediately seem right, but be careful. The test writers will usually put more than one reasonable answer choice on each question, so take a second to read all of them and make sure that the other choices are not equally obvious. As long as you have time left, it is better to read every answer choice than to pick the first one that looks right without checking the others.

⊘ Answer Choice Families

An answer choice family consists of two (in rare cases, three) answer choices that are very similar in construction and cannot all be true at the same time. If you see two answer choices that are direct opposites or parallels, one of them is usually the correct answer. For instance, if one answer choice says that quantity *x* increases and another either says that quantity *x* decreases (opposite) or says that quantity *y* increases (parallel), then those answer choices would fall into the same family. An answer choice that doesn't match the construction of the answer choice family is more likely to be incorrect. Most questions will not have answer choice families, but when they do appear, you should be prepared to recognize them.

⊘ Eliminate Answers

Eliminate answer choices as soon as you realize they are wrong, but make sure you consider all possibilities. If you are eliminating answer choices and realize that the last one you are left with is also wrong, don't panic. Start over and consider each choice again. There may be something you missed the first time that you will realize on the second pass.

⊘ Avoid Fact Traps

Don't be distracted by an answer choice that is factually true but doesn't answer the question. You are looking for the choice that answers the question. Stay focused on what the question is asking for so you don't accidentally pick an answer that is true but incorrect. Always go back to the question and make sure the answer choice you've selected actually answers the question and is not merely a true statement.

⊘ Extreme Statements

In general, you should avoid answers that put forth extreme actions as standard practice or proclaim controversial ideas as established fact. An answer choice that states the "process should be used in certain situations, if…" is much more likely to be correct than one that states the "process should be discontinued completely." The first is a calm rational statement and doesn't even make a definitive, uncompromising stance, using a hedge word *if* to provide wiggle room, whereas the second choice is far more extreme.

⊘ Benchmark

As you read through the answer choices and you come across one that seems to answer the question well, mentally select that answer choice. This is not your final answer, but it's the one that will help you evaluate the other answer choices. The one that you selected is your benchmark or standard for judging each of the other answer choices. Every other answer choice must be compared to your benchmark. That choice is correct until proven otherwise by another answer choice beating it. If you find a better answer, then that one becomes your new benchmark. Once you've decided that no other choice answers the question as well as your benchmark, you have your final answer.

⊘ Predict the Answer

Before you even start looking at the answer choices, it is often best to try to predict the answer. When you come up with the answer on your own, it is easier to avoid distractions and traps because you will know exactly what to look for. The right answer choice is unlikely to be word-for-word what you came up with, but it should be a close match. Even if you are confident that you have the right answer, you should still take the time to read each option before moving on.

General Strategies

⊘ Tough Questions

If you are stumped on a problem or it appears too hard or too difficult, don't waste time. Move on! Remember though, if you can quickly check for obviously incorrect answer choices, your chances of guessing correctly are greatly improved. Before you completely give up, at least try to knock out a couple of possible answers. Eliminate what you can and then guess at the remaining answer choices before moving on.

⊘ Check Your Work

Since you will probably not know every term listed and the answer to every question, it is important that you get credit for the ones that you do know. Don't miss any questions through careless mistakes. If at all possible, try to take a second to look back over your answer selection and make sure you've selected the correct answer choice and haven't made a costly careless mistake (such as marking an answer choice that you didn't mean to mark). This quick double check should more than pay for itself in caught mistakes for the time it costs.

⊘ Pace Yourself

It's easy to be overwhelmed when you're looking at a page full of questions; your mind is confused and full of random thoughts, and the clock is ticking down faster than you would like. Calm down and maintain the pace that you have set for yourself. Especially as you get down to the last few minutes of the test, don't let the small numbers on the clock make you panic. As long as you are on track by monitoring your pace, you are guaranteed to have time for each question.

⊘ Don't Rush

It is very easy to make errors when you are in a hurry. Maintaining a fast pace in answering questions is pointless if it makes you miss questions that you would have gotten right otherwise. Test writers like to include distracting information and wrong answers that seem right. Taking a little extra time to avoid careless mistakes can make all the difference in your test score. Find a pace that allows you to be confident in the answers that you select.

⊘ Keep Moving

Panicking will not help you pass the test, so do your best to stay calm and keep moving. Taking deep breaths and going through the answer elimination steps you practiced can help to break through a stress barrier and keep your pace.

Final Notes

The combination of a solid foundation of content knowledge and the confidence that comes from practicing your plan for applying that knowledge is the key to maximizing your performance on test day. As your foundation of content knowledge is built up and strengthened, you'll find that the strategies included in this chapter become more and more effective in helping you quickly sift through the distractions and traps of the test to isolate the correct answer.

Now that you're preparing to move forward into the test content chapters of this book, be sure to keep your goal in mind. As you read, think about how you will be able to apply this information on the test. If you've already seen sample questions for the test and you have an idea of the question format and style, try to come up with questions of your own that you can answer based on what you're reading. This will give you valuable practice applying your knowledge in the same ways you can expect to on test day.

Good luck and good studying!

Learner Development and the Learning Environment

Characteristics of Gifted Students

Characteristics and Needs of Intellectually Gifted Students

Some qualities that educators have found intellectually gifted students to exhibit include:

- Curiosity and an inquisitive nature (i.e. wanting to find out and know things, to understand processes, and to answer questions)
- Complexity in their thinking, personality, and behavior; possessing an extraordinary capacity for learning; more diversity among their interests in learning
- A preference for learning subjects holistically rather than in parts or analytically
- A tendency to learn more intuitively than methodically or logically
- Tendencies toward perfectionism; and a corresponding tendency to exhibit fear regarding risk-taking
- The need to reflect on their own thinking and learning (self-reflection)
- The need to achieve an understanding and an acceptance of the nature of giftedness; a need to develop healthy and positive skills for social interactions and relationships
- A need to solve problems in real life as a way to find meaning and connections in life

Emotional Characteristics

Gifted children often display emotional intensity by experiencing and expressing extremes of emotions. They likely exhibit more emotional sensitivity than other children. They may feel more anxiety, guilt, and sense of responsibility than other children their age. Despite their superior abilities, they can feel inadequate or inferior due to their extreme sensitivity, high standards, perfectionism, and tendency to internalize. They may be shy and timid, and as a result they may be lonely. However, they are also likely to show concern for other people. Their sense of right and wrong is often heightened, prompting strong reactions against dishonesty, hypocrisy, and injustices. They tend to retain stronger memories of emotional experiences. They may have difficulty adjusting to changes. Because of their emotional sensitivity, they are susceptible to depression. They tend to have a need for security. They may suffer from physiological symptoms of emotional states, such as getting a stomach ache from feeling anxious.

Social Characteristics

Because intellectually gifted students are proficient in understanding abstract concepts, they often show an interest in social and philosophical issues. They are typically concerned about seeing justice done and tend to object to actions or decisions they perceive as unfair. Developmental psychologists such as Jean Piaget and Lawrence Kohlberg would say that such children display advanced moral reasoning. Because they have high standards for themselves and others as well as the ability to do many things better than others, even achieving perfection in certain tasks, they tend to be perfectionists. They often have more internal motivation than external motivation to achieve. Desires such as wanting good grades and teacher approval are external, whereas desires such as wanting to learn about a subject or to beat one's own personal best on tests are internal.

Other prevalent characteristics include: good relational skills with parents, teachers, and age peers; well-developed senses of humor; energetic approaches; and emotional and physical sensitivity.

> **Review Video: Piaget's Cognitive Development Theory**
> Visit mometrix.com/academy and enter code: 100376

Aesthetic Characteristics in Terms of Intensity of Sensory Experiences

The Polish psychiatrist and psychologist Kasimierz Dabrowski (1902-1980) proposed intensities he termed "overexcitabilities" or "supersensitivities" in gifted children. His concept of sensual intensity involves heightened awareness and perception of the senses of vision, hearing, touch, smell, and taste. Gifted toddlers with this sensitivity may hate the feel of grass on their bare feet, gifted children may feel nauseated at the smells of certain foods, and/or they may overeat other foods that taste especially good to them. This characteristic is consistent with a craving for pleasure and a need or desire for comfort, two additional characteristics of gifted children with sensory sensitivities. These children often are more sensitive to air pollution and/or to the discomfort of labels/tags in clothing. Another aspect of this sensitivity involves the aesthetic appreciation of beautiful jewelry, visual art, music, literature, and the beauties of nature. Children with this sensitivity often can be moved to tears by beauty.

Characteristics of Imagination

Dabrowski identified the following sensitivities gifted children: psychomotor, sensual, emotional, intellectual, and imaginational. Many gifted children have very vivid imaginations. They are likely to have vivid dreams and to recall them. Because their imaginations allow them to conceive of diverse possibilities, to see things from different viewpoints, to look at things in new/different ways, to be inventive, and to generate original and unusual ideas, these children are likely to develop and utilize good senses of humor. They also are likely to daydream and have imaginary friends. They tend to love fantasy, poetry, drama, and music. They are more likely to have strong visualization skills as well as mental images with more detail than the mental images of other children. Because they can imagine all sorts of possibilities, they can envision the worst-case scenarios for any situation. This characteristic can promote fear of the unknown, of taking risks, and of new situations.

Intellectual Characteristics

Many gifted children have stronger reasoning abilities than do other students, and gifted children are better able to understand abstract concepts at earlier ages. Also, they often do not need to reinforce what they have learned with as much repetition as other children need. They should not simply be asked to recite or repeat something they have learned. Instead, they should be asked to use the higher cognitive skills they possess. For example, for comparison-contrast, you can ask the child the similarities and differences in words, familiar people, characters in a story, familiar songs, holidays, seasons of the year, birds and butterflies, etc. For categorizing, ask the child to group things, e.g. books, foods, toys, clothes, friends, or feelings. For sequencing, ask the child what happened in the beginning, middle, and end of a story. For summarizing, ask the child the most important events during a party, trip, or other activity with varied experiences.

Profiles of Types of Gifted Students

Challenging Gifted Students

Gifted students described as "challenging" are "divergently gifted." In other words, they are highly creative and unconventional. Schools often do not identify such students for gifted programs unless such programs have been implemented for a sufficient number of years and teachers have received enough in-service training. These children do not learn to use the system to their own benefit as more "successful" gifted students do. They tend to question authority and challenge teachers in class. Consequently, they are rarely rewarded for their abilities and often experience conflict. Those children who challenge their peers are not accepted, while others are liked for their originality and humor. They can be disruptive in class due to their spontaneous behaviors. Frustration and low self-esteem are risks for these students. Additionally, they may risk delinquency, drug use, and dropping out of high school if they do not receive suitable intervention by the time they reach middle school/junior high school.

Dropout Gifted Students

Researchers identify a salient characteristic of the "dropout" gifted student as anger. These students have experienced long-term failure of the system to meet their needs. Disappointment with themselves and with adults along with their feelings of rejection can lead to depression. In these students, this depression may manifest as social withdrawal or as defensive acting-out behavior. These students often have abilities and interests in unusual areas not included in school curricula, so they are not affirmed or rewarded for these abilities and interests. School may seem irrelevant or even antagonistic to those students with very different gifts. Many dropout students were not identified as gifted until later, e.g. in high school. This long-term lack of recognition and appropriate educational programming engenders resentment, bitterness, and low self-esteem. Educational experts recommend that these students need individual and group counseling, a close working relationship with a trusted adult, and diagnostic testing for possible remedial areas. Experts also state that traditional programming is not indicated for "dropout" gifted students.

Successful Gifted Students

Researchers have estimated that about 90 percent of students identified as gifted fit the profile described as "successful." These children are most often identified as gifted because they have learned which behaviors adults prefer; as a result of this learning, these children demonstrate the adults' preferred behaviors. . They typically achieve high scores on IQ, aptitude, and achievement tests. They are not likely to display problem behaviors because they crave adults' approval of and know which behaviors will obtain this desired result. Although many people expect such children to succeed independently, such success is often not the case. The researchers find these children tend to depend on adults for direction. Bored with regular curriculum, these children often "work the system" in order to achieve with minimal effort, not developing the autonomy necessary to pursue their own interests and gifts. Liked by peers and rewarded by adults, these students grow up socially well-adjusted but not prepared for life's changing demands; as adults, they may be underachievers.

Underground Gifted Students

Commonly researchers have found that middle school females often make up a group of students classified as the "underground" type of gifted student. In pre-adolescence and early adolescence, girls' need for group belonging and peer acceptance increases exponentially; as a result, many girls will hide their gifts or deny them to fit into a group. The researchers note that gifted boys in this category tend to go underground later, typically in high school, as a reaction to the pressure to join athletic teams and events and to their desire for identification with more popular "jocks" rather than less popular "nerds." Anxious and insecure, "underground" students have needs that conflict with adult expectations. Adult pressure only worsens their denial and resistance. Experts find that they benefit more from acceptance. As such, experts advise adults neither to push nor to permit abandonment of all prior interests in order to fit in; instead, adults should help these students find alternatives to meet their academic needs during what is considered a period of transition.

Double-Labeled Gifted Students

Researchers identify "double-labeled" gifted students as those with both giftedness and physical, emotional, or learning disabilities. Although dual diagnosis is possible with thorough evaluation, most educational programs for the gifted neither identify such students nor afford them differentiated instructional programming that integrates and meets their specialized needs. Because of their combinations of gifts with disabilities, schools can frequently overlook these students, as many of them display behaviors that school personnel do not associate with giftedness. Students with learning disabilities can display poor organizational skills, problems with memory, difficulties with reading, poor handwriting, and etc. Those students with emotional or behavior disorders may exhibit disruptive behavior. Due to the contradictions of their abilities and disabilities, these students are often confused and stressed and suffer from low self-esteem. Often these students are either perceived as average and therefore ignored, or targeted for remediation of their disabilities while their respective gifts are overlooked.

Autonomous Learners

Educational researchers find that parents may observe "autonomous learner" types of gifted children exhibiting signs of this style at home, but these children typically demonstrate it somewhat later in school once they have learned the system. Unlike the "successful" type of gifted student, who seems to have high self-esteem but depends on adult direction and reinforcement, autonomous learners have strong internalized self-concepts. Rather than meeting the system's demands with as little work as possible as do "successful" gifted students, autonomous gifted learners employ the system to create new opportunities to meet their own needs. Self-directed and independent, these students are characterized by self-acceptance and risk-taking ability. They feel secure about forming personal and educational goals. They exhibit a strong sense of self-efficacy (belief in their ability to do things) and personal power. They are active rather than passive, and they express their needs, emotions, and goals with freedom, but also within appropriate limits.

Personality Characteristics of Persons with Various Creative Gifts

Jane Piirto (Understanding Those Who Create, 1998) found that when compared to others with creative gifts, artists are more impulsive and spontaneous. The author found that writers tend more toward nonconformity than do the other creatively gifted types. In addition, Piirto found that in comparison to other creative types, musicians tend more toward introversion. She discovered that architects are not as flexible as other creative persons. Furthermore, she concluded that creative engineers and inventors were likely to be more well-adjusted overall than were other creative types. These findings imply that specific personality traits may need to be considered in order to make predictions, since different personality traits are associated with different domains of creativity. Kerr and Gagliardi (2009) find this domain-specific approach more useful than "...seeking one creative personality type that fits all creative occupations." Indeed, the latter seems doomed to failure in light of the many types of creativity.

Creativity in Gifted Students as a Function of Cognition or Personality

Some researchers view creativity as a strictly cognitive process; others view it as a group of personality traits. Kerr and Gagliardi (2009) assert that while some students might be identified as creative in their thinking, without personality characteristics such as independence and persistence, these students may not produce any creative work. Hence they recommend that both aspects be considered. Divergent thinking is the most prevalent cognitive attribute studied in creativity research. With respect to personality, creativity has been most associated with the traits of autonomy, introversion, and openness to experience. (The latter two traits are included in the "Big Five" personality traits identified by McCrae & Costa and others.) Researchers have noted (e.g. King and Pope 1999, Feist 1999) that creative types are likely to work independently on their creative products and to avoid much social stimulation and group influence. Openness to experience affords the stimulation of new ideas, questions, and topics.

Individual Differences Within the Population of Gifted Students

Social contexts such as geographic residence, socioeconomic status, and cultural background affect personal, family, and community definitions of giftedness. Some groups place high value on academic success. Other groups place higher value on creativity, while yet other groups place higher value on adaptability, i.e. ability to adjust to changing circumstances, including fitting into a social group, more than excellence. Finally, some cultures place priority on the value of service to others. Multiple types of giftedness exist besides intellectual ability. Even within that one type, emotional and social factors are significant considerations. The range of measured IQs among gifted students is as large as the range in general education classrooms. Differences between a moderately gifted child and an extremely gifted child can mirror differences between a child of low-average ability and a moderately gifted child. Psychologically and socially, variation is as great among gifted students as between gifted students and others. Increased variation can increase social problems. Nonetheless, because all gifted students vary in social adjustment, educators are also cautioned against making assumptions about social issues.

Characteristics of Under-Represented Student Populations

Experts in the field of gifted education have emphasized the necessity of using multiple assessment instruments and criteria for determining student gifts requiring special educational programming. However, too often the need for additional assessments is determined by an initial standardized test score. Such tests can overlook many gifted students. Factors interfering with student performance on standardized tests and/or in the classroom include: difficult life circumstances, lack of parental support, minority cultural values and behaviors, lack of language proficiency, disabilities, depression, lack of faith or trust in schools, behavioral issues, and illness. When such factors prevent identification, gifted students lose opportunities to have their abilities acknowledged and cultivated and opportunities for social access with their intellectual peers. Even identified gifted students frequently have to adjust themselves to a program, instead of the program's adjustment to accommodate students' abilities, as should occur. Without individualization, "one-size-fits-all" programs can cause frustration and discomfort to immigrant, minority, low-income, and underachieving gifted students.

Salient Characteristics of Low-Income Black Parents of Gifted Children

Children Who Have Achieved Well in School

Various researchers have found that in low-income black families, the parents' amount of education did not influence their gifted children's achievement; rather, parents' attitudes and behaviors exerted the greatest influence on children's achievement. The parents of high-achieving students in this population assertively involved themselves in their children's education and kept track of the children's progress. These parents perceived themselves as competent in their coping skills and had optimistic attitudes. They established realistically high expectations for their gifted children. They supported the ideology of achievement, and their orientations toward achievement were positive. They established specific, clear, achievement-oriented norms for their children. They also created explicit and clear boundaries regarding roles. They purposefully practiced behaviors and provided experiences to promote their children's achievement. These parents' relationships with their gifted children were openly communicative, supportive, nurturing, trusting, respectful, and positive.

Children Who Were Underachievers in School

Educational researchers have found that while low-income black gifted students who achieved well in school had parents with positive, optimistic attitudes and high expectations for their children's success, those students who underachieved academically had parents who did not feel as optimistic, expressing attitudes of helplessness and hopelessness. Parents of underachieving students in this population were less assertive about involvement in their children's educations than the parents of high-achieving students in this population. As a result, they were not as engaged in their children's schooling. Parents of these underachieving gifted black students were more likely to have unrealistic and/or unclear or ill-defined expectations for their children. These low-income black parents of gifted students who underachieved in school also were found to have less self-confidence in their parenting skills than parents of higher-achieving students in this population.

Approaches to Development of Gifted Students

Research on Effective Practices in Gifted Education

The National Research Center on Gifted and Talented (NRC/GT) is seeking to find out "what works in gifted education" through a five-year plan beginning with the 2008-2009 school year. Their plan involves integrating the examination of systems of identification, reading and math curricula based on theoretical models, and assessments of giftedness. Researchers are concentrating on three areas:

- Developing a solid system of identification that will build upon prior research
- With students identified via both traditional criteria and expanded criteria, analyzing the effects of certain units of reading and math curricula
- Measuring student outcomes using standardized achievement tests, extended standards-based assessments, or structured performance assessments

Researchers aim to create a system of identification for students across socioeconomic and cultural groups. Such groups will feature "talent pools" of elementary-school students, identified using standardized tests and teacher ratings, participating in randomly assigned reading and math curricula based on models.

Benefits to School Districts for Participation

Research studies regarding effective teaching methods in gifted education often develop curriculum units to test in actual practice at schools. Such units are designed to challenge gifted students, differentiated for all student levels in general education classrooms and based upon national standards. Such units educationally benefit more students at more levels than non-differentiated instruction. Participating school districts often receive tools for the identification and the assessment of gifted students free of charge, which represents a financial benefit. Major research centers also provide support for educators' professional development, benefiting school districts financially and benefiting teachers, other school personnel, and students. This support often includes online technical assistance, an additional benefit addressing the increasing use of online resources and tools. Participation in a research study conducted by a center offering professional development courses for educators also gives priority to some members of school district staffs in registering for these courses.

Characteristics of Gifted Students Relative to Achievement Motivation

Researchers have discovered that when gifted students consistently bring high skill levels to schoolwork, externally imposed limitations that represent threats to their senses of self-determination are particularly likely to affect them negatively. Gifted children frequently know they have the ability to exceed their non-gifted peers in performance; therefore, they do not rely as much on external rewards, the contingencies for earning them, or feedback from teachers. A more important need for them involves preserving their internal motivation, which cannot be forced or learned, but can too easily be quashed. While research finds gifted students as typically highly motivated, it also finds that motivation in classrooms is problematic for them. This finding is attributable to gifted students not responding well to rigidly structured, specific tasks or assignments, which non-gifted students often need. Since gifted students are self-motivated instead of teacher-motivated, gifted students perform better when given choices, flexibility, and unstructured tasks.

INTRINSIC MOTIVATION PRINCIPLE OF CREATIVITY

While what Renzulli has termed "schoolhouse giftedness" is more easily identified via IQ test scores and more amenable to academic success than what he called "creative-productive giftedness, " which is not as easily identified via IQ test scores. Social psychologists conducting research into creative production over 25 years have found it associated with students' motivational orientations, and those orientations are influenced by environmental factors. They find that internal motivation encourages creativity, while external motivation discourages creativity—this finding is called the Intrinsic Motivation Principle of Creativity. Intrinsically motivated students do tasks for their own sake because they enjoy them, so their rewards come from within them. In contrast, extrinsically motivated students do tasks for a reward coming from outside them.

INFLUENCES OF ENVIRONMENTAL FACTORS ON EXPRESSION OF CREATIVITY

The influence of environmental variables can be seen historically through creative proliferation at certain times and places. For example, Florence, Italy in the 15th century; the Harlem Renaissance in 1920s and 1930s New York in America; and San Francisco, California in 1960s America all exhibited unusual amounts of creative inspiration and production. Some of the environmental factors that allow people with creative gifts to express them in meaningful and socially valuable ways include:

- Social support for a subculture consisting of creative persons
- Availability and accessibility of materials and resources for creative production
- A political and cultural climate that allows freedom of expression
- The existence of patrons with the means and interest to lend financial, material, and moral support to creative endeavors

Influences impeding creative expression include the race, gender, and socioeconomic status of some gifted individuals due to others' stereotyping and lowered expectations because of such environmental characteristics.

NURTURING STUDENTS' AREAS OF GIFTEDNESS

TEACHERS

Teachers can observe student behaviors in order to identify their personal interests and abilities. When they notice a student excelling in a certain subject area, teachers can provide enrichment activities for that student. Even in a general education classroom with no gifted programs, teachers can provide additional activities in preferred areas to students who show evidence of giftedness by asking for additional activities. Teachers can vary their instruction by offering activities and assignments at higher grade levels to gifted students not challenged or even bored at their class' grade level. Teachers pressed for time can arrange peer tutoring by older and/or more advanced students to allow younger gifted students more 1:1 interaction and individualized learning at the students' own pace. Teachers can help gifted students plan and develop special projects in their areas of interest, allowing them to learn about these areas in more depth and with more complexity.

Parents

Parents can begin reading to children regularly as soon as the children are able to attend. Furthermore, as children develop, parents can encourage children to read to them as well. As children grow, parents can observe and encourage their interests/aptitudes. Providing books for verbally precocious children is crucial (libraries offer a good option if funds are limited), since good writers begin as good readers. Parents can give children with mathematical talents numerical puzzles and games. For children interested in producing reactions by mixing substances, junior chemistry sets or household materials can be provided. Beginner telescopes and trips to the local planetarium are good for children fascinated with stars and planets. Parents can provide interested children with introductory geology sample sets and take them on local field trips to discover rocks, minerals, and/or fossils. Basic art supplies are important for children with artistic abilities. Parents should allow and encourage free expression, exploration, discovery, learning, skills development, and new insights.

Content Skills and Process Skills

Content skills involve acquiring and retaining the information presented in a specific instructional subject area. Examples include learning the correct spelling of words; knowing the correct meaning of vocabulary words; knowing factual material such as places, names, and dates in history or social studies; remembering mathematical equations or formulas, etc. In contrast, process skills involve more interpretation of information. For example, a student not only knows what reportedly happened in a historical event, but s/he also can interpret that event in terms of its historical context, such as the frame of reference and viewpoints affecting participants. Process skills include analyzing information through comparisons-contrasts; generalizations; finding cause-and-effect relationships; classifying and sequencing; summarizing; and drawing inferences, conclusions, and predictions. Such skills include applying critical thinking skills and systematic methods of inquiry, especially in sciences. Content and process skills are related because content must be learned to process it. Integrating the two is most effective.

Enrichment Activities to Develop Skills in Forming and Testing Hypotheses

Gifted children typically exhibit advanced abilities in conceptual thinking. Their skills should be developed with activities wherein they manipulate information rather than merely memorizing or recognizing it. To stimulate and practice hypothesizing, you can ask questions of a gifted child beginning with "What would happen if we...?" For example, what if we put a block into a glass filled with water? What if we put a glass over a lit candle? If we put tennis balls into a shoebox, how many could it hold?, etc. Then you can test these hypotheses by following through and performing the hypothetical action to see what happens. These activities suit children in Piaget's Concrete Operations stage. For children who can think abstractly without concrete objects, activities can be extended to imaginary events and fantasies, e.g. "What would happen if you could fly?... if you were invisible?... if snow were ice cream?... if you were twelve feet tall?", etc.

Developing Skills in Making Inferences, Math, Reading, and Language

One way young gifted children can be encouraged to exercise their cognitive abilities is through inferences, which require them to move beyond literal and concrete perceptions to more abstract thinking involving speculation based on existing information. For example, you can show a child a picture of people wearing uniforms and ask what their jobs may be, or show a picture of people with various facial expressions and ask what they might be feeling. In both cases, ask what could have happened before and after what is in the picture. For children with mathematical gifts, it is important to incorporate fun, game-like math activities into daily living routines. For developing reading readiness skills in young gifted children, you can label common household objects with their printed names on 3x5 cards. Start open-ended stories; let them make predictions and hypotheses about what will happen next and what will happen if that occurs.

Language Experience Stories to Develop Language Skills

Younger gifted children with advanced abilities in language often will enjoy activities using language experience stories. You ask the child to make up a story on any subject the child prefers. For example, the story can be about the child's pet; the child's best friend or circle of friends; a favorite relative; a trip they took on vacation that they especially enjoyed; a day trip to a museum, zoo, planetarium; a party they had or attended; or any other subject of the child's choice. The child tells the story aloud and you write it down. You have the child draw illustrations to accompany the story. You then read the story back to the child, aloud from the printed version. Record your reading. Play back the recording and listen together, having the child follow the printed words to associate spoken and written language. Make multiple stories into a book for the child.

Affective Development of Gifted Individuals

Need for Further Research

Educational researchers specializing in gifted education find that many aspects of the social and emotional development of gifted individuals have not been researched nearly as much as the intellectual and academic aspects of their development. They recommend that researchers, school psychologists, guidance counselors, and other professionals can contribute to exploration of the affective domain. Asynchronous development in cognitive vs. affective domains has long been observed in the gifted, but it demands further study, as does perfectionism in the gifted. Scientists also want more research into underachievement, depression, eating disorders, self-injurious behaviors, and substance abuse relative to giftedness, as well as responses to life events such as divorce, loss and grief, serious illness, injury, and relocating. Additionally, research into giftedness is lacking related to obsessive-compulsive disorder, sexual abuse, physical disabilities, Asperger's syndrome, serious conflicts between parents and their gifted children, and problematic developmental transitions.

Support

Gifted education programs, both inside and outside of general education classrooms, should incorporate curriculum elements designed to support emotional, social, and career development in gifted students. At all age/grade levels, school curricula can be proactive by including psychoeducational knowledge regarding the way in which giftedness influences these developmental domains. When teaching social sciences and literature, teachers can give assignments related to the psychosocial aspects of these subjects. Classes can have group discussions about developmental challenges. Career and talent development often present issues for gifted children at much younger ages than for other students, so these topics should be addressed in the curriculum. Viewing and addressing underachievement and high achievement from a developmental perspective can help both students and educators. Teachers should affirm student resiliency and personal strengths, which can be eclipsed by performance/underperformance. Advocates for legislation, funding, and services for gifted students also should emphasize affective considerations in their efforts.

Review Video: Early Childhood Developmental Domains
Visit mometrix.com/academy and enter code: 100380

Influence of Common Characteristics of Gifted Children

The developmental tasks for gifted children are the same as for all children. For example, all children must develop such concepts as a sense of identity, a sense of self-efficacy, differentiation of self, relationships with peers, autonomy in life and in school, and paths toward careers. But gifted children can experience these developmental milestones quite differently from other children. Researchers find gifted children are commonly more emotionally sensitive, intense, and overly excitable. They also are commonly more perceptive about human behaviors and personalities; along with their talents, their moral development is precocious, so they tend to have different concerns at higher cognitive levels and younger ages than other children. Even the faster cognitive processing of gifted youngsters can intensify their emotional responses to external stimuli. These common gifted characteristics may sometimes impede developmental processes. Therefore educators, parents, counselors, psychologists, and psychiatrists working with gifted students should possess adequate and accurate knowledge regarding these children's affective development.

Attitude of Experts

As many experts in gifted education assert, gifted students deserve for adults to attend not only to their gifts, talents, and performance, but also to their overall wellbeing. Gifted children go through developmental processes and achievements universal to all children, although they may experience these processes and achievements differently. They also have other developmental experiences unique to each individual. Because educators and other adults so frequently focus on the academic and creative potential of gifted students and their performance or lack thereof, they may not focus enough on the affective dimension of their development. Adults need to remember that gifted students' developmental progress is not only cognitive, but also emotional, social, and career-related. Moreover, progress in cognitive and academic areas also has emotional and social effects. Thus, organizations such as the National Association for Gifted Children take the position that teachers, administrators, and counselors in schools should deliberately, proactively nurture the emotional and social development of gifted students.

Stages in Team Problem-Solving

If a group of gifted students wants to solve a problem as a team, the first stage they should address involves understanding the nature of the specific problem. That accomplished, in the second stage they would brainstorm ideas for potential solutions to the problem. Once they had a number of possible solutions, the third stage would involve deciding what to do. Dr. E. Paul Torrance, who developed the most widely used standardized tests of creative thinking, founded the Future Problem Solving Program (FPSP) in 1974. Today it is used with hundreds of thousands of students, nationwide and in several other countries. The FPSP model contains three sections and six steps: Under the first section, Understanding the Problem, steps 1 and 2 are identifying challenges in the problem, and selecting an underlying problem. The second section, Generating Ideas, has step 3, producing solution ideas. The third section, Planning for Action, includes steps 4, 5, and 6: generating and selecting criteria, applying criteria, and developing an action plan.

Skills Developed Through Creative Problem-Solving Process

Participating in creative problem-solving develops the higher-order cognitive skills of gifted students, which helps them to apply their knowledge for solving problems. According to experts, there is more emphasis in this process on learning "how to think" than on acquiring information. Creative problem-solving helps gifted students enhance their analytical skills as well as their creative abilities. It builds their skills in spoken and written communication and encourages gifted students to develop skills for conducting research and improving these skills. When gifted students participate in groups to solve problems creatively as a team, the process contributes to their developing responsibility as group members. The creative problem-solving process provides gifted students with guidance that enables them to develop not only responsibility, but also more self-direction. This process also furnishes gifted students with a model for problem-solving they can incorporate into their lives. Moreover, it engages gifted students' interest in the future.

Challenges Faced by Gifted Students

Strengths and Potential Problem Behaviors

Intellectually gifted students often have advanced organizational skills. This advancement benefits them academically, since it facilitates learning. However, this advancement also can manifest in these students exhibiting a need to organize things and people beyond their own academic subjects. Positively, this characteristic contributes to leadership qualities; negatively, it contributes to making rules too complex for others and to being perceived as bossy. Intellectually gifted students often possess knowledge ahead of their peers in both level and breadth; they frequently have larger vocabularies and more facile use of their respective vocabularies. Problems associated with these strengths include boredom with school and classmates and the potential for using language to manipulate others. Intellectually gifted students tend to have high expectations both for themselves and others. While this strength is a motivational quality, its drawbacks include perfectionism, a lack of tolerance for their own and/or others' shortcomings, and a potential for developing depression due to disappointment over unmet expectations.

Intellectually gifted students often learn and remember new information more quickly than other students. A potential side effect of this facility involves impatience with other less gifted, as well as with routine procedures they find superfluous and limiting. The curious/inquisitive nature of intellectually gifted students as well as their need to seek meaning can result in questions that embarrass others; others' perceptions that the gifted students are nosy and/or rude; and perceptions that the gifted students go overboard in pursuing their interests. Another strength involves internalized motivation; however, as a downside, these students can seem overly willful and resistant to direction from others. Students with superior capacities for synthesis and conceptualization tend to enjoy solving problems and dealing with abstract ideas. However, these students are more likely to question/challenge teaching practices and routines. They also tend to focus on truth and fairness, so they may have excessive humanitarian worries and/or difficulty accepting inequitable realities in life.

Often intellectually gifted students are sensitive and promote empathy for others. The problem associated with this area of giftedness involves the students' need for the acceptance of others, as well as an accompanying oversensitivity to rejection and/or criticism. Creative and inventive students enjoy finding new ways to do things. This gift proves a boon to society in terms of innovation, but it also can be perceived as disruptive and abnormal. Intellectually gifted students often have longer attention spans than other students, can concentrate on one subject more intensively, and are more persistent in the areas interesting them. Many important accomplishments are attributable to these qualities. However, these qualities also can result in the neglect of other academic subjects and/or persons and relationships, ignoring interruptions, and being thought stubborn. Many intellectually gifted students are highly alert, enthusiastic, and eager to learn; in addition, these students may possess high energy levels. These assets can be misperceived as hyperactivity/overactivity. These students can also become frustrated when inactive.

Many intellectually gifted students are academically independent. Superior abilities for learning, knowing, and understanding afford them both the skills and the confidence for autonomy and self-direction in learning. These skills and confidence, plus their thinking and learning differently from their age peers, promote self-reliance in such students. They are likely to prefer individualized tasks. Because of these factors, these students may be seen by others as not conforming to accepted norms. They also may reject input from their peers, teachers, or parents, and these other individuals likely will not receive such rejection well. Greater amounts of versatility and diversity in their abilities and interests give these students more options, but these characteristics also can cause time-management issues and cause a disorganized impression. Strong senses of humor can be misconstrued by age peers, and as a result these students may evolve into "class clowns." Their tendencies to seek causal relationships can make them uncomfortable with irrational/illogical feelings or traditions.

Uneven Development in Intellectually Gifted Children

Educational researchers have found that intellectually gifted children do not always develop evenly across all domains of ability. While some gifted students excel in all areas, particularly in the higher grades, many more of these students demonstrate comparatively greater gifts in certain domains than in others. One example of uneven development very common among younger gifted children occurs when their cognitive and conceptual abilities develop far in advance of their physical motor skills. When this uneven development happens, while a young child is capable of more sophisticated ideation, he or she is incapable of executing his or her ideas physically due to less advanced motor abilities. This frustrating inequity proves frustrating and produces tantrums in many children. Another example of uneven development occurs when an intellectually gifted child uses his or her superior cognitive skills to interact with the environment almost exclusively, leaving his or her emotional and social skills underdeveloped from lack of practice.

Gifted Students' Motivation for Subjects at Odds with Their Actual Talents

Some students are gifted in certain areas, yet their interests lay elsewhere, where they are less talented and even exhibit weaknesses. For example, a parent and retired educator had a gifted child with talent in mathematics and playing violin. However, his passions were for soccer and singing, where he was not gifted or average, but comparatively weak. His parents did not press him to focus on his gifted areas or give up on what he loved because he did not excel. Despite shortcomings in favored fields, his passion and persistence eventually won him a place on his high school soccer team and he realized his goal of making All-State choir in senior year. He teaches and directs voice and coaches soccer as an adult, happy with his choices. This illustrates that gifted students need not confine their efforts to gifted areas and may succeed in other fields with passion and perseverance.

Contributing Factors for Underachievement in Some Gifted Students

Some gifted students express their gifts during the earlier parts of their childhood by pursuing areas of special interest to them, excelling in certain school subjects, and working on advanced projects. Some students suddenly drop all these activities, deny their previous interests, or claim they have lost interest or outgrown them. Experts have found girls most likely to exhibit this trend during middle school/junior high school, while boys are more likely exhibit this trend in high school. Researchers attribute the change to social and emotional needs, especially in school. Girls approaching and entering adolescence experience a great increase in their needs for peer acceptance and for a sense of belonging. Consequently, some gifted girls will hide or deny their giftedness in order to fit in with a non-gifted group of peers. Boys in high school often experience pressure to play sports, a celebrated skill, while academic excellence without athleticism is ridiculed.

Not identified as gifted earlier in school, some gifted students reach their high school years without any special educational interventions or programs designed for their unique abilities. These students may have been overlooked in the school system if their gifts exist outside of their schools' areas of curricula. While these gifted students may have the ability to perform well in certain subjects, teachers might find these students' different methods of achieving such performances unacceptable or invalid. Furthermore, such students may attend a school in which personnel lack sufficient training or experience with giftedness. By the time students receive neither acknowledgement nor support for their gifts in high school, they have felt rejected for years and are usually angry and/or depressed. Without support or appropriate curriculum, they will not achieve and may drop out of school.

Some gifted students figure out early on which behaviors are desired and rewarded by adults, and then these students use their superior abilities to produce these behaviors. They are successful according to adult standards and appear to have high self-esteem because of the adult reinforcement they receive. They are not identified with behavior problems because they comply with adults' wishes in order to succeed. However, such students, especially when placed in regular classes with mainstream curricula, often secretly feel bored with school. These students use their expertise to get through school by expending the minimal effort possible. As a result, they do not develop the independence and skills needed for self-direction, nor do they explore subjects of personal interest to them. Instead, they rely on adults for direction, guidance, and feedback. They often develop into adults who display competence but not originality or imagination. When they continue these behaviors in adulthood, they can become underachievers in relation to their ability.

Some gifted students have superior abilities that they can express congruently within the traditionally accepted framework of academic performance and achievement. Other gifted students have superior abilities best expressed outside of this framework. These students often think in more markedly different ways than other students, who often fail to understand them. They may also have talents not included in school curricula. They do not receive rewards for their gifts in the same manner as students with more traditionally acceptable gifts. As a result, the gifted students become frustrated. Due to the unconventional nature of these students' gifts, educators often do not identify them as gifted, so they receive little instructional support. They also are often highly creative. Their spontaneity can be perceived as disruptive in school. With their self-esteem compromised and their gifts not nurtured, such students likely underachieve in school and exhibit increased risk for dropout if they do not receive specialized instructional attention.

Contributing Factors to Underachievement in Minority Gifted Students

Low self-esteem in general hampers student achievement. Researchers also find that poor self-concepts specific to academics and social interactions interfere. Some researchers have emphasized the need to consider the strength and/or positivity of a gifted minority student's sense of racial/ethnic identity. Students whose racial identities are not positive can be more susceptible to counterproductive peer pressure. They also may associate academic achievement with the dominant culture, hence with betraying their minority culture, i.e. "selling out" or trying to "act white." This view results in less effort, which results in less achievement. Psychologically, with a high internal locus of control, a student attributes his or her achievement to ability and effort and is more likely to achieve. Minority students who expect external factors such as discrimination and injustice to block their success demonstrate a high external locus of control and are less likely to achieve up to their potentials.

Researchers have found that among gifted black students, for example, underachieving students have reported experiencing less positive teacher-student interactions, less supportive classroom climates, insufficient time to understand lesson material, and feeling uninterested and unmotivated toward school. They also attributed part of their lack of interest to their schools' lack of multicultural education. Teachers often have lowered expectations of minority and low-income students, especially for teachers with inadequate preparation in both gifted education and multicultural education. Such teachers are less likely to refer minority students for gifted education services, and with lower expectations they are also less likely to identify these students as underachievers. Without access to suitable educational services that address their individual strengths and needs, minority gifted students can become frustrated, bored, lose interest in school, and become underachievers.

Review Video: Multiculturalism/Celebrating All Cultures
Visit mometrix.com/academy and enter code: 708545

Underachievement Due to Mismatches Between Learning and Teaching Styles

The predominant cultural values in America favor individualism, competition, and excellence in individual achievement, both in society and in school. In contrast, many other countries have cultures that value collectivism, cooperation, and placing the good of the group ahead of one's individual concerns. Therefore, many students belonging to minority groups in the United States have cultural values that more closely reflect the values of other countries of origin than the majority American values. These students tend to be more social and cooperative in their attitudes and behaviors, and less individualistic and competitive. Teaching styles in America tend to place emphasis on competing with others to be the best. Too much emphasis on competition can interfere with minority gifted students' achievement: rather than increasing their motivation, competition can decrease motivation by provoking anxiety and by negatively influencing students' social and academic self-images.

The majority of teaching methods in public schools tend to use the verbal modality, to deal in abstract concepts, and to teach concepts and skills in isolation, i.e. taken out of context. These methods contrast markedly with the learning styles of many minority students. For example, research finds that black students are more likely to be visual rather than verbal learners, i.e. they learn better using visual images than words. In addition, black students are more likely to be field-dependent rather than field-independent learners, meaning that they rely on the surrounding context to understand the material presented and will not grasp it as well (or at all) when it is presented out of context. Finally, the research indicates that black students tend to learn more concretely rather than abstractly, so teaching abstract concepts through using concrete objects rather than presenting such concepts only in abstract terms would enhance their learning. Mismatched teaching methods produce confusion and frustration in students with these learning styles, thereby leading to underachievement.

Supportive Strategies to Promote Achievement and/or Reverse Underachievement

Educators should give minority gifted students opportunities to talk about their concerns with teachers and counselors. In addition, educators should employ more collaborative and cooperative group learning methods, as well as verbal and other positive reinforcements. They should reduce norm-referenced and competitive contexts, set high expectations for minority gifted students, and teach for mastery. They should try different teaching modalities such as concrete/abstract, visual/auditory, etc. to identify students' learning styles, strengths, and needs. They should accommodate their instruction to student learning styles. Educators should attend to issues students may have with self-perceptions, self-efficacy (self-perceived ability to accomplish tasks), and motivation. Classrooms should be student-centered and address affective needs. Teaching and counseling techniques should be multicultural. Educators also should enlist significant involvement by students' parents and other family members and engage role models and mentors for their minority gifted students.

Developing Internal Motivation, Self-Efficacy, Academic Motivation, and Performance

For intrinsic motivation and self-efficacy, educators should give minority gifted students consistent and constructive feedback, concentrate on individual students' interests, and provide them with choices. In addition, they should alternate their teaching styles to accommodate different student learning styles and furnish projects, simulations, internships, case studies, role plays, and other activities that promote experiential, active, hands-on learning. Educators can provide mentors and role models for students, as well as relevant, inspirational biographies. They can also use bibliotherapy. Teachers should work to establish classrooms with affirming and nurturing atmospheres for minority gifted students and all other students, as well. Teachers should use multicultural instruction that is meaningful personally, relevant culturally, and promotes self-understanding and insights. Some remedial strategies to improve student performance in specific deficit areas include counseling, tutoring, teaching study skills, test-taking skills, organizational and time-management skills, assigning journaling, making learning contracts, and teaching individually and to small groups.

Issues Related to Timely Homework Completion

Problems result when gifted students are given both general and gifted education homework, thus doubling their load. When such doubling is not the case, some gifted students still can have time management issues with homework. Here are some factors to consider: many gifted students are perfectionists. As such, they can expend excessive, unnecessary time trying to perfect their homework. Also, while some gifted students process information faster than non-gifted students, many do not. In fact, researchers have found that measures of working memory and processing speed on standardized IQ tests are poor indicators of giftedness. Timely homework completion is a skill that develops over time. If problems have developed over time, such problems also are resolved over time. These problems are addressed in the Specially Designed Instruction section of the GIEP. While teachers or local school districts may require homework completion to pass a course, many State Departments of Education do not.

Complications for Students with Both Giftedness and Co-Existing Disabilities

Some gifted students also have a co-existing physical, emotional, psychiatric, behavioral, or learning disability. This co-existing occurrence of giftedness and disability complicates diagnosis. For example, intellectually gifted children can exhibit a number of behaviors that appear very similar to the behaviors of children with attention deficit hyperactivity disorder (behaviors such as high energy and activity levels, impulsive actions, rapid speech, etc.). They may exhibit compulsive organizing and possible obsessive-compulsive disorder. Most educational programs for gifted students do not address concomitant disabilities, while conversely most programs for disabled students do not address giftedness. Researchers are endeavoring to remedy these errors. At times teachers might overlook these students' areas of giftedness and instead focus on the behaviors produced by the students' disabilities. Teachers may not consider that a child with messy handwriting or disruptive classroom behavior, for example, might exhibit giftedness in areas such as art, science, music, dance, or athletics.

Characteristics and Challenges for Students Gifted in Math

Often children with mathematical gifts can grasp new concepts very quickly. In the general education classroom, they end up without recourse to additional intellectual exercise while they wait for the rest of the students to understand and master the new math ideas presented. Some consequences of letting gifted students go unchallenged are boredom, less than optimal thinking skills, and undesirable study habits. One way to offer them challenges is through differentiated instruction. The teacher can present math problems with graduated levels of difficulty and complexity. When students have a choice of problems at different levels, they have the opportunity to try to solve problems just within their current cognitive capacity. Such methodology challenges students with problems that are not too easy, without overly frustrating them by being out of range of their ability; it cultivates their passion for math; and it stimulates their cognitive growth and development.

Many mathematically gifted students enjoy challenges that engage their superior abilities for calculating and solving problems. However, gifted students who only have experience with effortless school work become uncomfortable confronting challenges and/or frustration inherent in learning more difficult material. In addition to teaching advanced students, teachers are charged with the job of helping them realize that confining their education to easy pursuits deprives them of many rewards, and a life without struggle leads to less achievement and fulfillment. Teachers can give students examples illustrating challenges to adults. One educator (Zaccaro, 2008) would tell his students about the time he did not calculate whether his rope was long enough to rappel off a cliff and reach the ground, and he had to jump 15 feet. He also gave them problems to work where mistakes were common so they could see that making errors was not the end of the world.

Things to Avoid in Order to Not Interfere with Development of Gifts

Parents

In general, toddlers are prone to tantrums due to frustration. Gifted toddlers are even more likely to demonstrate this characteristic when their cognitive development outpaces their physical development and they can conceive of actions but cannot perform them. Parents should not punish such tantrums as they allow emotional venting and reduce tension. Researchers have found that parents who are overly directive and controlling tend to influence children to become less exploratory and curious, less independent and self-directed, less internally motivated, and less creative. Total permissiveness is not ideal, since children need appropriate limits, boundaries, structure, and guidance. Detached or uninvolved parents are not helpful. Parents should avoid punishing or disapproving of gifted children's actions as abnormal just for being unusual or unfamiliar. Parents should not avoid activities with their gifted children from insecurity regarding their own preparation or competence. Activities confer important bonding experiences as well as children's learning and positive reinforcement.

Teachers

When a child exhibits giftedness in certain areas, the teacher should not prohibit or curtail the child's interest in preferred subjects and activities. If a gifted child prefers some subjects to the exclusion of other, required curriculum, the teacher can arrange behavioral contracts or contingencies; e.g., completing an assignment in a non-preferred area can be rewarded with more time exploring a preferred interest. Teachers should not punish or disapprove extensive interest in certain subjects, a characteristic of gifted students. Teachers should not force gifted students to follow traditional procedures for learning and performing if they learn best with different procedures. As a student, Albert Einstein reputedly was failed in math by a teacher for not following the prescribed procedures, even though he got the right answers. Fortunately, he overcame this deterrent through his intellect, curiosity, and persistence. Teachers should not ignore gifted students who grow bored or who clamor for more material.

General Mental Health Considerations

Research finds gifted students no more prone to experience mental health problems than are other students. Nonetheless, if educators and counselors have limited knowledge and experience of gifted students, their perceptions can be influenced by exclusively positive stereotypes of the gifted. Such a perception can be dangerous, in that adults may not recognize, and hence not address, counseling needs and/or developmental issues in gifted students. Some gifted characteristics can become liabilities in this sense. Also, adults unfamiliar with gifted students' specific characteristics may incorrectly interpret some divergent behaviors as pathological symptoms. Another consideration is that gifted students, wanting to preserve their competent reputations and avoid disappointing invested adults, often do not request needed assistance. Adults who are both uninformed regarding the complexity of gifted students' concerns and also dazzled by the gifted students' abilities are less objective, can overlook students' vulnerabilities, and cannot work effectively with them. Adult respect for gifted students is more appropriate than awe. As in curriculum and instruction, differentiation in counseling services is indicated for the gifted.

Prevailing View of Student Gifts and Talents as Assets

While superior intellectual abilities and/or creative talents may seem obvious assets, a number of factors have contributed to this view's overshadowing the recognition of less beneficial aspects of giftedness. Accordingly, samples selected for quantitative research studies have not covered a wide enough range of the gifted population. By not including sufficient socioeconomic, cultural, and performance factors in sampling, studies do not reflect the true range of issues for gifted students. In addition, such research findings inform the development of instruments for assessment and intervention, which in turn will not adequately represent "non-asset" aspects of giftedness. Also, due to the paucity of qualitative studies on gifted students, researchers are limited in understanding feelings and thoughts that gifted students have not expressed to others. Other factors include our society's emphasis on equality, and legislation mandating educational accountability and achievement, both of which are not conducive to addressing gifted students' emotional and social needs.

Review Video: Equality vs Equity
Visit mometrix.com/academy and enter code: 685648

Preparation Needed by Counselors

Giftedness has significant impacts on the emotional and social development of young people. They encounter the same universal developmental transitions and challenges as all children, yet they are likely to experience them quite differently. In addition, they experience other, individualized developmental issues. They will be concerned with moral, academic, and career issues at younger ages than other students. They may also have concerns that other students do not experience at any age. The issues that concern these gifted students have ramifications for their overall wellbeing. Thus school counselors and outside, private counselors must possess knowledge regarding the characteristics of gifted students. Knowing about the emotional intensity and hypersensitivity of many gifted students keeps counselors from misinterpreting these as abnormal. Knowledge of gifted students' characteristics can explain classroom and/or social problems and afford more perspective on developmental issues. This knowledge also should inform counselors' case studies and intervention plans.

Learning Environments

Relationship Between Gifted Education and Special Education

Many students with gifts in specific areas and/or global giftedness also have disabilities. This complicates the circumstances of the best educational programming for them. One consideration is that disabilities can prevent some gifted students from being identified as gifted. For example, if a student has visual impairment and does not receive appropriate classroom accommodations, it might not be discovered that this student also has superior language and reading abilities. Another consideration is that instruction must be differentiated in certain ways to accommodate the needs of students with disabilities, and in other ways to accommodate the needs of gifted and talented students. The challenge for educators is to combine and coordinate both types of differentiation for these doubly/multiply exceptional students. An additional aspect is that federal laws exist to guarantee education to disabled students but not to gifted students. Therefore, many US state regulations for gifted education are modeled upon federal laws protecting the rights of disabled students.

Relationship Between Gifted Education and General Education

One factor important to consider in both gifted education and general education, since it affects both, is that compared to the numbers of special schools for gifted and talented students, there are many more public schools attended by gifted and talented students. Additionally, while some public schools include self-contained classes composed entirely of identified gifted and talented students, many more have such students mainstreamed into general education classrooms along with non-gifted students. Many public schools have pull-out programs for gifted students wherein they attend resource rooms to participate in special, individualized activities with instruction from a gifted education teacher. However, pull-out programs only involve a portion of the students' school time, typically a half-day or one day at most. Therefore, it is crucial for general and gifted education teachers to coordinate their curricula and activities. Each must know what the other is doing to facilitate the student's educational progress.

Cognitive Process Models

Educational scientists develop theoretical models and then apply the models to instructional approaches and methods. Some models focus on a particular domain, such as affective or cognitive. Cognitive process models focus on the cognitive domain, i.e. mental processes by which students learn and think. Bloom's Taxonomy, created by Benjamin Bloom in 1956, remains one of the most famous and popularly used cognitive process models. This taxonomy contains six ascending levels of cognitive processes:

1. **Knowledge**: Students can recall (retrieve from memory) or recognize (identify upon presentation) specific information they have learned.
2. **Comprehension**: Students not only remember, but understand, information they learn.
3. **Application**: Students can learn ideas, principles, and theories and then apply them to other contexts.
4. **Analysis**: Students can break information down into component parts.
5. **Synthesis**: Students can take constituent parts and think originally and creatively to combine them into a whole.
6. **Evaluation**: Students develop standards and criteria and apply these to concepts, methods, and materials presented to judge their value.

Review Video: Bloom's Taxonomy
Visit mometrix.com/academy and enter code: 755020

Affective Process Models

The affective domain relates to the emotions, emotional responses to the environment, and interactions with the social environment, including an individual's motivation, attitudes, perceptions, and values. Some process models used in gifted education focus on this domain. Krathwohl's Taxonomy of the Affective Domain is one such model. It contains five levels:

1. **Receiving**: Students show awareness of and attention to stimuli presented by teachers.
2. **Responding**: Students commit to discovery, seek out learning activities, and feel satisfaction from participating in the process.

3. **Valuing**: Students demonstrate decision-making about a value, their engagement with it, and their commitment to it. At this level, students may endeavor to convince others to commit to a value they have chosen.
4. **Organizing**: Students construct a belief system/value system, including attitudes, which they organize by the interrelationships of its components.
5. **Characterizing by a value or set**: Students have organized and internalized their value system and can apply it to many circumstances as a philosophy of life.

VIRTUAL LEARNING ENVIRONMENT

A virtual learning environment is a computer-based environment where learning materials can be delivered to students via the Internet. By computer information technology, teachers can differentiate their instruction for gifted and talented students. Enhancing school projects by using online databases, scanning images, and incorporating hyperlinks and video clips into them is generally more motivating to students with all levels of ability. VLEs are useful for developing cultural experiences in the visual, performing, and/or creative arts. Students can visit museums, art galleries, government agencies, various industries, and institutions using VLEs. Teachers can acquaint students with a variety of ideas through online exposure to famous and/or controversial individuals. In subjects incorporating research activities, VLEs can give opportunities to gifted students for more advanced learning. Because of the virtually limitless amounts of information accessible on the World-Wide Web and the way it is instantaneously transmitted, using VLEs is a method that students find motivational and exciting.

ENVIRONMENTAL CONSTRAINTS THAT STIFLE CREATIVITY

Researchers (e.g. Amabile, 1983a, 1996; Hennessey, 1996) have identified five environmental constraints that destroy internal motivation and creativity:

1. **Expected Reward** – students work to receive some externally bestowed reinforcement, rather than being internally motivated to be creative for its enjoyment.
2. **Expected Evaluation** – students limit creative exploration, working instead to score well on a test.
3. **Competition** – rather than exploring a subject creatively to see where it leads, students focus on besting other students by obtaining the highest scores. Such competition limits creativity, since students' pursuits are narrowed to traditional academic tasks and to achieving the best among typical student responses rather than anything original or different.
4. **Surveillance** – when students know they are being observed, they feel less free to engage in creative exploration or find divergent solutions. They are more likely to conform and less likely to be creative.
5. **Time Limits** – when students know they are being timed, they feel pressured. Finishing on time interferes with the additional learning and production afforded by creativity.

ENVIRONMENTAL INFLUENCES ON MOTIVATION

Although one might expect gifted students' exceptional abilities to support them in their classroom performance, research finds that gifted students are also very sensitive to influences they encounter in the classroom environment. While enthusiasm for learning and for subject content is a common characteristic of gifted children, teachers can dampen this enthusiasm when they insist that students conform to traditional classroom procedures and behaviors. Because gifted children often think and do things differently, trying to make them conform can ruin their motivation. They lose interest and get bored. In addition, many gifted children, especially younger ones, frequently do not know how to handle adults' high expectations, how to conduct successful interpersonal interactions, or how to set suitable goals for themselves. All of these factors in combination can contribute to academic underachievement. Underachievement actually is one of the most frequent problems among gifted students.

Social psychologists and other educational researchers have amassed a body of literature over 30 years regarding intrinsic motivation, creative performance, and how to promote these attributes in the classroom. Research increasingly has produced evidence that educational reforms to make our schools more conducive to internal motivation and creativity can benefit all students, not merely gifted students. Some steps that have been suggested (Hennessey, 2005) to accomplish such reforms include the following: Teachers need to make every effort to create atmospheres in their classrooms wherein students feel in control of their learning processes. Teachers and school administrators need to attain some distance and perspective in order to make objective, critical reviews of their schools' current reward systems and the types of incentives used. In addition, when external rewards are being used, educators need to help students achieve distance from the limitations these impose. Educators must help students develop proficiency in knowing their own weaknesses and strengths.

Environmental and Personal Influences on Implementation of Curricula

A number of factors in the environment and within the individual teacher can influence the way teachers implement curriculum units in reading and math. While curriculum units based on theoretical models adhere to principles of the applicable model, their implementation can vary as it is shaped by personal and environmental variables. For example, the grade level of students being taught will make a difference in the way that teachers implement curriculum. The school subject and department also will influence what elements are emphasized or minimized. Even the school building can make a difference in how teachers carry out their curricula. Variables at the school district level also affect teachers' understanding of a curriculum and how they implement it. Teachers' personal variables include their duration of classroom experience, their beliefs about learning and teaching, their particular approach to classroom management, and the grade level(s) and subject(s) they teach.

Defining Giftedness

Defining the Concept of Giftedness

Educators and advocates agree that no universal consensus exists regarding the definition of giftedness. The National Association for Gifted Children (NAGC) asserts that the concept of giftedness, like the concepts of intelligence and talent, is fluid in nature. Depending upon culture and other contexts, such concepts can be manifested and perceived differently. Moreover, the term "gifted" has a variety of meanings and subtleties within each meaning, even in school systems and within individual schools. In any given school, individual educators likely hold a range of different personal beliefs regarding this term. The NAGC finds that individuals showing "...aptitude (...exceptional ability to reason and learn) or competence (documented performance or achievement in top 10% or rarer) in one or more domains" (2008) are gifted. They define domains as structured activity areas within symbol systems such as language, math, or music, and/or within sensorimotor skill sets such as art, dance, or sports.

Differentiation Between Definitions of Giftedness and Talent

Canadian psychology professor/researcher Dr. Francoys Gagné (not to be confused with American educational psychologist Dr. Robert M. Gagné), in his "A Differentiated Model of Giftedness and Talent (DMGT)" (1985, updated 2000), clearly distinguishes giftedness from talent using the criteria of competence/ability/aptitude versus performance/skill/achievement. He finds that

"...superior natural abilities (called aptitudes or gifts), in at least one ability domain..." that constitute giftedness are "untrained and spontaneously expressed." He defines talent as "...superior mastery of systematically developed abilities (or skills) and knowledge in at least one field of human activity..." The differences are (1) that talent requires methodical development and learning, while giftedness needs no training; and (2) that gifts are in "ability domains" while talents are in "fields of human activity." He designates both as placing an individual in the top 10% of age peers in a given domain or field. His ability/aptitude domains include Intellectual, Creative, Socioaffective, and Sensorimotor.

Roles of America's Federal and State Governments in Defining Giftedness

While America has federal laws governing special education services for students with disabilities, these laws do not contain specific provisions that mandate each state to offer special education services for gifted and talented students. As a result, each American state can create its own definitions of giftedness and talent and its own programs for gifted and talented students. A state's definition will inform how it identifies such students; how it decides eligibility for services; and the kinds of educational programs it develops. Indiana, Nebraska, and Washington use the term "high ability student." Eighteen states use "gifted," while the other twenty-five states use "gifted and talented." Four states—Massachusetts, Minnesota, New Hampshire, and South Dakota—have no state definition of giftedness or talent. Giftedness and talent are defined by the state legislatures in 25 states, while the remaining 21 states have each mandated or authorized their state Boards of Education to define these terms.

Characteristics Necessary to Demonstrate Gifted Behavior

Dr. Joseph Renzulli and colleague Dr. Sally Reis, both from the University of Connecticut, created a Schoolwide Enrichment Model (SEM) (1976, 1977, 1985, 1997) for academically gifted and talented students and for all schools to develop students' strengths and talents. Renzulli focuses more, as do other behaviorists, on students' actions—i.e. gifted behavior—than on students' abilities/potentials. He proposes that three groups of characteristics must interact to produce gifted behavior: (1) above average abilities, either general or specific; (2) high levels of motivation; and (3) high levels of creativity. He identifies any child who succeeds either in having or in developing this combination of characteristics and applying it to any "potentially valuable" field of human activity as gifted or talented. Renzulli states in the SEM that gifted behaviors exist "in certain people (not all people), at certain times (not all the time), and under certain circumstances (not all circumstances)."

Domains of Ability or Aptitude

Domains of aptitude (identified by F. Gagné) are Intellectual, Creative, Socioaffective, Sensorimotor, and "others." A student who is gifted in the Intellectual domain might demonstrate this giftedness through superior learning, academic and/or otherwise, as evidenced by extent, breadth, depth of knowledge and/or speed and ease of learning; through superior achievement in school grades and standardized tests; and/or facility beyond grade level in reading or mathematics, etc. Gifts in the Creative domain might be demonstrated by advanced learning and understanding of principles in music, art, etc.; superior musical interpretation, performance, and/or composition; superior composition and execution in visual arts; originating mathematical/scientific formulas; or producing inventions. Socioaffective gifts might appear in a student's heightened ability in making friends, helping peers resolve conflicts, disarming bullies/hostility, and empathy for others. Sensorimotor gifts can emerge in athletic abilities or physical abilities for certain crafts and arts. "Others" includes extra-sensory perceptions such as precognition, clairvoyance, and communicating with spiritual realms.

Individual and Group Differences Among Gifted Children

Researchers have pointed out that such individual factors as genetic composition, life experiences, personality, and personal development, as well as the influences of families, interpersonal relationships, and educational experiences result in individual variations in the ways in which gifted children respond to and express their special abilities. While the research has acknowledged individual differences among gifted children for at least 50 years, less work has been done to identify various groups among the gifted.

Roeper (1982) theorized five types of gifted children based on their approaches for coping with and expressing their feelings. These types include: (1) the Perfectionist; (2) the Child/Adult; (3) the Winner of the Competition; (4) the Self-Critic; and (5) the Well-Integrated Child.

Betts and Neihart (1988) identified six "profiles" of gifted students based on their needs, feelings, and behaviors: (I) The Successful; (II) The Challenging; (III) The Underground; (IV) The Dropouts; (V) The Double-Labeled; and (VI) The Autonomous Learner.

Fluency, Flexibility, Originality, and Elaboration in Creativity

Fluency, flexibility, originality, and elaboration are four qualities considered by many experts as key components of creativity. The original version of Torrance's creativity scales measured these four qualities. Fluency refers to an individual's ability to generate a large number of concepts or of alternate solutions to a problem. Flexibility refers to an individual's ability to approach a problem from a variety of perspectives, therefore enabling the individual to come up with ideas and solutions to problems in a variety of categories. Originality refers to an individual's ability to generate unique or uncommon ideas. Fluency, flexibility, and originality are hallmarks of creative thinking. These qualities also are reflected in divergent thinking, a key characteristic of creativity involving generating many different possibilities rather than narrowing ideas down to one conclusion, as in convergent thinking. Elaboration in creative thinking involves the ability to add details to embellish one's ideas or results.

Convergent Thinking and Divergent Thinking

Convergent and divergent are opposites. In convergent thinking, different thoughts narrow/come together (converge) on one conclusion. An example is forensic detective work. If a suspect's fingerprints are found on the murder weapon, his DNA is found on the victim, and eyewitnesses place him at the scene of the crime at the time of death, then these pieces of evidence converge to show that suspect's guilt. Considering whether this suspect was framed or whether the evidence was circumstantial would involve some divergent thinking in which different thoughts proliferate/separate (diverge) into many possibilities. Some creativity tests ask test takers to generate as many different uses as possible for a brick, tin can, paper clip, etc. Listing all the things you can build with a brick is not considered an instance of divergent thinking, because building is one category. Holding papers/cloths/leaves together with paper clips is convergent; using paper clips as snowshoes for mice is divergent.

Theoretical Models of Gifted Instruction

By studying theories of gifted education, researchers study theoretical models to address areas that include: intelligence, identification, evaluation, alternative assessment, curriculum, programming, and professional development. Some common research questions among studies include these: Researchers want to know whether students from under-represented groups such as students with identified disabilities and abilities, students from economically disadvantaged populations, and Blacks and Latinos, will be identified in greater numbers by expanded criteria than by traditional criteria for identification. Researchers want to discover whether students identified as gifted by both traditional and non-traditional methods perform better on standardized achievement tests, extended standard-based assessments, and/or structured performance assessments when given the model-based curricula, than such students given their schools' general education curricula. Additionally, researchers want to know if students identified using traditional criteria outperform students identified by expanded criteria on standardized and performance-based measures.

Determination of Eligibility for Gifted Educational Services in Public Schools

A major difference between determining eligibility for special services to disabled students versus special services to gifted students is that federal laws, such as IDEA 2004 and Section 500 of the Americans with Disabilities Act, specifically provide for special services to students with disabilities. The IDEA contains 13 categories of specific disabilities that qualify for special education services. Each covered disability has criteria to meet for a positive diagnosis. Section 500 of the ADA has a general definition of disability, and any student whose condition interferes with education according to that definition is eligible for services. However, the federal laws do not address giftedness as they do disabilities. Each state Department of Education decides how to address giftedness. Most departments begin with their definition of "gifted" to create rules. Local school districts comply with state eligibility rules. Some districts assign each school a gifted eligibility team to administer eligibility procedures.

Chapter Quiz

Ready to see how well you retained what you just read? Scan the QR code to go directly to the chapter quiz interface for this study guide. If you're using a computer, simply visit the online resources page at **mometrix.com/resources719/nesincgifted** and click the Chapter Quizzes link.

Assessment, Curriculum, and Instruction

Research and Statistics in Gifted Education

Research Methodology

Popular conceptions of research methodologies characterize quantitative methods as using hard data, numbers, objective information, and findings that can be generalized to the larger populations represented by study samples; and qualitative methods as using "soft" data, words, subjective impressions, and findings more specific to the study's subjects but not generalizable to larger groups. Each method has its own strengths and weaknesses. Rather than choosing one or another method by personal preference, many researchers (cf. Neill, 2006), believe the nature of the research question should dictate the most applicable methodology. Neill also points out that qualitative and quantitative methods are not opposing paradigms; rather, each has its use, and the existence of mixed-methods studies proves they can be used together. Researchers are more likely to use qualitative methods earlier in a study to learn more comprehensively about a topic, using quantitative methods later on to seek precise answers to more specific questions.

For educators who want to determine the grade level at which a gifted student is reading, for example, quantitative methods are best for measurements that can be represented numerically and somewhat discretely. If a gifted child in a regular second-grade class is tested as reading at a sixth-grade level, this finding helps teachers select reading material for that child that is intellectually more suitable, yet still age-appropriate emotionally, socially, and experientially. Quantitative measures are used in standardized tests of IQ, knowledge, and academic achievement. Qualitative methods are more helpful for determining which content areas are an individual gifted student's favorites. Such methods also are useful for discovering a gifted student's particular learning style as well as the student's academic strengths and learning needs. Qualitative data collection methods such as interviews, observations, and self-reports can yield thorough profiles of each gifted student as a whole person, incorporating intellectual, psychological, emotional, social, and behavioral characteristics.

Qualitative Research

One type of qualitative research is the case study. This method seeks to gain insights into a phenomenon such as giftedness by studying one individual case of the phenomenon in great depth and detail. The case could be an individual gifted student, a specific class of gifted students, a school for gifted students, or a particular event involving gifted students. Phenomenology is another type of qualitative research. Phenomenology refers to the process wherein the researcher describes the structures of his or her experiences as they are apprehended by the researcher's consciousness, without using theories, assumptions taken from other fields/disciplines, or deductive reasoning to influence that description. Another kind of qualitative research is represented by ethnography. In ethnography, the researcher makes detailed field observations of sociocultural events or characteristics, typically within a particular community or population. This type of research can lend itself to studying groups of gifted students and gifted educational programs.

Methods for Collecting and Analyzing Data

Qualitative research is descriptive, experiential, and interpretive rather than statistical or numerical, as is quantitative research. Qualitative research demands rich, detailed descriptions to reveal the research process and to communicate implicit knowledge. As such, qualitative research uses three methods of data collection and analysis: observations, interviews, and self-reports. In observation, the researcher observes the nonverbal and verbal behaviors of study subjects (avoiding influencing the subjects' behavior insofar as is possible) and records descriptions of observed behaviors. Interviews are interactive with the subjects: the researchers first ask the participants to describe specified events or phenomena orally, and then the researcher records the participants' responses. Researchers also may ask participants to write down descriptions of their experiences; these are self-reports. Researchers analyze the initial data they collect to inform and direct further data collection. All these methods can be used to obtain data from gifted students, their parents, teachers, non-gifted peers, etc.

DISADVANTAGES AND ADVANTAGES

Because quantitative forms of research using statistical analysis are the predominant methods used in educational and psychological research as well as in other social sciences, critics of qualitative types of research often regard these methods as more subjective. However, as Myers (2002) states, "Since we maintain our humanity throughout the research process, it is largely impossible to escape the subjective experience…" This humanity includes intuitive realizations and "aha moments." Qualitative research demands extensive time and effort. Furthermore, because of the subjective nature of qualitative research results, these results obtained with samples cannot be generalized to larger populations in the same manner as can the results from statistical studies. However, Myers and other researchers (e.g. Neill, 2006) find qualitative methods to transcend those drawbacks with other redeeming qualities, such as in-depth descriptions with sufficient detail for readers to realize the idiosyncrasies of the individual research situation, and providing the researcher's perspective on that situation.

QUANTITATIVE RESEARCH

Qualitative methodologies tend to be inductive, i.e. they proceed from the specific to the general and generate new theories. Quantitative methods tend to be deductive, i.e. they proceed from the general to the specific and test existing theories. Qualitative methods incorporate more subjective aspects, while quantitative methods restrict findings to objective facts and figures. For example, if you wanted to find out which of two curricula is preferred by individual gifted students in a general classroom, you likely would use qualitative methodology and ask students which curricula they liked better—thus introducing a subjective element. If you wanted to find out which curriculum resulted in higher scores on standardized achievement tests taken by the gifted students in the general classroom, you likely would use quantitative methodology to determine differences in test scores and to discover whether a correlational or causal relationship (or both) exists between the curricula and the test scores.

One quantitative research design is descriptive, which seeks to obtain more information about a specific attribute or phenomenon within a field. Descriptive designs can be used to defend existing practices, identify problems, develop theories, develop opinions, or identify others' work in the same field. Descriptive designs do not look for causal relationships or manipulate variables. Experimental designs represent the paradigm for using the scientific method. As such, main elements of experimental designs are randomization, manipulation, and control. Experimenters randomly select participants, i.e. each has an equal chance of selection. Experimenters manipulate some variable(s) in the study, and some participants receive some kind of intervention/treatment. Experimenters also control some variables. A common form of experimental design is the before/after or pre-test/post-test design. Quasi-experimental designs are used when control is unfeasible and/or to protect validity when randomization, manipulation, or control is missing. Correlational/ex post facto designs look for relationships (NOT causality) without manipulating variables.

Qualitative and Quantitative Research of Giftedness and Gifted Education

Quantitative research methods use statistical procedures to measure or quantify phenomena in giftedness and gifted education, while qualitative research methods do not use such measures. Qualitative research is interpretive in nature. Implicit in the qualitative approach is the assumption that one must investigate giftedness as a whole in order to understand it. Quantitative research typically analyzes components of giftedness/gifted education. Proponents of qualitative research argue that such piecemeal examinations overlook important parts of the holistic appreciation they advocate. Rather than an absolute reality posited in quantitative research, qualitative methods propose multiple realities, which themselves vary across different times and places. Holistic understanding of the complexity, richness, and depth of giftedness/gifted education often reveals meanings that help researchers gain new insights. While all quantitative research is conducted according to an overall structure, qualitative research methods vary in their individual theoretical orientations relative to the specific topic or phenomenon under study.

One kind of qualitative research is grounded theory. In this approach, a theory is developed inductively (rather than deductively, which uses the reverse process of formulating a hypothesis and then collecting data to test it) from a body of data. While simpler quantitative statistical tests such as analysis of variance yield only the main effects of one variable upon another, grounded theory takes a case-oriented rather than a variable-oriented approach, assuming that variables interact in more complex ways and function as a whole within a case. Grounded theory also has a comparative orientation, based on John Stuart Mill's methods of similarities and differences, to uncover the causes. Another type of qualitative research is historical. The researcher collects data about past events, and objectively evaluates these events to test his/her hypotheses about their trends, causes, and/or effects, which can help to explain current related events and predict future related ones.

Mean, Median, and Mode

Statistically, **mean**, **median**, and **mode** are measures of central tendency, meaning they quantify trends wherein the majority of values fall near the center/middle. The mean/arithmetic mean is an average of all values obtained. For example, if in a group of 11 gifted students, four score 100% on a test, three score 96%, two score 94%, one scores 92%, and one scores 90%, the mean = 96%. If one student scored 70%, this would corrupt or skew the mean. The median represents the midpoint of all scores. In this example, with this distribution: 100+100+100+100+96+96+96+94+94+92+90, the midpoint is 96. Median does not inform the other values; if one student scored 70%, the median would not change. The mode is the most frequent value; in this example, 100. Mode does not reflect non-central, extreme values. If this example had four scores of 100% and four of 96%, it would have a bimodal distribution.

Bell Curve and Normal Distribution

A **bell curve**, aka a normal curve or Gaussian curve, graphically visualizes a normal distribution. Most values obtained fall near the median (middle/center), and fewer fall higher or lower, resulting in a curve with a bell shape – higher in the center, sloping downward toward the edges, and symmetrical, with equal numbers above and below the middle. With normal distributions, the mean (average of all values), median (the middle of all values) and mode (the value occurring most often) should be equal or nearly so. If a standardized IQ test is administered to a general education class including a few gifted students and the scores are plotted on a graph, the overall distribution of all scores is likely to be normal; however, the few gifted students' scores are likely NOT to be found near the median with most other student scores, but at one extremity, among the fewest and highest values.

When data from a group can be graphed as a bell curve, the data have a normal distribution. The largest number of scores will fall on or around the mean or average. In normal distributions, approximately 68% of the values fall somewhere within 1 standard deviation above or below the mean; about 95% of the values fall within 2 standard deviations above or below the mean; and about 99% fall within 3 standard deviations above or below the mean. A steep curve with most values near the mean shows a small standard deviation; flatter curves show larger standard deviations with more values spread away from the mean. If the average IQ score in a regular classroom is 100, with one gifted student having a score of 150, that score represents 1% of the population, as it is more than 3 standard deviations (typically 15 points with IQ tests, x 3 = 45) above 100.

Standard Deviation and Variance

In statistics, **standard deviation** shows how much the numbers in a given set vary within their distribution and how close to or spread away they are from the mean/average. Standard deviation is the square root of variance. **Variance** is calculated by squaring each variation from the mean and averaging the squares. Standard deviation indicates how much variation around the average is expected; greater variations are statistically significant. In IQ scores, the most common standard deviation is 15 points; variations of + 2 standard deviations, i.e. 30 points above or below the mean, are statistically significant. Thus, a student scoring 134 does not necessarily have a higher IQ than one scoring 130 on the same IQ test. However, a student scoring 160 compared to another scoring 130 on the same test shows a significant difference of 30 points, or two standard deviations. This difference is sometimes used for labeling levels or degrees of giftedness.

Review Video: Standard Deviation
Visit mometrix.com/academy and enter code: 419469

Reliability, Validity, Internal Validity, and External Validity

In scientific research, reliability refers to whether a measurement can be repeated with consistent results, regardless of the administrator. For example, a reliable standardized achievement test given to the same gifted student should yield similar scores each time, even when different teachers/personnel administer the assessment. Validity refers to whether an instrument or procedure measures what it claims to measure. For example, a standardized achievement test is not a valid instrument for measuring IQ; conversely, a standardized IQ test is not a valid instrument for measuring academic performance. Internal validity refers to whether the findings of an experimental study are attributable to the intervention or treatment used in the study and not to any other variables. For example, students could test better due to being taught a different curriculum or to having a different teacher. External validity refers to how much a study's findings can be generalized to populations beyond the study's sample.

Test Ceiling

A **test ceiling** means a test's upper limit, i.e. the highest score it is capable of yielding. Most intelligence and achievement tests used in schools cannot accurately measure gifted student levels if they exceed the limits the test can measure. For example, many IQ and achievement tests direct administrators to stop when the student gets three consecutive items wrong. The disadvantage: a student can get two wrong, one right, one wrong, etc., never meeting the stopping criterion of three wrong consecutively. The student does miss a number of items, yet never hits the test's ceiling. An additional disadvantage: the student never reaches the point when items become too difficult to answer, which represents the true ceiling. Therefore, that student's score may be accurate, a bit too low, or much too low, but this is impossible to determine. The only certainty is that the student's score is his/her lowest possible score.

Safeguards for Identifying, Assessing, and Finding Services for Gifted Students

While federal law provides that students with designated disabilities are guaranteed a free appropriate public education (FAPE), it does not address gifted students. Thus each individual state determines the procedural safeguards for gifted students' identification, assessment, and eligibility for services, just as each state also determines its definition of giftedness and gifted programs. Some examples of procedural safeguards include: requiring school districts to give parents prior written notice before identifying, evaluating, placing, changing, or providing a FAPE to their child; obtaining written parental informed consent before initially evaluating their child to determine eligibility and before initially providing services for gifted children; parents' right to examine their child's school records and participate in educational planning meetings for their child; parents' right to due process hearings to resolve disputes related to identification, evaluation, or placement of their child or provision of a FAPE; and many others.

Measuring Intelligence

Naglieri Nonverbal Ability Test®, 2nd Edition (NNAT®-2)

According to the test's author, the NNAT®-2 is "culturally neutral," thereby making it suitable for testing culturally diverse student populations. It is nonverbal, making it a good choice for ESL/ELL and nonverbal students. It can be used with ages 5 through 17 years and grades K through 12. It has seven levels corresponding to grades K; 1; 2; 3-4; 5-6; 7-9; and 10-12. It takes 30 minutes and is easy to administer. Students do not need good reading skills, math skills, well-developed vocabularies, or factual knowledge to respond to the test items. For identifying gifted/talented students whose socioeconomic backgrounds have limited their development of verbal skills and acquisition of information, this test is a useful instrument. Among tests of ability, the NNAT®-2 has the most recent norms, from 2008. Its administration and instructions are facilitated by pictures. Its graduated difficulty range allows identification of advanced as well as gifted and talented students.

Online Version

The NNAT®-2 offers both pencil-and-paper and online administration options. The online version saves teachers and administrators a great deal of time compared with the time required for the pencil-and-paper version. It also saves money, as schools do not have to pay for printed paper tests. Furthermore, this test saves time, space, money, and human energy by relieving schools of the need for storing, distributing, organizing, and shipping test booklets. It has minimal system requirements, enabling more users and computers to access it. The test's publisher, Pearson, uses a secure browser, protecting the safety of student information. Paperless, this test offers a more environmentally friendly option than does the traditional paper-and-pencil test. The online version yields instant results, allowing teachers to spend more time with students requiring additional, more focused instruction. Online reporting allows teachers to tailor data disaggregation and filtering to their district's needs. The online format is appealing and motivating to students, promoting test completion for fuller measurement. One item per screen helps students focus.

WISC-IV, 2003

Subscales

According to a number of educational researchers who have analyzed its content and results, the Wechsler Intelligence Scales for Children, 4th edition (WISC-IV) is a useful diagnostic tool for giftedness. They note that although it seldom gives scores above the 140s and has a score ceiling of 160, it also indicates ability beyond these limits. WISC-IV's ten required subtests include: Similarities, Vocabulary, Comprehension, Matrix Reasoning, Picture Concepts, Block Design, Letter-Number Sequencing, Symbol Search, Digit Span, and Coding. Optional supplementary subtests include: Arithmetic, Word Reasoning, Picture Completion, and Cancellation. The WISC-IV gives four Composite Scores from subscale groups: Verbal Comprehension, Perceptual Reasoning, Working Memory, and Processing Speed. Expert analyses find Verbal Comprehension (a composite of Similarities, Vocabulary, and Comprehension subscales) and Perceptual Reasoning (a composite of Matrix Reasoning, Picture Concepts, and Block Design subscales) very good indications of giftedness, as they assess abstract and visual thinking. Working Memory and Processing Speed are the subscales least correlated with giftedness.

Researchers at the Gifted Development Center recommend, often subscales required by the WISC-IV, using only the following six to identify giftedness: Vocabulary, Similarities, Comprehension, Matrix Reasoning, Picture Concepts, and Block Design. The first three subscales comprise the Verbal Comprehension Index; the last three subscales comprise the Perceptual Reasoning Index. The researchers find these two indices most relevant to measuring giftedness. The General Ability Index (GAI) is recommended by Flanagan and Kaufman (2004) as an additional measure, computed from the six subscales/two indices named. Dumont and Willis provided the Dumont-Willis Indices (DWI); the DWI-1 is similar to the GAI, computed from the Verbal Comprehension and Perceptual Reasoning indices. The DWI-2 averages Working Memory and Processing Speed. They advise only computing both DWI-1 and DWI-2 for gifted students if scores are similar. Advantages include greater efficiency, time- and cost-effectiveness, and accuracy without Working Memory and Processing Speed scores, which confound results for gifted students.

The Arithmetic subscale of the WISC-IV is found the strongest indicator of general intelligence (g); (Keith et al, 2004) and the strongest index of giftedness (Silverman, Gilman, and Falk, 2004). Vocabulary, Information, and Similarities, in that order, were identified by Keith et al as the next best indices of g. "Fair" measures of g were the Matrix Reasoning, Block Design, Word Reasoning, Comprehension, Letter-Number Sequencing, Picture Completion, Picture Concepts, Symbol Search, and Digit Span subscales, in that order. They found the Coding subscale "poor," and the Cancellation subscale the "poorest" measure of g. While Keith et al ranked Letter-Number Sequencing higher than Digit Span in their factor loading on g, Silverman and colleagues note that student responses to Digit Span are more predictable and interpretable, whereas Letter-Number Sequencing can seriously confuse and slow down some gifted students. They sometimes substitute Arithmetic for Letter-Number Sequencing with non-math-phobic students.

Using FSIQ Score

Researchers at the Gifted Development Center observe that since the Wechsler Intelligence Scales for Children, 4th edition (WISC-IV) includes more emphasis on processing skills than earlier versions, this confounds the identification of giftedness because gifted students tend to score higher on abstract thinking measures but lower on processing measures. This characteristic reflects the asynchronous development typical of gifted children. Averaging these measures lowers the Full-Scale IQ (FSIQ) score. The researchers find abstract thought a better index of intelligence than processing speed or working memory. They also point out that many educators mistakenly assume gifted students are naturally quicker processors. Some are, but many others are perfectionists and/or reflective thinkers, which slows down processing time. Also, many gifted students perform well on meaningful tasks, but not on tests of short-term memory containing material with no meaning for them. Flanagan and Kaufman (2004) recommend not reporting the FSIQ score if the difference between the highest and lowest Composite scores is 23 points or more.

Researchers compared Wechsler Intelligence Scale for Children (WISC-IV) scores of a gifted student group with scores of a control group from the WISC-IV's normative sample. The normative sample had little IQ variation—only 4 points between highest and lowest subscale scores. Working Memory and Processing Speed scores were not lower enough than Verbal Comprehension and Perceptual Reasoning scores to lower their Full-Scale IQ (FSIQ) averages. In contrast, the gifted sample averaged 27.4 points difference between highest and lowest subscale scores; the greatest variation was 69 points—over four standard deviations. Almost 60% of gifted students had 23-point differences between Verbal Comprehension and Processing Speed Composites. Gifted students scored 25 points higher than the norm group in Verbal Comprehension, but differed by below 2 points in Processing Speed. This trend implies gifted students are superior in verbal abstract reasoning but not processing; as a result, the WISC-IV's FSIQ should not be used for gifted identification.

Using the DWI-1 and Flanagan and Kaufman's GAI

At the Gifted Development Center, Silverman, Gilman, and Falk (2004) found that gifted students' WISC-IV Composite Scores in Verbal Comprehension and Perceptual Reasoning were typically high enough to qualify them for gifted educational services, but their scores on Working Memory and Processing Speed subscales were typically below qualifying levels. Additionally, since the Full-Scale IQ (FSIQ) score average incorporates these lower scores, they drag the average down, and also are individually not good indicators of giftedness. Consequently, the FSIQ identifies neither gifted strengths nor relative weaknesses. The Dumont-Willis Index-1 (DWI-1) computes a score combining the Verbal Comprehension and Perceptual Reasoning Composites using only six WISC-IV subscales, which these researchers find an excellent option for schools to identify gifted students. Flanagan and Kaufman's General Ability Index (GAI) averages the same two Composite scores; Harcourt Assessments (PsychCorp) trainers support this. Another solution involves basing identification on assessments of reasoning, delivering gifted services/accommodations, and adding accommodations for relative weaknesses.

WPPSI-III

The **Wechsler Preschool and Primary Scales of Intelligence** (WPPSI-III) is for ages 2.6 to 7.3 years. It includes 14 subscales: Block Design, Information, Matrix Reasoning, Vocabulary, Picture Concepts, Symbol Search, Word Reasoning, Coding, Comprehension, Picture Completion, Similarities, Receptive Vocabulary, Object Assembly, and Picture Naming. By various combinations of subtests, measures can be computed for verbal IQ, performance (fluid) IQ, processing speed quotient, general language composite, and full-scale IQ. Verbal IQ, performance IQ, and full-scale IQ are computed from core subtests. The WPPSI-III features short activities to accommodate attention spans of the youngest children in the age range. Activities are colorful and game-like, appealing to and interesting young children. Varied samples, second chances, and layered scoring enabling partial credit help children do their best. With children aged 6.0-7.3, the WISC-IV, for ages 6:0-16:11, is recommended for identifying giftedness, the WPPSI-III for general academic reasons. Because they are similar, these should not be administered successively to avoid practice effects.

Disadvantages

The WPPSI-III is a standardized instrument with proven validity and reliability. However, it does have some disadvantages. In testing the youngest children, the WPPSI-III's subscales reflect an expectation for IQ scores to jump significantly every 2-3 months. To qualify children for gifted services, experts advise scheduling testing optimally for ruling in/out such qualification. They also warn that a retest can take up to two years, so if a child has taken the WPPSI-III and needs re-evaluation sooner, they should use a different test. Another consideration about the WPPSI related to the youngest children is that IQ results are not as stable at earlier ages. Therefore, administering the WPPSI-III near the end of the kindergarten year is recommended to allow greater maturation and pre-academic/academic skills development. An exception is when earlier testing is indicated, e.g. a child displays signs of extreme giftedness at a very young age.

MDSD

The **Multi-Dimensional Screening Device** (MDSD) (Kranz, 1978) is based on the idea that intelligence is multidimensional in nature, not reflected by any one measurement. The author designed this instrument to facilitate better initial identification of giftedness among "the less accepted school population." A staff development program for teachers required to participate in the screening process is part of this instrument. In fact, the first step in its implementation is staff development. Other steps include rating students individually and forming a local screening committee to select individual students for screening. The MDSD's categories of giftedness are: visual arts ability; performing arts ability; demonstrated creative/productive thinking; discipline-specific academic ability; general intellectual ability of 1 in 100 or more; leadership characteristics, organization, and decision-making; psychomotor history and ability; history and use of spatial and abstract thought; wide difference between performance and general intellectual ability; and talent related to cultural heritage.

GRS

The **Gifted Rating Scales** (GRS) are norm-referenced, based on a multidimensional model of giftedness, and informed by current giftedness theories as well as federal and state definitions and guidelines. The GRS-P form, for ages 4 years to 6 years, 11 months, includes domains of intellect, academic readiness, motivation, creativity, and artistic talent. The GRS-S form, for ages 6:0 through 13:11 and grades 1-8, includes the same five domains as the GRS-P, except for an academic domain rather than academic readiness and the additional sixth domain of leadership. Administration takes 5-10 minutes. Relative strengths and specific gifted areas can be identified. Statistical validity studies positively correlate the GRS with the Wechsler Preschool and Primary Scales of Intelligence (WPPSI-III), Wechsler Intelligence Scales for Children (WISC-IV), and Wechsler Individual Achievement Test (WIAT-II). These standardized scales are designed to help qualify students for placement in gifted/talented programs. Domain-specific identification guidelines are included. Teacher form completion is easy and quick.

Measuring Creativity

Difficulty in Measuring Creativity

Although many researchers agree about common elements of creativity such as the originality, applicability, and value to society of creative work, they find it much more difficult to agree about which methods to use to make their definitions operational, and about which instruments of measurement to use. Creativity is such a complex quality that most measures cannot sum it up alone. Experts advise using multiple measures, but even this tactic can fail to achieve a comprehensive representation. Forty years ago, researchers found that the absence of any one unified and broadly accepted theory of creativity caused problems with understanding creativity's relationship to other abilities, the ramifications of different testing instruments and administrations, and operational definitions. Researchers find the same problems today. Meanwhile, so many creativity tests have been developed with varying degrees of psychometric credibility that difficulties in focusing on criteria have only increased.

Guilford Battery of Tests for Creative Thinking

Psychologist Joy Paul Guilford (1897-1987) formulated his Structure of the Intellect model in 1962, identifying 180 different kinds of thinking, many of them divergent. He found that the types of divergent thinking most pertinent to creativity were the abilities to generate new information from existing information and to transform knowledge or experience into new patterns and configurations. Based on this model, Guilford developed a battery of tests for creative thought. This battery's ten tests each measure divergence in producing the following:

- Names for Stories - semantic units
- What to Do with It - semantic categories
- Similar Meanings - semantic relationships
- Writing Sentences - semantic systems
- Kinds of People - semantic implications
- Make Something Out of It - figural units
- Different Letter Groups - figural categories
- Making Objects - figural systems
- Hidden Letters - figural transformations
- Adding Decorations - figural implications

The Guilford Battery contains ten tests of different types of divergent thinking, a cognitive process associated with creativity. Half of the tests are verbal measures, and half are nonverbal/figural measures. The verbal measures portion of the battery asks students to offer as many solutions as they can in the following categories: names for stories, verbal classes/categories, synonyms, sentence structures, verbal inferences about categories, figures, categories of figures, systems of figures, transformations of figures, and inferences about the figures. Each test is timed and scored for fluency by number of responses and for originality by statistical infrequency of responses. Not much validity research exists regarding these tests. Follow-up studies by Meeker (1978) found that students identified as creative by Guilford's tests in elementary school also had high creativity scores in high school. Michael and Bachelor (1990) found limited confirmation of Guilford's findings through conducting factor analyses.

Identifying and Predicting Aspects of Creativity

Researchers find that many instruments designed to measure creativity can identify the characteristics of fluency in ideation and divergence in thought, commonly accepted as components of creativity. However, they find that these measures do not predict future creative behaviors in a student identified as creative. Some scientists attribute this characteristic not to psychometrics but poor methodology—e.g. some studies were not continued long enough, data not having normal distributions did not receive adequate statistical procedures, or the criteria for outcomes in longitudinal studies were not well operationalized. Some researchers also note that while personal definitions and theories of creativity are not included, they should be. These researchers have proposed that individuals acting creatively are directed by their personal beliefs about the nature of creativity, how to nurture and measure creativity, and that these beliefs may differ substantially from the theories that experts in the study of creativity have developed.

Intelligence vs. Creativity Measures for Indicating Giftedness

Traditionally, standardized intelligence tests were used to determine whether a student was gifted. IQ scores above certain numbers (e.g. above 120, 130, etc.) qualified a student as gifted. However, IQ scores are an indication of intellectual giftedness rather than of creativity. Traditional standardized intelligence tests typically feature questions or problems with only one right answer. When taking this kind of intelligence test, the student must use convergent thinking to narrow down the possibilities to the correct one. In contrast, many measures of creativity test divergent thinking, which generates multiple ideas and possible responses. During the 1960s, J. P. Guilford and E. P. Torrance both developed standardized tests of divergent thinking that are still popular today. Because the traditional standardized intelligence tests require convergent thinking and little or no divergent thinking, and because divergent thinking is identified as a key characteristic of creativity, scientists have come to hypothesize that intelligence and creativity are separate constructs.

Torrance Tests of Creative Thinking

In order to operationalize creativity for research purposes, E.P. Torrance focused on its problem-solving aspect. His tests include nonverbal and verbal forms. "Thinking Creatively with Pictures" features three activity groups: namely, drawing lines elaborating on one shape, drawing lines finishing an incomplete picture, and drawing as many different pictures as possible using the same shape. "Thinking Creatively with Words" features six activities involving generating questions, alternate uses for things, and guesses. All these activities are timed and scored for fluency, flexibility, and originality. In addition, the nonverbal forms are scored for elaboration. Torrance's tests apply to grade levels from kindergarten through graduate school and are the most widely used creativity tests. They also have the most research supporting their validity worldwide, as they have been translated into many languages. While their longitudinal predictive validity is not high (.62 for males, .57 for females), Torrance indicates they match or exceed rates for intelligence measures.

Models of Instruction

General Goals of Good Gifted Education Programs

Good gifted education programs seek to facilitate the gifted student's mastery of basic reading and math skills at paces and depths suitable to the student's abilities; to foster abilities of reasoning and critical thinking; to create an environment conducive to divergent thought; to promote inquiry; to promote challenging attitudes relative to learning; to develop higher level skills in spoken and written language; to develop skills and methods for doing research; to cultivate students' comprehension of issues, problems, themes, and systems of knowledge that structure the extrinsic environment; to foster student development of self-understanding; to enable learning experiences outside of school that fit the individual student's educational needs; to provide or improve opportunities for future student development and planning; to develop creative thinking and problem-solving skills; to foster effective social skills for interpersonal interaction and coping; and to develop the student's skills of metacognition for self-direction and independent learning.

Reading Curriculum Units to Research Gifted Education

Three instructional models are: Carol Ann Tomlinson's Differentiation of Instruction model, which focuses on varying teaching methods; Sandra N. Kaplan's Depth and Complexity model, which focuses on attributes of deeper understanding and more complex knowledge; and Joseph S. Renzulli and Sally M. Reis' Schoolwide Enrichment Model (SEM), which uses educational enhancements that simultaneously benefit all students and address the special needs of gifted students. The National Research Center on Gifted and Talented (NRC/GT) has a longitudinal study basing curricula on these instructional models. By sampling school districts nationwide that implement gifted and talented programs, these studies' findings represent diverse populations, socioeconomic levels, and urban, suburban, and rural settings. These sample schools are selected from nominations by educators who develop curriculum models; state gifted education directors; and representatives from state and national organizations. Outcomes are measured by:

- state standards extended for advanced reading and math achievement
- performance-based measures of investigative and problem-solving skills

Research of Curricula Used in Gifted Education

Some research teams, including teams on a nationwide level, are interested in examining comparisons of different criteria for identifying gifted students, the effects of such criteria on assessment results and on under-represented populations, and comparisons of the effects of general education curricula and model-based curricula on gifted students. They ask research questions such as: When comparing standardized and performance-based measures of reading and math, whether the criteria for identifying giftedness interact in any ways with the type of instructional method (i.e. general education curricula vs. theoretical model-based curricula) delivered. They want to discover if students not identified as gifted are helped or harmed in achievement by model-based curricula, and if non-identified students in their non-treatment and treatment classes perform the same or differently on standardized reading and math achievement tests. These researchers are also interested in how teacher implementations of model-based curricula are affected by personal and environmental variables.

Experimental Research Design to Investigate Teaching Methods

Introduce two teaching methods, neither one normally used with the students. Divide students into two experimental groups and one control group by random sampling; i.e. they all have an equal chance of being in any group, preventing biased selection. One experimental group gets a lecture on a new topic followed by a question-and-answer/discussion session; the other gets a hands-on activity on the same topic followed by a question-and-answer/discussion session. The control group contains comparable students receiving no treatment; e.g., they receive the same teaching method normally used in your school, on the same topic as the experimental groups. The control group helps rule out the influences of extraneous/confounding variables on differing results between experimental groups, supporting the experimental treatments' differing influences. All groups receive the same pre-test and post-test on the topic. The teaching method is the independent variable, which was manipulated. The dependent variable is post-test score.

Collaborative Consultative Model of Education

The collaborative consultative model of education posits three component entities: the Consultant, the Mediator (the consultee), and the Target (usually the student). This model views the consultant and consultee as equal partners. They bring varying expertise to the collaboration and have mutual responsibility for identifying problems, planning strategies for interventions, and carrying out recommendations through combining their respective knowledge and skills. Disagreements between consultant and consultee are regarded as constructive opportunities to extract the most helpful information. This model assumes that consultant and consultee will both work directly with the target or student. Educational researchers have found in surveying teachers that while time shortages and scheduling issues can interfere with the success of collaborative consultative services, most teachers find them acceptable as alternatives to resource room services; furthermore, some teachers find them very desirable as alternatives. This model addresses special student needs, including giftedness as well as disabilities.

One of the benefits of using collaborative consultative models in gifted education involves the congruence of such models with recent trends in educational reform. Another benefit affords professional development for all those participating as they contribute and share their expertise. Collaboration also allows many more ideas to be produced than any individual could generate in isolation. In addition, consultative methods make the most of the opportunity for the adult participants to use their individual differences toward achieving constructive goals. Another advantage of the collaborative consultative model is that it is amenable to the school administrator's taking the role of facilitator. Moreover, using collaboration and consultation between teachers, parents, and others from outside of the school affords the benefit of parents' satisfaction through their direct involvement, contributions, learning from others, and seeing their children's knowledge and social skills improve.

Potential Issues to Consider

While there are many definite advantages for using the collaborative consultative model to meet students' special needs, including those of gifted students, there are also a few potential issues to consider. First, teachers, parents, and other participants from outside the school may have little or no training collaboration, unless the school institutes such training. If the school does so, another consideration is the time, expense, and human energy involved in providing training. Another very real consideration is that any or all of the potential collaborators may not have sufficient time to interact with one another. In addition, some educators prefer working with students, and would rather not work with other adults, especially if they lack relevant experiences. Moreover, implementation of collaborative consultative methods requires firm support from the school administrator. Finally, while collaborative consultation is effective, visible results take time, so patience is needed.

Curriculum Development

Selecting Curriculum Materials

Curriculum Design Features to Consider

Gifted students need greater breadth and depth of knowledge and processes than are afforded by school textbooks. When selecting curriculum materials for gifted students, teachers should consider the following curriculum design features:

1. The purpose and rationale of the curriculum design should be clear.
2. Selected materials should address objectives for each lesson.
3. Materials should include appropriate, stimulating, and challenging activities for gifted students.
4. Materials should include instructional strategies suitable for gifted students that teachers can use.
5. The materials should include valid and reliable assessment procedures teachers can use to assess the effectiveness of instruction using those materials.
6. References for additional materials and resources should be provided.
7. Ideas for extension of the curriculum, activities, and materials should be given.
8. Technology should be incorporated in the materials. Today many materials are available on websites, which are most likely to adhere to the preceding guidelines.

Special Needs of Gifted Students to Consider

When teaching gifted students, teachers will find that while these students often master textbook content easily, they also demand broader and more in-depth knowledge of a subject than textbooks afford. As they seek additional curriculum materials for gifted students, teachers should consider their special needs. Specifically, students with higher levels of ability need to be presented with more sophisticated ideas than others and more challenging activities than those usually offered in general education classrooms. Choosing activities that can be individually tailored to any specific student will give teachers more options for optimally meeting individual gifted students' educational requirements. Curriculum materials chosen for gifted students should require more use of higher-order cognitive skills than for other students. Teachers should select materials that incorporate relevant major themes, contain high levels of abstraction, allow student exploration according to their interests, and enable them to create products.

Aspects Within Areas of Content and Process to Consider

As Renzulli (2000) defines them, content equals authentic knowledge and process equals teaching techniques. Within the area of content, when selecting curriculum materials, teachers should consider: the organization of the content, the depth in which the content covers its subject, the accuracy of the content, and the degree to which the content moves from concrete topics to abstract concepts. Within the area of process, teachers should consider: opportunities to use/learn problem-solving skills, opportunities to use/develop communication skills, activities that exercise skills of reasoning, relevant connections among parts of the subject area, providing multiple representations of concepts to be taught, opportunities for students to verify their speculations when indicated, opportunities for students to work both individually and in groups, and opportunities for students to use divergent thinking in responding to a lesson, exercise, or activity.

Common Difficulties in Writing Curricula for Gifted Students

Curriculum writing can be quite difficult and time-consuming. Difficulties include trying to comply with state curriculum guidelines, feeling pressured to include activities currently popular in the educational community, trying to achieve a balance between content (information/knowledge) and process (teaching/learning), and juggling all these demands. Moreover, the results of these efforts often do not further education or impart meaning to it. Seeking to improve curriculum writing and believing that teachers need time and tools to create meaningful teaching units based on desired outcomes named in a curriculum guide, Renzulli et al (2000) of the University of Connecticut's National Research Center on the Gifted and Talented produced the Multiple Menu Model of curriculum development. Differentiating this model from more traditional approaches are its stronger emphases on encouraging original inquiry by students, on examining the organization and interrelatedness of knowledge, and on arriving at a balance between content and process.

Multiple Menu Model of Curriculum Development

While its authors originally conceived of the Multiple Menu Model of curriculum development as a means for differentiating instruction to address the needs of gifted and talented students, Renzulli remarks that teachers can also use it to promote original inquiry and creativity in students at all levels. This model uses the term "menu" to indicate that teachers are able to choose from among many options within each menu. The six component menus are: the Knowledge Menu, addressing the specific subject areas; the Instructional Objectives and Student Activities Menu, Instructional Strategies Menu, Instructional Sequences Menu, and Artistic Modification Menu, all of which address various aspects of pedagogy, i.e. instructional techniques; and the Instructional Products Menu, consisting of the interrelated Concrete Products and Abstract Products Menus, which address the kinds of products the student may create based on the knowledge acquired, and how students as primary inquirers construct this knowledge.

Components of Curriculum Writing

In curriculum writing, the stated instructional objectives and the specified student activities are concerned with the processes students use in constructing knowledge (for example, analysis, synthesis, and application). These processes are both cognitive and affective in nature. When curriculum writers include both variety and balance among these processes in the activities they design, they enable gifted students to practice using a fuller range of the encoding, decoding, and recoding processes involved in learning new ideas, principles, and information. Instructional strategies represent another area wherein curriculum writers should provide variety. Teachers can use class discussions, student dramatizations of topics, and independent study projects, for example, affording gifted students different ways to learn and utilizing broader ranges of abilities and learning styles. The Multiple Menu Model of curriculum development's Instructional Sequences

Menu is a rubric teachers can use with any teaching technique/strategy to help them present lessons in the most effective order.

Traditional vs. Progressive Models of Curriculum Development

In developing curricula, teachers must select topics that illustrate a subject's fundamental principles and characteristic concepts. Both traditional models of curriculum development and more progressive ones, such as the National Research Center on the Gifted and Talented's Multiple Menu Model of curriculum development (Renzulli et al, 2000) take into account the students' ages, maturity levels, prior knowledge, and levels of experience. These methods differ in that traditional instructional models typically require teachers to cover a whole textbook with their classes by the end of the term or year; however, the Multiple Menu Model asks teachers instead to narrow down, from all potential texts, chapters, or other sources of information, those few that best represent the concepts and principles of the subject area. This model's authors recommend using a three-phase approach to choosing content: intensive group coverage, extensive group coverage, and intensive individual or small group coverage.

Curriculum Units with Differentions for Academically Diverse Students

Some research groups interested in determining which methods of identification, testing, curriculum, and instruction are most effective for gifted students develop curriculum units to use in their studies. They then compare test scores of students taught using different curricula. Some researcher-developed curriculum units feature differentiated instruction in order to tailor teaching to the individual needs of "academically diverse students." These units place emphasis on problem-solving skills, conceptual thinking, and "real-world disciplinary inquiry" (e.g. using the scientific method to investigate subjects in various fields applied to real life). Curriculum units also function as tools for assessing individual students' learning needs. In addition, they help students attain progressively higher levels of expertise. Researchers believe that their work will foster both fairness and achievement in school systems nationwide and will nurture student gifts by focusing on gifted identification, model-based math and reading curriculum units, and traditional and performance-based assessments.

Program Evaluation

Evaluation plans are crucial elements in the provision of services and programs for gifted students. Formative evaluations are made during the implementation of a program for educators to see that their programs accomplish their intended goals. Summative evaluations are made following full program implementation to assess the extent to which the program attains its goals and objectives. To enable both formative and summative assessment of a gifted education program, the element of evaluation should be built into the original program plan. A common error made in some programs involves waiting to plan the evaluation until the program has been in use for a year or two. Educators may wait this period in order to ensure their program is fully implemented prior to assessment, but planning should be done initially to allow both formative and summative assessments and to assure that the services offered can be evaluated in both these ways.

Review Video: Formative and Summative Assessments
Visit mometrix.com/academy and enter code: 804991

Guidelines

Some of the guidelines given by the National Research Center on the Gifted and Talented for program evaluation involve the following. In program development, educators should incorporate evaluation procedures into the earliest planning stages. They should develop a specific plan for how they will use their evaluation results. They should use multiple sources such as students, teachers, parents, administrators, and school board members, for information to develop clear program goals and descriptions. They should allow enough time and funds for evaluations. They must also prepare/train their school staff to conduct assessments and analyze the results. Educators should identify clearly all parties needing, and/or interested in, evaluation findings, and engage them in the process of evaluation. Because the results of gifted education programs are complex, educators must find or create appropriate assessment instruments. Data collection methods should reflect the organization and objectives of gifted programs, e.g. portfolio assessments, out-of-level testing, product ratings with inter-rater reliability, etc. Educators should report evaluation findings timely to all those involved, including follow-up recommendations.

General Purpose Regarding the Relationship of Program Planning and Implementation

An important reason to evaluate gifted programs is to ascertain whether the school's/educators' implementation of their program is congruent with their initial program plans and/or to what degree. To determine this, they can examine: identification of gifted/talented students, services provided to them, data available showing how effective their screening/identification systems are, criteria for screening and identification to prevent overlooking special populations, available curriculum options for meeting student academic needs, data available showing how effective the curriculum is, whether/how acceleration is used, how effective their acceleration options are, how program goals and objectives are implemented, how these are connected to district philosophy and mission statements, impacts of the program on the regular education program(s), opportunities available for advanced training to all teachers, how formal and informal feedback is used for program quality improvement, student educational outcomes, curriculum approach implementation at different grade levels, and evidence showing the value of current service delivery models.

Differentiated Instruction

Principles Related to High Quality of Gifted Classroom Instruction

1. To be of sufficiently high quality, classroom instruction for gifted students should accomplish the following:
2. It should adapt, modify, or differentiate the grade-level curriculum and teaching practices to address the special educational needs of gifted students;
3. It should give gifted students ways in which they can show their proficiency in the required curriculum, and thereafter give them educational opportunities that present them with appropriate challenges;
4. It should be made up of curriculum options, resource materials, and teaching approaches that are differentiated and reside along a continuum;
5. It should allow for flexibility in educational arrangements for gifted students, to include such options as the use of compacted material for accelerating or advanced students; subject and/or whole-grade acceleration; independent study agreements and research projects; and
6. It should be designed with the goal of increasing the depth and breadth of knowledge that learners with high ability acquire.

Types of Differentiated Instruction

With acceleration, the master educational standard has fewer tasks assigned. Students are assessed prior to instruction. Acceleration clusters are determined by higher-order cognitive skills. With complexity, multiple higher-level thinking skills are used. Use of multiple resources is required.

More variables are added to study. With depth, students study multiple applications of a concept they have learned. They might conduct original research into subjects they study, or they may develop an original product. With challenge, students make use of advanced resource materials or work with more sophisticated content in subjects they study. They can apply their learning across different academic disciplines. Furthermore, they are expected to be able to explain their process of reasoning to others. With creativity, students might design and/or build a model based upon principles and/or criteria they have learned. Alternatives for various academic tasks, products, and assessments are made available. Oral and written communication to the real-world audience is emphasized.

Acceleration

Positive Effects and Forms of Acceleration

Although acceleration must be decided for each individual student, research finds many benefits of acceleration for gifted students. Those students who exhibit advancement for their age far beyond their grade can even develop poor study habits, behavioral problems, become bored and daydream in school, or avoid attending school if they are forced to stay with their age-grade level. Especially in math, science, and English, some gifted students are more gifted than in other subjects. Such students may attend class with higher grades in their most gifted subject(s), but stay with their age's grade level for other subjects. Another form of acceleration is tutoring, either individually or in small groups. Some high school students gifted in math, for example, might be in their school for all other subjects, but a group of them would attend advanced math classes with a local university's math professor a couple of days each week.

Addressing Concern That Acceleration Can Hurt Students Academically

For those who worry that accelerating a gifted student will cause academic harm, they should be reassured that the majority of research shows that accelerated students get higher grades than gifted children who are not accelerated. Also, their grades compare positively with grades of the older students in the class. Researchers find that gifted students who accelerate report greater enthusiasm for and an interest in school as well. Another academic concern is that students who skip grades in a subject or skip whole grades will have gaps in their knowledge. This does occur, but less often than people think, because regular curricula contain so much redundancy. Gaps also do not present substantial problems for gifted children as they learn more quickly and thoroughly and can catch up more easily. Accelerating gifted students should not be penalized for unfamiliarity with any missed material, but should be allowed to cover it.

Addressing Concerns Regarding Effects of Acceleration on Child's Wellbeing

The most common worry of parents and educators about accelerating a gifted student to a higher grade is the impact it might have on the student's emotional and social development and wellbeing. They fear that while the child's intellectual development is undoubtedly at the higher grade level, his or her social and emotional development might lack the same levels of advancement. They worry about the child interacting with older children. However, researchers find children who are emotionally well-adjusted and socially comfortable before acceleration will report after accelerating that they have two circles of friendships: one from their newer class of older students, and another from their previous age-level class and/or other children their age, with whom they maintain friendships. While gifted children who have trouble making friends may experience difficulty in older classes, many gifted students prefer friendships with older children, finding more in common with them due to their advanced development in many areas.

Attitudes of Educators Toward Academic Acceleration

The majority of research studies show that academic acceleration for gifted students affords them many benefits in both academic and social domains. However, despite these positive findings, most educators are reluctant to adopt or even consider acceleration as an option for fear that acceleration will result in problems in the students' emotional and social development. In contrast, educators who specialize in the education of the gifted student, and teachers and parents who have had personal experience with the acceleration of gifted students tend to have much more positive attitudes about accelerating and are more willing to select this option when a gifted student's profile indicates it. Pushing a student to accelerate can cause problems, as can accelerating an emotionally immature student or one continually getting negative responses from peers or educators. Having a small support group of similarly accelerated students eases the acceleration process.

Students' Perception of Their Status Relative to the Class or Group

Many gifted students in regular classes at their age level perceive that they are the smartest student in their class. When they are far enough beyond grade level to accelerate, the student often finds after acceleration that they are not the smartest in the group anymore. This change in status can require considerable adjustment, especially for students who have become accustomed to everything being too easy for them. In this situation, parents and teachers should not pressure students trying to adjust to unfamiliar circumstances. They should give them emotional support rather than pushing too much too soon for academic performance. They should also make clear to the student that a choice to accelerate can always be reversed if it seems unsuitable emotionally, socially, and/or academically for them. Adults should also help gifted students understand that reversing acceleration does not represent a failure on the part of the student.

Criteria and Process

If a student's scores on standardized achievement tests are many grades above age/grade level, or are so high that they are off the tests' charts, the student is a candidate for acceleration. If a formerly enthusiastic student begins exhibiting boredom and/or behavioral problems not due to other factors, this is another criterion. The student, parents, and school personnel ideally should all agree that accelerating would benefit the student. Early in the process, the IEP team and school psychologist should be involved. Classroom teachers should be consulted, as well as others who know the student best, e.g. the school's gifted and talented coordinator, principal, and/or guidance counselor. The school psychologist should evaluate the student relative to acceleration. Parents can consult state Department of Education coordinators of gifted education. Support from involved teachers and coordination and continuity from school officials is important. Acceleration decisions are usually made by the principal and/or IEP team/committee.

Considerations Regarding Acceleration in Only One Subject

On one hand, many educators are more receptive to accelerating a gifted student in one subject because the student learns the remaining majority of subjects with age-level classmates. These educators often feel this type of acceleration can avoid social and/or emotional problems for the student. On the other hand, certain factors must be considered when a gifted student is accelerating in only one subject. One is continuity. If educators do not carefully coordinate the student's programming, the student could learn accelerated materials one year, only to repeat these the following year. Teachers and curriculum specialists can help by defining what is taught in each grade for each subject. Another consideration is that elementary school students might need to attend a junior high/middle school, junior high/middle school students a high school, and high school students a college course, to accelerate in one subject. Transportation can present worse problems than academic or social concerns.

Examples of Testing Policy

In some districts, rules differ for a student's first and subsequent years of subject acceleration. In the first year, if a test exists at the accelerated-subject grade level, testing is required for students whose overall/age-level grade is third-grade or higher; whose accelerated-subject grade-level is fourth-grade or higher; and the accelerated subject is reading or math. Testing is more likely optional if the accelerated subject is science, social studies, or writing; and if the student's overall level is second-grade or lower and the accelerated subject is third-grade or higher. If no test exists at the accelerated grade level and one exists at the student's overall grade level, testing may be optional. In subsequent years of acceleration, if a test exists at the accelerated grade level, testing is usually required. If no test exists at the accelerated-subject grade level and one exists at the student's overall grade level, districts may prohibit testing.

Examples of Provisions in Acceleration Plan to Skip Grades

If the school has determined a gifted first-grader can do third-grade work, the written whole-grade acceleration plan should include such provisions as these: The third-grade teacher should report and discuss any signs of academic and/or emotional stress in the student to the school staff person assigned to monitor plan implementation. The monitor should check with the third-grade teacher weekly on student progress. A gifted intervention specialist and/or third-grade teacher should obtain/develop curricula and assessments that compact only the second-grade standard the student has never experienced to make up anything he will miss by skipping second grade. He will complete these standards/skills during free time at school and/or home with his parents helping him as needed to master them. Upon successful transition, he remains in the accelerated grade until additional acceleration options are indicated. By middle school, the student's program should be reviewed to see if dual-enrollment options might benefit him.

Curriculum Compacting

Compacting is a way to streamline regular curricula for gifted students who learn faster. Compacting also can fill instruction gaps for students accelerating to higher grades and for those using the time saved by compacting to pursue enrichment activities. Sequential steps in the curriculum compacting process include: identifying pertinent learning objectives for the subject or grade level; locating or creating pre-test instruments for these objectives; identifying student candidates for compacting; pre-testing these candidates to ascertain their learning levels of the identified objectives; get rid of teaching, drilling, and/or practicing time for students who have already mastered the objectives; for objectives students have not mastered, streamline their instruction for the gifted students' faster rates of mastery; offer options of enrichment or acceleration for students who have exhausted the regular curriculum; and maintain records of the entire process and of instruction options available for students participating in compacted curricula.

Virtual Learning

Thematic Units

Teachers use thematic units as a way of incorporating complex, abstract concepts into the curriculum. Thematic units are organized around a particular theme or topic. This organization provides a focus for learning abstract ideas and appeals to areas of student interest. One way that a teacher can employ both thematic units and information technology is to select the content for an integrated thematic unit and then develop a virtual learning environment (VLE) for teaching it. Today there are many Internet websites containing teacher resources, including those for thematic units. For example, the site A-Z Teacher Stuff offers thematic units on topics such as magnets, oceans, Martin Luther King Jr., Harry Potter, and many other themes, including lesson plans for teachers, class activities, etc. The website of the C.O.O.R. Intermediate School District in Michigan provides additional examples of integrated thematic units.

Websites

Once teachers have selected the content for a lesson or unit they want to deliver in a virtual (computer) environment, they can take advantage of such websites as The Educator's Reference Desk, where they can find lesson plans for any grade level or school subject. In addition to getting help creating and delivering lesson plans, teachers can incorporate hyperlinks from these sites in the virtual learning environments they create for students. Students can follow these links to access virtual lessons providing content enriching the teacher's basic lesson or unit. In addition to lesson plans, teachers can find online student projects and activities, instructional materials, and virtual "field" trips. In virtual trips, students can visit otherwise inaccessible nations, museums, galleries, institutions, organizations, and corporations all over the world. Education World, Eduscapes' Digital and Virtual Museums, and the Museum of Science and Industry are examples of websites offering virtual museum tours.

Fostering Creative Performance of Gifted Students

Educational researchers find that modifying curriculum, using alternative materials, encouraging brainstorming, and teaching strategies for thinking "outside the box" are all necessary, these strategies alone are not sufficient. Teachers, students, parents, and administrators need to collaborate to affect changes in the entire climate of our schools at every level, as well as in the environments of individual classrooms. Some gifted education programs developed in recent decades can be individualized to meet the needs and interests of each specific student. Instead of identifying only students who excel in traditional school subjects, programs taking this alternate approach acknowledge student talents and strengths across a broader range of dimensions. Researchers find the motivation of gifted/talented students is especially susceptible to classroom environmental influences, even more so among the culturally diverse and/or economically deprived. Experts call for educational reform that does not require money so much as commitment to change and willingness to collaborate to make school environments nurture internal motivation and creativity.

Self-Contained Classes

The primary value of self-contained classes for gifted students is the academic rigor possible when all students in a class are at similar intellectual levels. The general classroom teacher will not have to differentiate instruction specifically for gifted students by offering more in-depth study of subject content, materials at higher grade levels for acceleration, compacted curriculum, alternative activities, etc., if no gifted students are present. However, one inherent pitfall is that some general education teachers, relieved of the necessity to differentiate instruction for gifted students, may fail to differentiate instruction for their existing students. Such failure reflects that these teachers do not understand (or observe) that differentiation is intended to customize teaching for the needs of every individual student, not just every individual gifted student. Varying difficulty levels, paces, prior knowledge, interests, and learning styles also require differentiation among non-gifted students.

Ability Grouping

Ability grouping should not be equated or confused with cluster grouping, heterogeneous grouping, or tracking. Ability grouping involves dividing the students within one classroom and grouping them according to their ability levels, which can differ broadly within one general education classroom. This grouping by ability is not rigid but fluid, and it can be changed as needed at any time. For example, a student might be placed into a high ability group for math and participate in a group of middle ability for reading. If that student's reading improves, the student could move into the high ability group for reading. Conversely, if a student develops problems in an individual subject, s/he can move into a lower ability group to address his or her academic needs best. The flexibility of ability grouping allows gifted students more options to receive the most appropriate instruction and to adjust for needs that change over time.

INDEPENDENT STUDY

Independent study gives gifted students encouragement and preparation for initiating, implementing, and successfully completing their own scholastic activities in their areas of interest. As such, it provides them with a structural context for making choices and decisions about what and how they learn. It also teaches them how to communicate what they have learned. When gifted students have independent study projects, these also benefit teachers by helping them to fulfill the roles of facilitating students' progress, listening to students, and clarifying ideas and objectives. Many gifted students underachieve; this can be related to lack of interest in assigned topics, frustration at not being able to study subjects in more depth, boredom with the mainstream class pace and/or types of assignments. Independent study of a topic a student is passionate about can alleviate these factors and increase task commitment. Planning and executing projects stimulates inquiry, builds motivation and self-discipline, improves study skills and habits, and promotes positive attitudes and self-concepts.

Teachers should ensure that any independent study program for a gifted student will meet their individual instructional needs as well as their particular personal interests. In self-selected studies, the gifted student chooses a topic s/he wants to study that will meet these needs and interests. In related studies or "spin-off" studies, the gifted student is acquainted with a subject in the usual teacher-directed class lessons, and then selects a topic within that subject that particularly interests her/him to investigate in more depth and specificity through an independent study project. In curricular studies, the teacher will have made a list of topics based on the subject content for the whole class to study. Gifted students can select one topic from this teacher-made list and conduct an independent study of it. Curricular topics may be studied independently by individual gifted students; or they may also collaborate on these in small group settings.

PURPOSES AND POSITIVE OUTCOMES

Independent study projects allow gifted students to explore a variety of subjects and areas in which they are interested. Planning, developing, and carrying out an independent study project can serve as the student's introduction to the methods used to organize, research, and present the results obtained to others. With guidance and support from teachers, independent study can encourage gifted students to develop individual qualities of initiative as well as their intellectual and creative abilities. Independent study activities stimulate gifted students' skills in critical thinking, logical reasoning, and continuity in focus. By working on independent study projects, gifted students develop a sense of personal responsibility for pursuing their goals. In addition, when they pursue and successfully attain their goals through independent study, gifted students attain a sense of satisfaction and achievement.

PROCESS

The gifted student chooses a topic of special interest and reads extensively about it, developing a knowledge base. With a general grasp of the topic and knowing what s/he wants to discover, the student asks questions to answer. Students utilize and develop higher-order cognitive skills as they learn to identify and use resources in the forms of places and persons, establish goals and objectives, develop and carry out plans to accomplish these, make self-evaluations of their own work, and identify avenues whereby they can communicate their discoveries, conclusions, and knowledge. Students can use fact cards to record information they collect on the topic. By analyzing the information they gather, students can develop questions reflecting a problem to solve; for example, the student can ask what methods s/he could use to get a specific species of wildlife off the endangered list. This process demands student analysis of information, creation of novel and unusual plans, and expression of their opinions. It also involves them in authentic research, products, and audiences.

Categories of Research

One category of research that gifted students can use for independent study is historical research, which endeavors to reconstruct the past objectively. Some sources for gathering information include old newspapers, written records, oral history, baby books, folk songs, poems, and stories. Students could study the history of the school, the community; some aspect of the US Constitution or Bill of Rights, etc. Another category is developmental research, which examines trends, change, continuity, sequences, and patterns. Developmental psychology and human growth and development are examples of developmental research areas. Students can investigate such topics as human biological development, cognitive development in children, personality development over the lifespan, etc. Another category is descriptive research, which is quantitative. Numerical statistics are depicted using graphs, charts, and tables. Students can conduct opinion or fact-finding surveys, or observational or interview studies.

In experimental research, the researcher seeks to discover whether one variable causes changes in another variable. Statistical methods of multivariate analysis can also be applied to study the effects of and on multiple variables within the same experiment or set of experiments. For example, gifted students use independent study projects to research whether a plant responds differentially to various stimuli or which combinations of substances will produce a certain chemical reaction. Experimental studies involving human subjects include such research questions as whether the amount of sleep the night before an exam affects student test performance, whether one school curriculum is more conducive to student motivation than another, or whether internal or external rewards have greater positive influences on student performance. Experimenters establish a treatment group receiving the intervention being tested, and a control group receiving no treatment to control for extraneous variables. By manipulating the independent variable being tested, researchers can see if it affects the selected dependent variable(s).

Correlational research is a type of quantitative research method that compares quantitative data obtained to discover whether a relationship exists between two or more variables. Specifically, it seeks to find whether one variable affects another variable and how. A positive correlation means that as one variable increases or decreases in amount or number, so does the other variable. A negative or inverse correlation means that as one variable increases, the other decreases, and vice versa. Statistics also show the strength of the correlation, or the degree of relationship. Some examples include whether the seasons affect school attendance, whether an individual's head size and foot size are related, or whether school attendance affects achievement test scores. Correlations do not imply causations: two variables may increase or decrease together or oppositely, but this does not mean that either variable causes the other. To determine causation, experimental research must be used.

Enhancing Instruction Via Online Educational Games

Gifted and talented students tend to enjoy activities that they find stimulating and challenging. One way in which teachers can enhance their education is by offering students online educational games they can play wherein they apply the concepts they have learned in a lesson or unit. Online gaming has become so popular that it is a good choice for gifted students to extend and apply their knowledge and skills while having fun. For example, the About.com website has action games that address the content of various school subject areas. The Education World website's Online Game Archives has such games for students as Wacky Wordplay and Math Bingo. For teachers to evaluate student progress toward learning objectives they have developed for a unit, and evaluate the objectives themselves, they can find free assessment rubrics at websites like RubiStar. Teachers can customize RubiStar's rubric templates, including for assessment of virtual learning lessons/units.

Issue of Homework

Gifted children commonly start out in regular classes. Even after identification as gifted, the majority of gifted students are in regular classes most of the time with a small portion in supplementary gifted services like pull-out programs. They can end up with twice the homework: regular class assignments, plus gifted education assignments. Even students receiving accommodations in regular classrooms can receive double homework unless specific accommodations substitute gifted for regular homework. Having doubled work feels punishing, making students resent being identified as gifted. The excess can mean not doing all homework, damaging grades. Solutions include assigning more advanced work taking the same time but applying lesson knowledge instead of repeating it, which gifted students often do not need. For example, a student could do ten advanced math problems instead of 100 rote problems. Instead of writing simple sentences including spelling words, a student could write a poem or short story using them.

Individualized Education Programs

IEP for Gifted Student in General Education Classroom Setting

Gifted children do not have gifts only part of the time; they are the same individuals all the time. As a result, their educational needs also are constant. Such rationale also extends for addressing those needs throughout the school day/year. Each school district has the responsibility not only to place a gifted student in a gifted program, but also to make whatever accommodations and modifications in the regular education setting, curriculum, and instructional methods are necessary and specified in the gifted IEP (GIEP) to meet the student's individual educational needs. Parents should know that if district administrators tell them a gifted pull-out program is the "only" accommodation available, this constitutes a severe misrepresentation of the district's responsibilities and the student's and parents' rights. Parents should inform administrators they are aware of these responsibilities and rights and should hold administrators responsible for addressing and fulfilling these rights. Parents can advocate for their child at GIEP meetings and/or request due process hearings.

In general, the gifted IEP is a guide for the teacher to help focus instruction on the student's educational needs and goals. It is not a rigid directive forcing the teacher to adhere to specific activities determined months before instruction. At the beginning of the school year, the student's gifted IEP should establish the student's main educational goals and a schedule within the school year for their attainment. Because goals are more general than short-term learning objectives, they allow time for teacher and student to collaborate in determining a school subject for a given goal that is compatible with the student's abilities and preferences. After arriving at a subject, the teacher and student can collaborate further in developing individual short-term learning objectives according to the schedule previously established. These objectives specify the smaller increments/steps toward achieving a goal, permitting the teacher to adjust to the student while also assuring progress.

Considerations for Development of IEP

In part because federal law addresses special education needs for disabled students but not for gifted students, in part because of emphases on inclusive education, and for other reasons, most public schools do not have many (or any) classrooms with all gifted students. Many schools have pull-out gifted programs, which comprise a very small part (about 5%) of the gifted students' school hours. Thus, the general classroom should be the focal area for modifications or accommodations included in a gifted IEP. In addition, if any school problems arise in gifted students, such problems are likely to arise in regular classrooms. Gifted students who learn more quickly and/or with less repetition can become bored and/or impatient with the class pace and come to dislike school. Although such problems may be minor in elementary school, they still should be addressed early to prevent the development of larger problems by high school. Simple general classroom changes in gifted IEPs can make tremendous differences.

Issues Many Parents Commonly Experience

Many parents of gifted children have commonly expressed several repeated experiences across public school districts. First, many parents report being told that their children must make up assignments in the general education classroom they missed due to the gifted pull-out program. Furthermore, some parents are told that since their child earns As in school, s/he needs no special attention or supplementary educational services. Parents often express concern that their child is growing comfortable with levels of schoolwork too low for his/her ability, that school is not offering challenges to their child, and/or that their child is developing bad study habits. Many parents are surprised and disappointed that their school district seems averse or avoidant to acknowledge and address their child's giftedness, since parents often expect for school districts to welcome superior learners. Parents often express perplexity or resentment at not knowing about available educational programming for their gifted children.

Recurring issues that many parents of gifted students in public school districts have reported include the following: when invited to IEP meetings, many parents report they were not informed of their status as equal partners in IEP planning, not informed that IEP meetings are working meetings, or not informed that parents should bring their own ideas to meetings. Many parents report they were not informed that accommodations to general classrooms could be written in gifted IEPs. If parents find their school has not assessed a student's present level of educational performance, many express that they were not informed how to request testing or that assessment results could be used to develop their child's gifted IEP. Parents often state they are told that acceleration in grade or subject violates the school district's policy, and that their gifted program is an "enrichment only" program. They also say districts often indicate their pull-out program as their entire gifted program.

Considerations Expressed by Experts

Two main concepts regarding gifted education (as expressed by McIntyre and Mery, 2004) are:

- Educationally, "gifted" does not mean that a student necessarily demonstrates superior academic performance in the regular, general education classroom. Rather, it means that the student has an educational need. The gifted child learns differently enough from others that regular classroom, grade-level teaching methods and practices are insufficient.

- Once this educational need is identified, the school must plan for the student's individual education to meet his or her specific needs. This planning is reflected in the development of an IEP. In addition to the need to individualize the student's educational planning, the authors emphasize that gifted "pull-out" programs alone are insufficient, as students still spend around 95% of their time in regular classes. Pull-outs should be used together with modifications to the regular program. Also, accommodations/services must not be limited to group programs, precluding individualization.

IEP Planning Meeting

A gifted IEP planning meeting should be student-centered and should be used for developing the IEP, not simply for reviewing a previously written IEP with no input from the meeting. Because school IEP team members will have prepared for the meeting, parents may misinterpret this preparation as the school presenting a predetermined plan. However, all members, including the parents and the student, should contribute to IEP development during the meeting. If a certain class or pull-out program is proposed, for example, but parents know it will not challenge their child (or already does not), they should indicate this. If parents find that the proposed IEP does not meet a certain educational need for their child, they should bring this up for the school to define and the team to find ways to meet it. Parents also can advocate for courses initially not offered by the school or not at their child's grade level.

For a Gifted IEP (GIEP) meeting, educators typically will prepare some provisional educational goals, courses, and activities they deem appropriate for the student. Furthermore, educators should avoid using technical jargon so parents can understand it. Parents should bring their ideas to the meeting. They can inform educators of their child's interests, likes and dislikes, and behavior, and bring suggestions for educational programs and/or materials they want for their child. They also should ask questions about anything they do not understand or if they need more information. When educators present parents at the meeting's end with a document to sign, often called a Notice of Recommended Assignment (NORA), parents should not assume they must sign it immediately. State laws allow a number of days for them to decide. Parents can request additional and/or amended wording. They can also write exceptions to parts they do not accept, and then sign, or they can reject the entire GIEP.

PLEP and Assessment

Generally, objective assessments are needed to establish a student's **Present Levels of Educational Performance** (PLEP). While subjective teacher observations, or checklists showing student strengths and weaknesses in the curriculum, are helpful for developing a gifted IEP, they should not be used to define PLEP, which requires objective testing instruments for accuracy. Ideally, such objective measurements are taken at least annually, or more often as needed. However, in the reality of public schools, this schedule is seldom followed with gifted students. Gifted IEP teams often wrongly use report cards, which measure learning of material taught in the past rather than in the present, and do not indicate student ability—a student may get As in a class which is still three grade levels below his/her capacity, or a student may be so uninterested in this lower level as to get Cs or even Fs. Either way, the student would not be functioning at his/her present level of educational performance.

Goals and Objectives

Goals are the long-term targets for a student's education, while objectives represent short-term targets, but this is not the only difference. Goals need not be specific or measurable, whereas objectives should be both specific and measurable. While goals are more general and global, they still must be specific to the individual student rather than assigned to that student based on his or her class or group. First, identifying the individual student's educational needs and the final outcomes desired are the ways of determining the student's educational goals. Short-term learning objectives then specify the smaller steps the student must achieve toward eventually meeting the associated goal. Objectives are also the IEP team's means of measuring student progress toward a goal. Objectives quantify criteria for attainment and state when these criteria are to be met. Goals and objectives should be congruent with one another: when read together, they should "make sense" to parents as well as to educators.

FOUR MAIN PARTS

When developing a Gifted IEP (or any IEP in general), the first part should indicate the student's Present Levels of Educational Performance (PLEP). Because asynchronous development is characteristic of gifted students, they have relative strengths and weaknesses as other do students, and they also may be extremely gifted in specific areas. Therefore, the PLEP must reflect school performance in all school subjects. This establishes a baseline wherefrom subsequent educational programming proceeds. The second IEP part should state the student's educational goals. Goals are more general and global; they do not include specific ways of achieving them. A third IEP part includes short-term learning objectives. These objectives do specify the time frames in which to achieve them and exactly what measures will demonstrate the learning. These are steps in achieving goals. A fourth part outlines specially designed instruction for the gifted student and explains teaching methods for attaining student short-term outcomes and long-term goals.

ABOVE GRADE LEVEL

By itself, the phrase "above grade level" contributes no meaning to establishing a gifted student's Present Levels of Educational Performance (PLEP) or to developing that student's IEP. Some gifted advocates opine this phrase should not be included in gifted IEPs. If it does appear, both the student's current grade level in school and the grade level at which the student performs must be defined. In some US states, State Departments of Education require these determinations by law. Objective, standardized achievement tests have established norms for each grade level, so these definitions can be determined through test scores and norms. The description "above grade level" without such specific grade-level information is analogous to going clothes shopping for a child with only the information that s/he is "taller than four feet." The child's actual height must be measured; so must the student's actual performance grade level be measured, as well.

RELATIONSHIP OF GENERAL EDUCATION TEACHER TO GIEP

If a gifted student is in a general education classroom for any part of the school day, the general education teacher needs to be familiar with the content of the student's GIEP. None of the privacy laws protecting the privacy/confidentiality of student records applies to either general or gifted education teachers' access to the GIEP. Some school districts have their own privacy procedures, such as having general education teachers sign a log to read a GIEP, but teachers are still allowed to read the GIEP. They cannot align with the GIEP's goals, objectives, activities, and materials without knowing them. Familiarity with the GIEP facilitates general teachers' coordinating their instruction with gifted teachers/programs. If parents believe their child's teacher does not know about the GIEP, and/or that their child is identified as gifted, they should ask the teacher. Bringing their child's gifted written report and GIEP to parent-teacher conferences is advisable.

GENERAL EDUCATION TEACHER'S INVOLVEMENT

Advocates observe that engaging general education teachers in the GIEP process represents the best way of developing and implementing a GIEP. The general education teacher should attend the GIEP meeting. Since a teacher familiar with the student always should attend IEP meetings, the primary general education teacher also is likely to be on the IEP team and attend the meeting. If a school/district does not include the general education teacher, parents can request the chairperson of the GIEP team or local educational agency (LEA) to include her/him. All teachers must comply with the GIEP. If a teacher refuses to implement the whole GIEP or any part(s) of it, e.g. pre-testing, giving differentiated classwork and/or homework, etc., parents either should call for another Team meeting or pursue due process proceedings. Teachers can make written objections to a GIEP on record. However, team-proposed, parent-approved GIEPs always must be implemented.

SDI Section

The **Specially Designed Instruction** (SDI) section of the GIEP is, in general, the section where classroom activities are designed to match the individual gifted student's needs. Any specific educational challenges or issues for that student, including any problems the student has in the general education classroom, should be addressed here. Any educational programming that the student and his/her parents think should become part of the school district's gifted program should also be included in the SDI section. Three considerations relative to general education teachers and GIEPs are:

- gifted education and general education for gifted students are not separate entities: gifted students' needs must be met in BOTH district gifted programs AND general education classrooms
- general education teachers cannot refuse to implement GIEPs; parents have recourse (i.e. another GIEP meeting/due process) if teachers do refuse to implement
- general education teachers have access to all parts of GIEPs

Instructional Accommodations That Can Be Requested

The only constraints on accommodations one might request in school for a gifted student are that such accommodations be reasonably expected to provide the student with meaningful educational value using the school's curriculum. Any accommodations meeting these criteria can be written into a student's gifted IEP. A common response from school/district administrators for students, parents, and advocates to consider is that no one ever has asked for a certain accommodation before, or no others are requesting a particular change. This happens more frequently in schools using only pull-out gifted services and/or those schools not normally providing accommodations to general education classrooms. Administrative responses even can give students/parents/advocates the impression that their request is inconvenient and/or unnecessary. However, rejecting a request simply because it sets a precedent is not valid. The only criteria for validity are the reasonable expectation of meaningful educational value and its educational appropriateness for the individual student.

Differentiated Homework

Since gifted students most often are placed in general education classrooms and given supplementary gifted services, they could be assigned the same homework as the regular class, plus another set of homework from their gifted program. Thus, gifted students can end up feeling punished rather than rewarded by having to complete a double amount of homework. Differentiated homework can avoid this problem by substituting homework more appropriate to the student's gifts instead of the regular class homework rather than in addition to it. Differentiated homework also can eliminate excessive rote work/repetition beyond the gifted student's needs. For example, assigning math puzzles instead of memorization lets gifted students apply their knowledge. Assigning a gifted student an additional vocabulary list, with homework only on the extra list, and/or having a gifted student write two longer stories per week instead of five shorter stories are other examples.

Independent Study Agreements

In public schools, gifted students are not commonly enrolled in completely separate gifted programs/"tracks" where all classes differ from general education classes in order to accommodate the gifted students' learning needs. Such gifted students most often are placed in general education classrooms for part/all of the school day. They may have pull-out programs for gifted instruction, but such programs represent a minority of the student's school day/week. Due to asynchronous development, some gifted students are farther ahead of the regular curriculum in some subjects than in others. Also, some gifted students still may find the regular curriculum relevant, but they simply may finish their class work sooner. Independent study agreements offer gifted students ways to occupy their free time instead of waiting for the rest of the class to catch. They can work on one big project incrementally, or on a series of smaller projects. Such projects should be designed to meet goals written in the student's gifted IEP.

Pre-Testing

Gifted students often have mastered the content of a lesson or subject at their grade level before teaching has begun in that class. Making them sit through instruction in material they already know only bores and/or frustrates them and damages damaging their motivation; moreover, they are prevented from learning new things in the subject at a higher level and at their own pace. The first section of the gifted IEP (GIEP) specifies the student's resent Levels of Educational Performance. When the GIEP team determines these, they can determine the need for pre-testing. Students whose pre-tests demonstrate mastery of material can be given alternate assignments that challenge them and allow them to learn new material. Students whose pre-tests demonstrate they have almost mastered a subject can be given only the parts they have not mastered to study, thereby saving time and redundancy. These students can use the rest of their class time for independent work on alternative assignments.

Acceleration

Acceleration is considered a more serious choice than other forms of accommodations for gifted students. Considerations for the student include the student's levels of emotional and social maturity, which can cause adjustment difficulties if a student is placed in chronologically older classes and is emotionally and/or socially unprepared. Historically, students skipped whole grades. While some cases still warrant such practices, students also can accelerate in individual subjects according to their levels of ability and performance. They can even work across grades if their learning levels dictate "straddling" two grade levels. Though accelerating is not always best, research finds gifted students more often benefit from ability-appropriate materials. Objective data on the student's current performance and potential are important to decisions to accelerate. Many school districts frown on acceleration, but they cannot have a policy prohibiting it. Attitudes against acceleration should be challenged when acceleration represents the only way to benefit the student.

Procedures If GIEP Is Not Working and/or If Student Has Problems in School

GIEP meetings exist in order to review the efficacy of the plan, not the student. Accordingly, "The Plan fails the child; the child does not fail the plan." (McIntyre, 2004) Some students may have had a GIEP for years that has not met their needs. If a student is in danger of failing in any subject or in school, the GIEP meeting should be reconvened. GIEP team members discuss the problem, appraise the circumstances, discuss available alternatives, and arrive at a solution for the individual student, changing the GIEP accordingly. The team can even write a provision into the GIEP for problems, specifying that if the student is potentially failing a subject, is unlikely to meet a GIEP goal(s), or his/her performance becomes substantially worse, the GIEP team will reconvene, including the teacher of the subject involved, and the GIEP will be modified to address the problem(s).

The main purpose of the GIEP is to address the needs of the individual gifted student. By definition, a gifted student learns differently enough from others that standard teaching methods and curricula are unsuitable. The different nature of the gifted student's learning and needs is the reason for a GIEP. The nature of the GIEP is not a class(es) or program(s) in which the gifted student participates. Instead, the GIEP offers a plan for the student's education. As such, the GIEP must be monitored: the student's educational needs will evolve/change over time, and the plan then must be adapted to continue meeting them. If problems persist after modifying a GIEP, the team should revisit the student's Present Levels of Educational Performance, ascertain what additional assessment data and other information are needed, and develop a new, more suitable/effective GIEP. Teams should obtain outside expert consultations if needed.

Review Video: Assessment Reliability and Validity
Visit mometrix.com/academy and enter code: 424680

Parental Access to School Records and About IEP Planning Meetings

Parents have the right to request and receive copies of all of their children's school records, including the results of any tests. These may not all be in one place. For example, the guidance counselor might maintain records of students' IEPs and educational programs, while IQ and other test results would be maintained by the school psychologist. Gifted advocates advise that parents of gifted students should obtain copies of current tests used to identify their child as gifted and of tests used to determine the student's achievement levels. Common misconceptions among all parents, including those with gifted children, is that the school IEP team already has created the IEP, that it cannot be altered, and that they are attending the meeting only to review and approve/disapprove its content. As such, parents must be informed of their roles as equal team members in contributing to, developing, and/or modifying their child's gifted IEP.

Assessment Methodology

Assessment Methods

Effective teaching requires multiple methods of assessment to evaluate student comprehension and instructional effectiveness. Assessments are typically categorized as diagnostic, formative, summative, and benchmark and are applicable at varying stages of instruction. **Diagnostic** assessments are administered before instruction and indicate students' prior knowledge and areas of misunderstanding to determine the path of instruction. **Formative** assessments occur continuously to measure student engagement, comprehension, and instructional effectiveness. These assessments indicate instructional strategies that require adjustment to meet students' needs in facilitating successful learning and include strategies like checking for understanding, observations, total participation activities, and exit tickets. **Summative** assessments are given at the end of a lesson or unit to evaluate student progress in reaching learning targets and identify areas of misconception for reteaching. Such assessments can be given in the form of exams and quizzes or be project-based activities in which students demonstrate their learning through hands-on, personalized methods. Additionally, portfolios serve as valuable summative assessments in allowing students to demonstrate their progress over time and provide insight regarding individual achievement. **Benchmark** assessments occur less frequently and encompass large portions of curriculum. These assessments are intended to evaluate the progress of groups of students in achieving state and district academic standards.

Assessment Types

- **Diagnostic:** These assessments can either be formal or informal and are intended to provide teachers with information regarding students' level of understanding prior to beginning a unit of instruction. Examples include pretests, KWL charts, anticipation guides, and brainstorming activities. Digital resources, such as online polls, surveys, and quizzes are also valuable resources for gathering diagnostic feedback.
- **Formative:** These assessments occur throughout instruction to provide the teacher with feedback regarding student understanding. Examples include warm-up and closure activities, checking frequently for understanding, student reflection activities, and providing students with color-coded cards to indicate their level of understanding. Short quizzes and total participation activities, such as four corners, are also valuable formative assessments. Numerous digital resources, including polls, surveys, and review games, are also beneficial in providing teachers with formative feedback to indicate instructional effectiveness.
- **Summative:** Summative assessments are intended to indicate students' levels of mastery and progress toward reaching academic learning standards. These assessments may take the form of written or digital exams and include multiple choice, short answer, or long answer questions. Examples also include projects, final essays, presentations, or portfolios to demonstrate student progress over time.
- **Benchmark:** Benchmark assessments measure students' progress in achieving academic standards. These assessments are typically standardized to ensure uniformity, objectivity, and accuracy. Benchmark assessments are typically given as a written multiple choice or short answer exam, or as a digital exam in which students answer questions on the computer.

Review Video: Formative and Summative Assessments
Visit mometrix.com/academy and enter code: 804991

Determining Appropriate Assessment Strategies

As varying assessment methods provide different information regarding student performance and achievement, the teacher must consider the most applicable and effective assessment strategy in each stage of instruction. This includes determining the **desired outcomes** of assessment as well as the information the teacher intends to ascertain and how they will apply the results to further instruction. **Age**- and **grade-level**-appropriateness must be considered when selecting which assessment strategies will enable students to successfully demonstrate their learning. Additionally, the teacher must be cognizant of students' individual differences and learning needs to determine which assessment model is most **accommodating** and reflective of their progress. It is also important that teachers consider the practicality of assessment strategies and methods they will use to implement the assessment for maximized feedback regarding individual and whole-class progress in achieving learning goals.

Assessments That Reflect Real-World Applications

Assessments that reflect **real-world applications** enhance relevancy and students' ability to establish personal connections to learning that deepen understanding. Implementing such assessments provides authenticity and enhances engagement by defining a clear and practical purpose for learning. These assessments often allow for hands-on opportunities for demonstrating learning and can be adjusted to accommodate students' varying learning styles and needs while measuring individual progress; however, assessments that focus on real-world applications can be subjective, thus making it difficult to extract concrete data and quantify student progress to guide future instructional decisions. In addition, teachers may have difficulty analyzing assessment results on a large scale and comparing student performance with other schools and districts, as individual assessments may vary.

Diagnostic Tests

Diagnostic tests are integral to planning and delivering effective instruction. These tests are typically administered prior to beginning a unit or lesson and provide valuable feedback for guiding and planning instruction. Diagnostic tests provide **preliminary information** regarding students' levels of understanding and prior knowledge. This serves as a baseline for instructional planning that connects and builds upon students' background knowledge and experiences to enhance success in learning. Diagnostic tests allow the teacher to identify and clarify areas of student misconception prior to engaging in instruction to ensure continued comprehension and avoid the need for remediation. They indicate areas of student strength and need as well as individual instructional aids that may need to be incorporated into lessons to support student achievement. In addition, these tests enable the teacher to determine which instructional strategies, activities, groupings, and materials will be most valuable in maximizing engagement and learning. Diagnostic tests can be **formal** or **informal** and include pre-tests, pre-reading activities, surveys, vocabulary inventories, and graphic organizers (such as KWL charts). These tests are used to assess student understanding prior to engaging in learning. Diagnostic tests are generally not graded, as there is little expectation that all students in a class possess the same baseline of proficiency at the start of a unit.

Formative Assessments

Formative assessments are any assessments that take place in the **middle of a unit of instruction**. The goals of formative assessments are to help teachers understand where a student is in his or her progress toward **mastering** the current unit's content and to provide the students with **ongoing feedback** throughout the unit. The advantage of relying heavily on formative assessments in instruction is that it allows the teacher to continuously **check for comprehension** and adjust instruction as needed to ensure that the whole class is adequately prepared to proceed at the end of the unit. To understand formative assessments well, teachers need to understand that any interaction that can provide information about the student's comprehension is a type of formative assessment which can be used to inform future instruction.

Formative assessments are often a mixture of formal and informal assessments. **Formal formative assessments** often include classwork, homework, and quizzes. Examples of **informal formative assessments** include simple comprehension checks during instruction, class-wide discussions of the current topic, and exit slips, which are written questions posed by teachers at the end of class, which helps the teacher quickly review which students are struggling with the concepts.

Summative Assessments

Summative assessment refers to an evaluation at the end of a discrete unit of instruction, such as the end of a course, unit, or semester. Classic examples of summative assessments include end-of-course assessments, final exams, or even qualifying standardized tests such as the SAT or ACT. Most summative assessments are created to measure student mastery of particular **academic standards**. Whereas formative assessment generally informs current instruction, summative assessments are used to objectively demonstrate that each individual has achieved adequate mastery of the standards in question. If a student has not met the benchmark, he or she may need extra instruction or may need to repeat the course.

These assessments usually take the form of **tests** or formal portfolios with rubrics and clearly defined goals. Summative assessments are usually high-stakes, heavily-weighted, and they should always be formally graded. These types of assessments often feature a narrower range of question types, such as multiple choice, short answer, and essay questions to help with systematic grading.

Project-based assessments are beneficial in evaluating achievement, as they incorporate several elements of instruction and highlight real-world applications of learning. This allows students to demonstrate understanding through a hands-on, individualized approach that reinforces connections to learning and increases retainment. **Portfolios** of student work over time serve as a valuable method for assessing individual progress toward reaching learning targets. Summative assessments provide insight regarding overall instructional effectiveness and are necessary for guiding future instruction in subsequent years but are not usually used to modify current instruction.

Review Video: Assessment Reliability and Validity
Visit mometrix.com/academy and enter code: 424680

Benchmark Assessments

Benchmark assessments are intended to quantify, evaluate, and compare individual and groups of students' achievement of school-wide, district, and state **academic standards.** They are typically administered in specific intervals throughout the school year and encompass entire or large units of curriculum to determine student mastery and readiness for academic advancement. Benchmark assessments provide data that enable the teacher to determine students' progress toward reaching academic goals to guide current and continued instruction. This data can be utilized by the school and individual teachers to create learning goals and objectives aligned with academic standards. It can also be used to plan instructional strategies, activities, and assessments to support students in achieving these academic standards. In addition, benchmark assessments provide feedback regarding understanding and the potential need for remediation to allow the teacher to instill necessary supports in future instruction that prepare students for success in achieving learning targets.

Alignment of Assessments with Instructional Goals and Objectives

To effectively monitor student progress, assessments must align with **instructional goals** and **objectives**. This allows the teacher to determine whether students are advancing at an appropriate pace to achieve state and district academic standards. When assessments are aligned with specific learning targets, the teacher ensures that students are learning relevant material to establish a foundation of knowledge necessary for growth and academic achievement. To achieve this, teachers must determine which instructional goals and objectives their students must achieve and derive instruction, content, and activities from these specifications. Instruction must reflect and reinforce learning targets, and the teacher must select the most effective strategies for addressing students' needs as they work to achieve them. Assessments must be reflective of content instruction to ensure they are aligned with learning goals and objectives, as well as to enable the teacher to evaluate student progress in mastering them. The teacher must clearly communicate learning goals and objectives throughout all stages of instruction to provide students with clarity on expectations. This establishes a clear purpose and focus for learning that enhances relevancy and strengthens connections to support student achievement.

Clearly Communicating Assessment Criteria and Standards

Students must be clear on the purpose of learning throughout all stages of instruction to enhance understanding and facilitate success. When assessment **criteria** and **standards** are clearly communicated, the purpose of learning is established, and students are able to effectively connect instructional activities to learning goals and criteria for assessment. Communicating assessment criteria and standards provides students with clarity on tasks and learning goals they are expected to accomplish as they prepare themselves for assessment. This allows for more **focused instruction** and engagement in learning, as it enhances relevancy and student motivation. Utilizing appropriate forms of **rubrics** is an effective strategy in specifying assessment criteria and standards, as it informs students about learning goals they are working toward, the quality of work they are expected to achieve, and skills they must master to succeed on the assessment. Rubrics indicate to students exactly how they will be evaluated, thus supporting their understanding and focus as they engage in learning to promote academic success.

Rubrics for Communicating Standards

The following are varying styles of rubrics that can be used to communicate criteria and standards:

- **Analytic:** Analytic rubrics break down criteria for an assignment into several categories and provide an explanation of the varying levels of performance in each one. This style of rubric is beneficial for detailing the characteristics of quality work as well as providing students with feedback regarding specific components of their performance. Analytic rubrics are most effective when used for summative assessments, such as long-term projects or essays.
- **Holistic:** Holistic rubrics evaluate the quality of the student's assignment as a whole rather than scoring individual components. Students' scores are determined based upon their performance across multiple performance indicators. This style of rubric is beneficial for providing a comprehensive evaluation but limits the amount of feedback that students receive regarding their performance in specific areas.
- **Single-point:** Single-point rubrics outline criteria for assignments into several categories. Rather than providing a numeric score to each category, however, the teacher provides written feedback regarding the students' strengths and ways in which they can improve their performance. This style of rubric is beneficial in providing student-centered feedback that focuses on their overall progress.
- **Checklist:** Checklists typically outline a set of criteria that is scored using a binary approach based upon completion of each component. This style increases the efficiency of grading assignments and is often easy for students to comprehend but does not provide detailed feedback. This method of grading should generally be reserved for shorter assignments.

Communicating High Academic Expectations in Assessments

The attitudes and behaviors exhibited by the teacher are highly influential on students' attitudes toward learning. Teachers demonstrate belief in students' abilities to be successful in learning when they communicate **high academic expectations**. This promotes students' **self-concept** and establishes a **growth mindset** to create confident, empowered learners that are motivated to achieve. High expectations for assessments and reaching academic standards communicates to students the quality of work that is expected of them and encourages them to overcome obstacles as they engage in learning. When communicating expectations for student achievement, it is important that the teacher is aware of students' individual learning needs to provide the necessary support that establishes equitable opportunities for success in meeting assessment criteria and standards. Setting high expectations through assessment criteria and standards while supporting students in their learning enhances overall achievement and establishes a foundation for continuous academic success.

Effective Communication and Impact on Student Learning

Communicating high academic expectations enhances students' self-concept and increases personal motivation for success in learning. To maximize student achievement, it is important that the teacher set high academic expectations that are **clearly** communicated through **age-appropriate** terms and consistently reinforced. Expectations must be reflected through learning goals and objectives and must be **visible** at all times to ensure student awareness. Teachers must be **specific** in communicating what they want students to accomplish and clearly detail necessary steps for achievement while assuming the role of facilitator to guide learning and provide support. Providing constructive **feedback** throughout instruction is integral in reminding students of academic expectations and ensuring they are making adequate progress toward reaching learning goals. When high academic expectations are communicated and reinforced, students are empowered with a sense of confidence and self-responsibility for their own learning that promotes their desire to learn. This ultimately enhances achievement and equips them with the tools necessary for future academic success.

Analyzing and Interpreting Assessment Data

Teachers can utilize multiple techniques to effectively analyze and interpret assessment data. This typically involves creating charts and graphs outlining different data subsets. They can list each learning standard that was assessed, determine how many students overall demonstrated proficiency on the standard, and identify individual students who did not demonstrate proficiency on each standard. This information can be used to differentiate instruction. Additionally, they can track individual student performance and progress on each standard over time.

Teachers can take note of overall patterns and trends in assessment data. For example, they can determine if any subgroups of students did not meet expectations. They can consider whether the data confirms or challenges any existing beliefs, implications this may have on instructional planning and what, if any, conclusions can be drawn from this data.

Analyzing and interpreting assessment data may raise new questions for educators, so they can also determine if additional data collection is needed.

Using Assessment Data to Differentiate Instruction for Individual Learners

By analyzing and interpreting assessment data, teachers can determine if there are any specific learning standards that need to be retaught to their entire classes. This may be necessary if the data shows that all students struggled in these specific areas. Teachers may consider reteaching these standards using different methods if the initial methods were unsuccessful.

Teachers can also form groups of students who did not demonstrate proficiency on the same learning standards. Targeted instruction can be planned for these groups to help them make progress in these areas. Interventions can also be planned for individual students who did not show proficiency in certain areas. If interventions have already been in place and have not led to increased learning outcomes, the interventions may be redesigned. If interventions have been in place and assessment data now shows proficiency, the interventions may be discontinued.

If assessment data shows that certain students have met or exceeded expectations in certain areas, enrichment activities can be planned to challenge these students and meet their learning needs.

Aligning Assessments with Instructional Goals and Objectives

Assessments that are congruent to instructional goals and objectives provide a **clear purpose** for learning that enhances student understanding and motivation. When learning targets are reflected in assessments, instructional activities and materials become more **relevant**, as they are derived from these specifications. Such clarity in purpose allows for more focus and productivity as students engage in instruction and fosters connections that strengthen overall understanding for maximized success in learning. Aligning assessments with instructional goals and objectives ensures that students are learning material that is relevant to the curriculum and academic standards to ensure **preparedness** as they advance in their academic careers. In addition, it enables the teacher to evaluate and monitor student progress to determine whether they are progressing at an ideal pace for achieving academic standards. With this information, the teacher can effectively modify instruction as necessary to support students' needs in reaching desired learning outcomes.

Norm-Referenced Tests

On **norm-referenced tests**, students' performances are compared to the performances of sample groups of similar students. Norm-referenced tests identify students who score above and below the average. To ensure reliability, the tests must be given in a standardized manner to all students.

Norm-referenced tests usually cover a broad range of skills, such as the entire grade-level curriculum for a subject. They typically contain a few questions per skill. Whereas scores in component areas of the tests may be calculated, usually overall test scores are reported. Scores are often reported using percentile ranks, which indicate what percentage of test takers scored lower than the student being assessed. For example, a student's score in the 75th percentile means the student scored better than 75% of other test takers. Other times, scores may be reported using grade-level equivalency.

One advantage of norm-referenced tests is their objectivity. They also allow educators to compare large groups of students at once. This may be helpful for making decisions regarding class placements and groupings. A disadvantage of norm-referenced tests is that they only indicate how well students perform in comparison to one another. They do not indicate whether or not students have mastered certain skills.

Criterion-Referenced Tests

Criterion-referenced tests measure how well students perform on certain skills or standards. The goal of these tests is to indicate whether or not students have mastered certain skills and which skills require additional instruction. Scores are typically reported using the percentage of questions answered correctly or students' performance levels. Performance levels are outlined using terms such as *below expectations*, *met expectations*, and *exceeded expectations*.

One advantage of criterion-referenced tests is that they provide teachers with useful information to guide instruction. They can identify which specific skills students have mastered and which skills need additional practice. Teachers can use this information to plan whole-class, small-group, and individualized instruction. Analyzing results of criterion-referenced tests over time can also help teachers track student progress on certain skills. A disadvantage of criterion-referenced tests is that they do not allow educators to compare students' performances to samples of their peers.

Ways That Standardized Test Results Are Reported

- **Raw scores** are sometimes reported and indicate how many questions students answered correctly on a test. By themselves, they do not provide much useful information. They do not indicate how students performed in comparison to other students or to grade-level expectations.
- **Grade-level equivalents** are also sometimes reported. A grade-level equivalent score of 3.4 indicates that a student performed as well as an average third grader in the fourth month of school. It can indicate whether a student is performing above or below grade-level expectations, but it does not indicate that the student should be moved to a different grade level.

- **Standard scores** are used to compare students' performances on tests to standardized samples of their peers. Standard deviation refers to the amount that a set of scores differs from the mean score on a test.
- **Percentile ranks** are used on criterion-referenced tests to indicate what percentage of test takers scored lower than the student whose score is being reported.
- **Cutoff scores** refer to predetermined scores students must obtain in order to be considered proficient in certain areas. Scores below the cutoff level indicate improvement is needed and may result in interventions or instructional changes.

Formal and Informal Assessments

Assessments are any method a teacher uses to gather information about student comprehension of curriculum, including improvised questions for the class and highly-structured tests. **Formal assessments** are assessments that have **clearly defined standards and methodology** and which are applied consistently to all students. Formal tests should be objective and scrutinized for validity and reliability since they tend to carry higher weight for the student. Summative assessments, such as end-of-unit tests, lend themselves to being formal tests because it is necessary that a teacher test the comprehension of all students in a consistent and thorough way.

Although formal assessments can provide useful data about student performance and progress, they can be costly and time-consuming to implement. Administering formal assessments often interrupts classroom instruction and may cause testing anxiety.

Informal assessments are assessments that do not adhere to formal objectives, and they do not have to be administered consistently to all students. As a result, they do not have to be scored or recorded as a grade and generally act as a **subjective measure** of class comprehension. Informal assessments can be as simple as asking the students to raise their hands if they are ready to proceed to the next step or asking a particular question of an individual student.

Informal assessments do not provide objective data for analysis, but they can be implemented quickly and inexpensively. Informal assessments can also be incorporated into regular classroom instruction and activities, making them more authentic and less stressful for students.

Using Various Assessments

The goal of **assessment** in education is to gather data that, when evaluated, can be used to further student learning and achievement. **Standardized tests** are helpful for placement purposes and to reflect student progress toward goals set by a school district or state. If a textbook is chosen to align with district learning standards, the textbook assessments can provide teachers with convenient, small-scale, regular checks of student knowledge against the target standard.

In order be effective, teachers must know where their students are in the learning process. Teachers use a multitude of **formal and informal assessment methods** to do this. Posing differentiated discussion questions is an example of an informal assessment method that allows teachers to gauge individual student progress rather than their standing in relation to a universal benchmark.

Effective teachers employ a variety of assessments, as different formats assess different skills, promote different learning experiences, and appeal to different learners. A portfolio is an example of an assessment that gauges student progress in multiple skills and through multiple media. Teachers can use authentic or performance-based assessments to stimulate student interest and provide visible connections between language-learning and the real world.

Assessment Reliability

Assessment reliability refers to how well an assessment is constructed and is made up of a variety of measures. An assessment is generally considered **reliable** if it yields similar results across multiple administrations of the assessment. A test should perform similarly with different test administrators, graders, test-takers, and over multiple iterations. Factors that affect reliability include the day-to-day wellbeing of the student (students can sometimes underperform), the physical environment of the test, the way it is administered, and the subjectivity of the scorer (with written-response assessments).

Perhaps the most important threat to assessment reliability is the nature of the **exam questions** themselves. An assessment question is designed to test knowledge of a certain construct. A question is reliable in this sense if students who understand the content answer the question correctly. Statisticians look for patterns in student marks, both within the single test and over multiple tests, as a way of measuring reliability. Teachers should watch out for circumstances in which a student or students answer correctly a series of questions about a given concept (demonstrating their understanding) but then answer a related question incorrectly. The latter question may be an unreliable indicator of concept knowledge.

Measures of Assessment Reliability

- **Test-retest reliability** refers to an assessment's consistency of results with the same test-taker over multiple retests. If one student shows inconsistent results over time, the test is not considered to have test-retest reliability.
- **Intertester reliability** refers to an assessment's consistency of results between multiple test-takers at the same level. Students at similar levels of proficiency should show similar results.
- **Inter-rater reliability** refers to an assessment's consistency of results between different administrators of the test. This plays an especially critical role in tests with interactive or subjective responses, such as Likert-scales, cloze tests, and short answer tests. Different raters of the same test need to have a consistent means of evaluating the test-takers' performance. Clear rubrics can help keep two or more raters consistent in scoring.
- **Intra-rater reliability** refers to an assessment's consistency of results with one rater over time. One test rater should be able to score different students objectively to rate subjective test formats fairly.
- **Parallel-forms reliability** refers to an assessment's consistency between multiple different forms. For instance, end-of-course assessments may have many distinctive test forms, with different questions or question orders. If the different forms of a test do not provide the same results, the test is said to be lacking in parallel-forms reliability.
- **Internal consistency reliability** refers to the consistency of results of similar questions on a particular assessment. If there are two or more questions targeted at the same standard and at the same level, they should show the same results across each question.

Assessment Validity

Assessment validity is a measure of the relevancy that an assessment has to the skill or ability being evaluated and the degree to which students' performance is representative of their mastery of the topic of assessment. In other words, a teacher should ask how well an assessment's results correlate to what it is looking to assess. Assessments should be evaluated for validity on both the **individual question** level and as a **test overall**. This can be especially helpful in refining tests for future classes. The overall validity of an assessment is determined by several types of validity measures.

An assessment is considered **valid** if it measures what it is intended to measure. One common error that can reduce the validity of a test (or a question on a test) occurs if the instructions are written at a reading level the students can't understand. In this case, it is not valid to take the student's failed answer as a true indication of his or her knowledge of the subject. Factors internal to the student might also affect exam validity: anxiety and a lack of self-esteem often lower assessments results, reducing their validity as a measure of student knowledge.

An assessment has content validity if it includes all the **relevant aspects** of the subject being tested—if it is comprehensive, in other words. An assessment has **predictive validity** if a score on the test is an accurate predictor of future success in the same domain. For example, SAT exams purport to have validity in predicting student success in a college. An assessment has construct validity if it accurately measures student knowledge of the subject being tested.

Measures of Assessment Validity

- **Face validity** refers to the initial impression of whether an assessment seems to be fit for the task. As this method is subjective to interpretation and unquantifiable, it should not be used singularly as a measurement of validity.
- **Construct validity** asks if an assessment actually assesses what it is intended to assess. Some topics are more straightforward, such as assessing if a student can perform two-digit multiplication. This can be directly tested, which gives the assessment a strong content validity. Other measures, such as a person's overall happiness, must be measured indirectly. If an assessment asserted that a person is generally happy if he or she smiles frequently, it would be fair to question the construct validity of that assessment because smiling is unlikely to be a consistent measure of all peoples' general happiness.
- **Content validity** indicates whether the assessment is comprehensive of all aspects of the content being assessed. If a test leaves out an important topic, then the teacher will not have a full picture as a result of the assessment.
- **Criterion validity** refers to whether the results of an assessment can be used to **predict** a related value, known as **criterion**. An example of this is the hypothesis that IQ tests would predict a person's success later in life, but many critics believe that IQ tests are not valid predictors of success because intelligence is not the only predictor of success in life. IQ tests have shown validity toward predicting academic success, however. The measure of an assessment's criterion validity depends on how closely related the criterion is.
- **Discriminant validity** refers to how well an assessment tests only that which it is intended to test and successfully discriminates one piece of information from another. For instance, a student who is exceptional in mathematics should not be able to put that information into use on a science test and gain an unfair advantage. If the student is able to score well due to his or her mathematics knowledge, the science test did not adequately discriminate science knowledge from mathematics knowledge.
- **Convergent validity** is related to discriminant validity, but takes into account that two measures may be distinct but correlated. For instance, a personality test should distinguish self-esteem from extraversion so that they can be measured independently, but if an assessment has convergent validity, it should show a correlation between related measures.

Practicality

An assessment is **practical** if it uses an appropriate amount of human and budgetary resources. A practical exam doesn't take very long to design or score, nor does it take students very long to complete in relation to other learning objectives and priorities. Teachers often need to balance a desire to construct comprehensive or content-valid tests with a need for practicality: lengthy exams consume large amounts of instruction time and may return unreliable results if students become tired and lose focus.

Assessment Bias

An assessment is considered biased if it disadvantages a certain group of students, such as students of a certain gender, race, cultural background, or socioeconomic class. A **content bias** exists when the subject matter of a question or assessment is familiar to one group and not another. For example, a reading comprehension passage that discusses an event in American history would be biased against students new to the country. An **attitudinal bias** exists when a teacher has a pre-conceived idea about the likely success of an assessment of a particular individual or group. A **method bias** arises when the format of an assessment is unfamiliar to a given group of students. **Language bias** occurs when an assessment utilizes idioms, collocations, or cultural references unfamiliar to a group of students. Finally, **translation bias** may arise when educators attempt to translate content-area assessments into a student's native language—rough or hurried translations often result in a loss of nuance important for accurate assessment.

Authentic Assessments

An authentic assessment is an assessment designed to closely resemble something that a student does, or will do, in the real world. For example, students will never encounter a multiple-choice test requiring them to choose the right tense of a verb, but they will encounter contexts in which they have to write a narration of an event that has antecedents and consequents spread out in time—like narrating their version of what caused a traffic accident. The latter is an example of a potential **authentic assessment**.

Well-designed authentic assessments require a student to exercise **advanced cognitive skills** (e.g., solving problems, integrating information, performing deductions), integrate **background knowledge**, and confront **ambiguity**. Research has demonstrated that mere language proficiency is not predictive of future language success—learning how to utilize knowledge in a complex context is an essential additional skill.

The terms "authentic" and "performance-based" are often used interchangeably when describing assessments; however, a performance-based assessment doesn't necessarily have to be grounded in a possible authentic experience.

Performance-Based Assessments

A performance-based assessment is one in which students demonstrate their learning by performing a **task** rather than by answering questions in a traditional test format. Proponents of **performance-based assessments** argue that they lead students to use **high-level cognitive skills** since they focus on how to put their knowledge to use and plan a sequence of stages in an activity or presentation. They also allow students more opportunities to individualize their presentations or responses based on preferred learning styles. Research suggests that students welcome the chance to put their knowledge to use in real-world scenarios.

Advocates of performance-based assessments suggest that they avoid many of the problems of language or cultural bias present in traditional assessments, allowing more accurate assessment of how well students learned the underlying concepts. In discussions regarding English as a second language, they argue that performance assessments come closer to replicating what should be the true goal of language learning—the effective use of language in real contexts—than do more traditional exams. Critics point out that performance assessments are difficult and time-consuming for teachers to construct and for students to perform. Finally, performative assessments are difficult to grade in the absence of a well-constructed and detailed rubric.

Technology-Based Assessments

Technology-based assessments provide teachers with multiple resources for evaluating student progress to guide instruction. They are applicable in most formal and informal instructional settings and can be utilized as formative and summative assessments. Technology-based assessments simplify and enhance the efficiency of determining comprehension and instructional effectiveness, as they quickly present the teacher with information regarding student progress. This data enables the teacher to make necessary adjustments to facilitate student learning and growth. Implementing this assessment format simplifies the process of aligning them to school and district academic standards. This establishes objectivity and uniformity for comparing results and progress among students. It also helps ensure that all students are held to the same academic expectations. While technology-based assessments are beneficial, there are some shortcomings to consider. This format may not be entirely effective for all learning styles in demonstrating understanding, as individualization in technology-based assessment can be limited. These assessments may not illustrate individual students' growth over time but rather their mastery of an academic standard, thus hindering the ability to evaluate overall achievement. As technology-based evaluation limits hands-on opportunities, the real-world application and relevancy of the assessment may be unapparent to students.

Advantages and Disadvantages of Technology-Based Assessments

Technology-based assessments can have many advantages. They can be given to large numbers of students at once, limited only by the amounts of technological equipment schools possess. Many types of technology-based assessments are instantly scored, and feedback is provided quickly. Students are sometimes able to view their results and feedback at the conclusion of their testing sessions. Data can be quickly compiled and reported in easy-to-understand formats. Technology-based assessments can also often track student progress over time.

Technology-based assessments can have some disadvantages as well. Glitches and system errors can interfere with the assessment process or score reporting. Students must also have the necessary prerequisite technological skills to take the assessments, or the results may not measure the content they are designed to measure. For example, if students take timed, computer-based writing tests, they should have proficient typing skills. Otherwise, they may perform poorly on the tests despite strong writing abilities. Other prerequisite skills include knowing how to use a keyboard and mouse and understanding how to locate necessary information on the screen.

Portfolio Assessments

A **portfolio** is a collection of student work in multiple forms and media gathered over time. Teachers may assess the portfolio both for evidence of progress over time or in its end state as a demonstration of the achievement of certain proficiency levels.

One advantage of **portfolio assessments** is their breadth. Unlike traditional assessments, which focus on one or two language skills, portfolios may contain work in multiple forms, such as writing samples, pictures, and graphs designed for content courses, video and audio clips, student reflections, teacher observations, and student exams. A second advantage is that they allow a student to develop work in authentic contexts, including in other classrooms and at home.

In order for portfolios to function as an objective assessment tool, teachers should negotiate with students in advance of what genres of work will be included and outline a grading rubric that makes clear what will be assessed, such as linguistic proficiency, use of English in academic contexts, and demonstrated use of target cognitive skills.

Curriculum-Based Assessments

Curriculum-based assessments, also known as **curriculum-based measurements (CBM)**, are short, frequent assessments designed to measure student progress toward meeting curriculum **benchmarks**.

Teachers implement CBMs by designing **probes**, or short assessments that target specific skills. For example, a teacher might design a spelling probe, administered weekly, that requires students to spell 10 unfamiliar but level-appropriate words. The data from these assessments can be tracked over time to measure student progress toward defined grade-level goals.

CBM has several clear advantages. If structured well, the probes have high reliability and validity. Furthermore, they provide clear and objective evidence of student progress—a welcome outcome for students and parents who often grapple with less-clear and subjective evidence. Used correctly, CBMs also motivate students and provide them with evidence of their own progress; however, while CBMs are helpful in identifying areas of student weaknesses, they do not identify the causes of those weaknesses or provide teachers with strategies for improving instruction.

Textbook Assessments

Textbook assessments are the assessments provided at the end of a chapter or unit in an approved textbook. **Textbook assessments** present several advantages for a teacher: they are already made; they are likely to be accurate representations of the chapter or unit materials; and, if the textbook has been prescribed or recommended by the state, it is likely to correspond closely to Common Core or other tested standards.

Textbook assessments can be limiting for students who lag in the comprehension of academic English or whose preferred learning style is not verbal. While textbooks may come with DVDs or recommended audio links, ESOL teachers will likely need to supplement these assessment materials with some of their own findings. Finally, textbook assessments are unlikely to represent the range of assessment types used in the modern classroom, such as a portfolio or performance-based assessments.

Peer Assessment

A peer assessment is when students grade one another's work based on a teacher-provided framework. **Peer assessments** are promoted as a means of saving teacher time and building student metacognitive skills. They are typically used as **formative** rather than summative assessments, given concerns about the reliability of student scoring and the tensions that can result if student scores contribute to overall grades. Peer assessments are used most often to grade essay-type written work or presentations. Proponents point out that peer assessments require students to apply metacognition, build cooperative work and interpersonal skills, and broaden the sense that the student is accountable to peers and not just the teacher. Even advocates of the practice agree that students need detailed rubrics in order to succeed. Critics often argue that low-performing students have little to offer high-performing students in terms of valuable feedback—and this disparity may be more pronounced in ESOL classrooms or special education environments than in mainstream ones. One way to overcome this weakness is for the teacher to lead the evaluation exercise, guiding the students through a point-by-point framework of evaluation.

Chapter Quiz

Ready to see how well you retained what you just read? Scan the QR code to go directly to the chapter quiz interface for this study guide. If you're using a computer, simply visit the online resources page at **mometrix.com/resources719/nesincgifted** and click the Chapter Quizzes link.

Professional and Ethical Practice and Collaboration

Choosing a Program

The Quality of Gifted Programs or Schools

Parents should be able to identify the philosophy and goals of a gifted program and/or school. Because giftedness is a lifelong trait, gifted students' academic needs will have some continuity. If program goals differ by age, these differences should reflect instructional variation, which should be both age-appropriate and appropriate for gifted students. Gifted programs should include both acceleration, i.e. offering instruction at a faster pace more suitable for gifted students; and enrichment, i.e. extending the curriculum by increasing the depth of study of a subject appropriately to gifted students' abilities and needs. Another essential factor involves offering multiple options in gifted education. Students gifted in the language arts are different from those gifted in math; mildly gifted and profoundly gifted students differ from one another. Owing to individual differences such as personalities and learning styles, even students with similar levels of giftedness in the same subjects can be very different. As a result, it is critical to include multiple ways to address these multiple educational needs.

Many times, schools depend on a teacher's recommendation or results of a single standardized group test to identify a student for gifted placement. Such methods typically overlook gifted students who are underachievers, have learning disabilities, and/or belong to under-represented populations such as the economically disadvantaged and racial/ethnic/linguistic/cultural minority groups. For these reasons, for years educators have advocated using multiple assessment instruments and practices. Another factor is staff development: Teachers trained in gifted education provide more effective instruction to gifted students. A school/program's teachers of gifted students should have certifications/endorsements in gifted education, and schools should provide regular in-service trainings regarding gifted students. Because gifted students are different from other students, schools also should provide guidance services to address problems such as fitting in socially with non-gifted peers and gifted hypersensitivities to the ordinary stresses of growing up and attending school. Additionally, schools should confer equivalent honors to academic talents/achievements as to athletic talents/achievements.

Any good gifted education program or school should state its learning outcome expectations clearly for the student. Providing activities that students enjoy is important, but gifted students also must learn while having fun. Specifying learning objectives and designing instruction to facilitate reaching those objectives is an essential part of any gifted program. Gifted education programs/schools should provide curricula that stimulate and challenge their students. Gifted students often grow bored if instructional tasks are too easy and do not require them to "stretch" their minds. Flexibility is important to help gifted students receive suitable challenges and meet individual needs. For example, students who perform several years above grade level in one subject should not be made to do grade-level work. Programs should be flexible to let such students study higher-level material. Students with musical gifts could exchange some school time for participation in special music programs, or study with an "artist-teacher" musician.

Review Video: Learning Objectives
Visit mometrix.com/academy and enter code: 528458

ONLINE INFORMATION ABOUT COMMUNITY RESOURCES

Many websites offer information on community resources for gifted and talented students. One good resource is the website of the National Association for Gifted Children (NAGC). State associations can join NAGC as an affiliate. State affiliates then can offer NAGC Parent Affiliate Memberships to parents of gifted children. On the NAGC website, there is a Gifted by State page. As of its 2008 copyright, it linked to organizations for every US state except Alaska and Wyoming. Minnesota has two gifted organizations linked. Websites of state organizations for the gifted offer such information as local chapters, publications, webinars, audio recordings, upcoming events, recent news; the organization's mission statement; the state's definition of giftedness; programming standards; legislative updates; summer teacher professional development courses, workshops, institutes, conferences, etc.; e-stores; awards and scholarships; communicators; advocacy information; job postings; and more. State gifted organizations' sites also list and link to local community resources within their state, including other gifted associations; college/university programs; academic/enrichment opportunities including competitions, activities, programs, and journals.

PROGRAM PLACEMENT OPTIONS

REGULAR EDUCATION WITH RESOURCE SERVICES

The term "resource services" refers to the student in the general education classroom going to a separate resource room part-time, also called pull-out program or send-out classes, available in some middle schools and more prevalent in elementary schools. Typically, groups of 10-30 students attend a resource room for classes with a gifted teacher for one day or ½ day weekly. Gifted teachers may reserve one weekday for third-graders, and designate two other days for cross-grade groups of fourth- and fifth- and/or fifth- and sixth-graders in the resource room. They might visit regular classrooms to teach model lessons on a fourth weekday, and use the fifth day for completing their administrative duties.

One less common, but valuable, way to implement a pull-out program is with a multiple-year curriculum, which affords continuity. For example, using the theme of change and adaptation, fourth-graders could study environmental changes; fifth-graders could examine political changes under oligarchies, monarchies, and democracies; and sixth-graders could learn of changing family roles in different regions of our country. Another method involves extending the regular classroom curriculum by studying the same subjects or topics in more depth. A third approach is basing the pull-out curriculum on national or regional enrichment programs, e.g. Odyssey of the Mind, Science Olympiad, or the Future Problem-Solving Program, and adding activities focused on the underlying reasoning and creative skills whereby students succeed in such programs. In a fourth approach, the resource-room gifted teacher decides the pull-out curriculum. In this case, the quality of program content depends largely on the knowledge, experience, and skills of the individual teacher.

ADVANTAGES

Pull-out programs give gifted students the benefits of weekly classroom interactions with their intellectual peers and of sharing experiences involving their individual strengths. Many gifted students look forward to this so much that they will never miss school on their pull-out day. Pull-out classes often have open-ended enough curricula to allow freedom of creative exploration, enlisting the teachers' and students' skills and imaginations to design projects of interest and value, which is another advantage. Having gifted resource-room teachers is also financially advantageous to school districts, as these teachers usually work with all gifted students at various grade levels, teach lessons in regular classrooms, conduct in-service trainings for other teachers and staff, field parents' phone calls as delegated by their school principals, and perform other functions entailing intensive communication with varied audiences.

Disadvantages

One disadvantage of pull-out programs is that school personnel may not adequately coordinate their activities with the regular classroom curriculum. Consequently some teachers—and students—wonder how some pull-out activities relate to general education subjects. Another problem occurs if resource teachers base projects on their own interests rather than students' strengths. Many teacher resources are available for activities supporting higher levels of learning, but teachers often do not avail themselves of these curriculum guides and materials. The activities they design for gifted students should not only be fun and interesting for the students, but also develop their advanced cognitive skills. Rarely, some general classroom teachers resent gifted students' weekly absence and retaliate by scheduling class parties or field trips, important tests, and/or new topic introductions on pull-out days. This unprofessional behavior is uncommon but problematic. Also, some busy classroom teachers do not give gifted students other differentiated learning choices for the rest of the week, mistakenly thinking the pull-out program is enough.

Gifted Pull-out Programs vs. Inclusive, Regular Classroom-Based Gifted Instruction

Suppose that a school district has two schools served by a gifted resource teacher. A total of 60 gifted students are served, with 30 gifted students in each school. Each school has two classrooms per grade, and the gifted students are in second through fifth grades. Four grades x two classrooms = eight, x two schools = 16. With pull-out programs, the resource teacher can teach one group of students per grade level, or four groups at each school (eight total). The teacher can do this in two full school days, one at each school. In contrast, if this teacher had to go to sixteen separate regular classrooms to teach the gifted students, it would take more time, and that time would be more fragmented. The teacher likely could not see students as regularly. Researchers found when a school district switched from pull-out to in-class programs, it cost three times as much to hire three times as many specialists as they had needed with pull-out teaching.

Remediating Drawbacks of Pull-Out/Resource Room Programs

To remedy a lack of coordination between pull-out activities and regular classroom curriculum, the resource teacher can circulate a newsletter to classroom teachers explaining their resource room activities and how they connect with the regular curriculum. To provide both gifted resource teachers and general classroom teachers with reciprocal insights into each other's work and experiences, they can each trade places for a day or half-day. The gifted resource teacher can offer to teach a lesson for the regular classroom teacher, who can observe the teaching strategies the resource teacher uses for gifted as well as regular students. The gifted resource teacher also can propose that the two teachers work together to team-teach a regular class that includes gifted students. Educational researchers find that pull-out programs can succeed or fail depending on whether or not the regular and gifted teachers share mutual understanding, solid communication, and positive interactions.

Self-Contained Special Education Programs

Self-contained gifted classes consist entirely of gifted students. In districts having these, they are at the elementary school level. If middle and high school students are placed in each subject via ability grouping, these classes may function as self-contained. However, true self-contained gifted classes for all subjects do not exist in regular public secondary schools due to subject departmentalization. Advantages include the ability to design more gifted-appropriate instruction overall; higher gifted student achievement levels than those in pull-out gifted programs; usually no extra expense, as the gifted class will have the same number of students as a regular class at that grade level; the greater ability of gifted students to relate to their intellectual peers; and a more supportive classroom atmosphere, more conducive to freedom of expression and more encouraging relative to individual student strengths and weaknesses, which allows gifted students to perform better and more consistently.

CLUSTER GROUPING

One practice that schools employ to meet the educational needs of their gifted students is to use cluster grouping. This practice entails grouping all of the gifted children at one grade level inclusively in one regular classroom. For example, if a school has three separate fourth-grade classrooms and a total of six fourth-graders identified as gifted, these students would all be placed in one of those classrooms rather than being distributed among several fourth-grade classrooms. This works for students gifted in individual subjects; a student with verbal gifts can be in a different classroom than a student with mathematical gifts. Some benefits are that cluster grouping is inexpensive and that students can move fluidly in and out of cluster groups. A drawback of cluster grouping is that globally gifted students cannot attend multiple classrooms simultaneously to meet their advanced needs in multiple subjects. Another consideration is that teachers must differentiate their instruction for greater variations in ability levels within one class.

DISADVANTAGES

One disadvantage of self-contained gifted classes that continue for several years is that gifted students lack classroom interactions with non-gifted peers. One solution is to have activities such as lunch, physical education, art, and music include all students to provide interaction. Some school districts create "teams" of several classrooms, including the self-contained gifted class, so gifted and other students interact daily. Another problem occurs when either too few or too many gifted students are identified for the school's normal class size. A smaller gifted class would provoke resentment in teachers with normal, larger class sizes; a group too large would force schools to leave out some qualified gifted students. Self-contained classes also can lead to student, teacher, and parent perceptions of school elitism and isolationism. Also, though there is no proof that other students suffer, some teachers still feel that removing the gifted students leaves the other students with no role models.

Professionalism

RECENT ISSUES AND TRENDS IN GIFTED EDUCATION

Researchers in gifted education have identified issues in some gifted programs that reflect common concerns in gifted education. Programs including part-time pull-outs, cluster grouping within general education classrooms, and center-based gifted programs all share some common concerns. Even with well-established, exemplary curriculum units, a need exists to reconsider the organization and focus relative to progress in cognitive learning theory and to content standards. The emphasis on documenting how instruction supports students' learning requires educators to consider differentiated instruction in greater depth. Performance-based assessments have gained greater prominence in evaluating learning because they are more congruent with higher-order content standards such as enabling more student demonstration of reasoning and problem-solving skills in specific subjects. Implications include that assessment must play a more central role in program and curriculum planning rather than depending only on traditional standardized achievement tests. Furthermore, collection and reporting of performance-based student impact data as well as more integration of assessment techniques and economy in analyzing data are indicated to promote both learning and accountability.

NEEDS IN PROGRAM MANAGEMENT OF GIFTED EDUCATION PROGRAMS

Educational researchers have observed that in some gifted programs, little time and few resources are left for the crucial components of curriculum design, program evaluation, and staff development, because so much time and effort are disproportionately devoted to the identification of gifted students. Nonetheless, researchers have clarified that this observation reflects not a criticism of program managers but instead an insight about the unrealistic expectations and insufficient investment in quality programs for students with high ability. Because trends increasingly emphasize curriculum planning and student assessment for such quality programs, greater program management capacities are needed. Progress includes greater recognition and provision of a variety of service options at the program level to meet diverse student and community needs, program developers' responses to the National Association for Gifted Children's standards for conveying program expectations, and the positive perceptions by constituents of the quality of staff in good gifted programs.

JAVITS ACT

The Javits Act, passed in 1988, after Public Law 94-142, aka the Education for All Handicapped Children Act (EHA) passed in 1975, renamed the Individuals with Disabilities Act (IDEA) in 1997, most recently reauthorized in 2004, with final regulations released in 2006. IDEA provides for all children to be educated, but it does not specify services for the gifted as for people with disabilities. The Javits Act, initiated by then-Senator Jacob Javits of New York, funds educational programs for gifted children from low-income families. It states, "The term gifted and talented student means children and youths who give evidence of higher performance capability in such areas as intellectual, creative, artistic, or leadership capacity, or in specific academic fields, and who require services or activities not ordinarily provided by the schools in order to develop such capabilities fully." This legislation meets the need for special services to gifted students in order to fulfill their special abilities.

CHALLENGES TEACHERS FACE WITH GIFTED AND TALENTED STUDENTS

An ever-increasing challenge in our schools is that due to economic considerations, school budgets are being cut, and special or supplementary services to gifted students often are eliminated. As a result, general education teachers find they have more gifted and talented students in their classrooms. Their challenge involves meeting the educational needs of students with average ability, students with high ability, students with disabilities whose inclusion in regular classrooms is mandated by law, and students with both gifts and disabilities. Teaching the same curriculum to all students, i.e. teacher-centered instruction, is no longer feasible. Information technology recently has become popular for use with gifted students. As such, information technology can replace some existing delivery methods and be added to others to enhance them. Assistive technology also aids students with vision, hearing, physical, and other disabilities. Those students with both gifts and disabilities receive multiple benefits from technology. Students can work at their own paces, access multiple modalities, select preferred modalities, and learn in more depth through enriched learning experiences.

Review Video: Teaching Through Multiple Modalities
Visit mometrix.com/academy and enter code: 100371

PROCEDURAL SAFEGUARDS REGARDING EDUCATION OF GIFTED STUDENTS

While the federal government has mandated procedural safeguards for the educational placement of students with disabilities, federal laws do not specifically address the placement of students who are gifted without disabilities. Each state Department of Education issues its own set of procedural safeguards for the placement of gifted students. They typically derive these standards from the federal requirements for students with disabilities in that all students must receive a free, appropriate public education (FAPE). Some common safeguards across states include the following standards: districts must give parents prior notice of initiation or refusal to identify, evaluate, place, or provide a FAPE to a gifted student, in the parents' primary communicative mode. Parents must be given copies of procedural safeguards. Written informed parent consent is required before providing individual formal evaluation or initial service to a gifted student, and such consent is voluntary and revocable before the action. Parents have the right to view their child's educational records and participate in educational planning meetings.

Each state Department of Education writes its own procedural safeguards. Specifically, many states require that if parents obtain independent evaluations of their gifted children at their own private expense, the state's school districts must consider those evaluation findings in any educational decisions they make for those students. In addition, states commonly require that if an administrative law judge requests an independent evaluation as part of a hearing, the expense becomes a public responsibility. Usually the district must finance the evaluation. Another standard of state procedural safeguards, adopted from Federal disability laws, is the right of gifted students and their parents to a due process hearing regarding the student's identification, evaluation, or educational placement. States also commonly stipulate that students remain in their current placements while an administrative or judicial proceeding is pending.

Legal Issues Concerning Gifted Students

Federal laws protect the legal rights of students with disabilities but not the legal rights of gifted students without disabilities. Even the Jacob K. Javits Gifted and Talented Student Act (1994), which funds research and projects related to giftedness, does not protect gifted students' legal rights. Each US state has jurisdiction over its educational procedures. However, discrimination based on giftedness is equally as unlawful as discrimination based on race, color, national origin, gender, or disability. Despite the lack of specific federal mandates for gifted education, the US State Department of Education's Office of Civil Rights protects the educational rights of gifted students participating in government-funded programs and activities. From 1985-1995, this office has ruled in 86 cases involving gifted students regarding discrimination, identification, and program admissions. The American Civil Liberties Union has also filed discrimination suits; for example, against a school district for offering fewer Advanced Placement programs in schools with African-American and Hispanic populations with lower socioeconomic status.

Equity in Education

Equality vs. Equity

Equality refers to providing everyone with the same resources when working toward a goal, regardless of the unique needs or situation of the individual. **Equity** means considering an individual's needs and circumstances to provide the proper supports that allow the individual a fair opportunity to achieve a common goal. In the classroom, creating an equitable environment requires the consideration of students' individual learning styles, needs, and personal situations and using this knowledge to instill necessary supports to help each student achieve the same objectives relative to their peers. Equity in the classroom is especially important for closing the achievement gap, particularly in low socioeconomic areas, because many of these students come from disadvantaged situations and need additional help to gain a fair opportunity for academic success.

Review Video: Equality vs Equity
Visit mometrix.com/academy and enter code: 685648

Supports Utilized to Provide an Equitable Learning Environment

The nature of academic, physical, and behavioral supports depends largely on the needs of the individual student; however, some common supports are effective in addressing an array of needs to facilitate an equitable learning environment. Students with **learning disabilities** may benefit from academic supports such as preferential seating near the front of the room and minimized distractions to enhance focus. Modified test questions or alternate assignments, graphic organizers, scaffolded texts, extra copies of class notes, and individualized instruction are also valuable in enhancing focus, preventing students from becoming overwhelmed, and ensuring learning activities are aligned with students' capabilities. Students with **physical disabilities** may require wheelchair access, a sign language interpreter or scribe, braille text, enlarged fonts, or the use of technology devices to aid in reading and writing. Common **behavioral supports** in the classroom include opportunities for frequent breaks or movement as needed, a daily check-in with a caseworker or other dedicated staff member, or a behavior chart to allow students to self-monitor.

Establishing High Academic Expectations

In any classroom, establishing high academic standards is imperative for motivating and empowering students to succeed. By communicating high expectations clearly and frequently, the teacher demonstrates belief that each student can overcome obstacles and excel academically, thus inspiring student engagement, curiosity for learning, and an overall positive and productive learning environment. To create an environment of high academic standards, the teachers' expectations must be apparent in instruction. The teacher must provide lessons and activities that are rigorous but not so challenging that students are unable to complete them without assistance, as this would disempower and disengage students from learning. The teacher must set achievable learning goals based on knowledge of student abilities and encourage self-reflection. Additionally, the teacher must utilize knowledge of students' individual needs to instill necessary supports to help students in achieving tasks and create an equitable environment for learning. This will ultimately empower students to overcome obstacles and motivate them for academic success.

Legal and Ethical Obligations Surrounding Student Rights

Legal Requirements for Educators

Special Education Services

Establishing an inclusive, equitable learning environment for students with disabilities requires educators to adhere to strict legal guidelines regarding special education services. According to **IDEA (Individuals with Disabilities Education Act)**, educators must provide students with disabilities a **free and appropriate public education (FAPE)** in the **least restrictive environment (LRE)**. To do this effectively, educators are required to fully comply with students' **IEPs (Individual Education Plans)** at all times. This includes providing students requiring special education services with the necessary supports, accommodations, and modifications according to their IEPs throughout all stages of instruction. Educators must also document the academic and behavioral progress of these students in relation to the goals outlined in their IEPs to report to the designated case manager. In addition, the specifics of students' special education services must be kept confidential in order to protect their privacy. Adhering to these legal requirements promotes equity in the classroom by ensuring that the unique needs of students with disabilities are met, thus allowing them to effectively participate and engage in learning.

Review Video: Legal and Ethical Issues
Visit mometrix.com/academy and enter code: 934372

Review Video: IEPs
Visit mometrix.com/academy and enter code: 153484

Review Video: Development of the Individuals with Disabilities Education Act
Visit mometrix.com/academy and enter code: 100350

FERPA

Understanding and observing the legal requirements related to students' and families' rights is integral to maintaining their confidentiality and establishing a safe, secure learning environment. Educators are required to follow the guidelines of **FERPA (Family Educational Rights and Privacy Act)** regarding students' education records and personally identifiable information. According to FERPA, educators may not release students' education records or personally identifiable information except in authorized situations, such as when the student enrolls in another school or the information is requested by a financial aid institution to which the student has applied. In all other instances, the educator must have written permission to disclose this information. FERPA also provides students' parents or legal guardians the right to access their child's education records and request that the education records be amended. While educators may not disclose personally identifiable information, they are permitted to release directory information regarding the student, including their name, phone number, or student identification number; however, educators must provide an appropriate amount of time to allow for the refusal of such disclosure. It is also important to note that the rights guaranteed under FERPA become applicable only to students once they have turned 18 or begun postsecondary education.

Discipline Procedures and Student Code of Conduct

Adhering to legal requirements regarding student discipline procedures is necessary to ensure a safe, orderly, and unbiased learning environment. School districts are responsible for developing a **student code of conduct** to distribute among teachers, staff, students, and families. This document outlines expectations for student behavior as well as specific consequences for varying degrees of infractions that may occur on school grounds. Educators must strictly adhere to the guidelines stated in the student code of conduct when enacting disciplinary measures. This includes ensuring that consequences for student misbehavior align with the nature of the action and do not interfere with the student's right to a free public education. Disciplinary actions must be free of bias and must not endanger the student's physical, mental, or emotional health. In addition, the educator must document instances of student discipline and keep these records confidential to protect the student's right to privacy. Extended suspensions and expulsions must be reserved for instances in which all other disciplinary measures have been exhausted. In such cases, the student is entitled to a hearing at the board of education, and teachers must provide adequate instructional materials for the time that the student is out of the classroom.

Guidelines for acceptable student behavior on school property are outlined in a student code of conduct. Providing students with this reference helps to ensure that the school functions in a safe, orderly, and productive manner so as to create and maintain an environment focused on learning. This document typically addresses a number of topics related to **daily school procedures**, including student dress code standards, acceptable use policies for the internet and digital devices, attendance, grading policies, and academic integrity. Student codes of conduct also address **potential behavioral issues**, such as acceptable conduct while riding school buses, the use of illegal substances on school property, and harmful or disruptive behavior, including bullying, harassment, or fighting. The expectations iterated in student codes of conduct are typically accompanied by an ascending matrix of classroom, administrative, and district-level **consequences** that coincide with the severity and frequency of student infractions.

Establishing an Equitable Learning Environment for All Students

An **equitable environment** is one in which students receive the individual support necessary to facilitate their success in learning. Establishing such an environment requires educators to adhere to several legal guidelines to ensure all students are provided with fair access to learning opportunities. Educators must be sure that all students are included in the educational program, and may not discriminate based upon students' races, religions, genders, backgrounds, disabilities, or any other differentiating characteristics. All students must be provided with equal access to learning materials, resources, technologies, and supports. In addition, educators must fully comply with all accommodations outlined in students' **IEPs**, **504 plans**, and **Behavior Intervention Plans (BIP)**, and implement all required supports to provide them with equitable access to learning.

Review Video: 504 Plans and IEPs
Visit mometrix.com/academy and enter code: 881103

Child Abuse

One of the primary responsibilities of an educator is to ensure the safety of all students. In order to do so, it is important that educators understand and follow all legal requirements related to child abuse. Within the classroom, educators are responsible for establishing a safe, secure learning environment. All interactions with students must be appropriate and refrain from harming students' **physical**, **mental**, or **emotional health**. Educators must also recognize the signs of potential **child abuse** or **neglect** among their students. If any abuse or neglect is suspected, educators are legally required to report it immediately to the proper agency according to their state and local laws regardless of whether there is concrete evidence, as waiting to report it may place the student in continued danger. Reports of potential child abuse or neglect must be **confidential** so as to protect the students' privacy. Depending on the protocols established by individual school districts, educators may be required to notify their school's administration and resource officer of the report.

Significance of Understanding and Adhering to Legal Requirements

Understanding the legal requirements for educators ensures that teachers know what is expected of them to maintain professionalism and establish a safe, secure learning environment. This avoids misconception regarding the teacher's **roles** and **responsibilities** within the educational program so that teachers understand how to adhere to legal guidelines properly. When teachers are aware of the legal requirements they must follow, they are more effectively able to implement the appropriate protocols for addressing specific education-related situations. This includes instances related to establishing an equitable learning environment, providing special education services, interacting appropriately with students, colleagues, and families as well as protecting students' privacy. In addition, understanding the legal requirements for educators ensures that they are aware of their own professional rights and how to protect themselves in various education-related situations.

Ethical Guidelines

Confidentiality

Adhering to ethical guidelines in relation to confidentiality is an important part of demonstrating professionalism as well as protecting the privacy of students, their families, and others in the school building. Teachers are required to follow all standards outlined by **FERPA** regarding student and family privacy. This includes preserving the confidentiality of all **personally identifiable information** about students, such as grades, medical history, discipline records, or special education services, except in authorized situations. By following these guidelines, teachers ensure that they do not release any information that may compromise the safety of students or their families. In addition, when students and families feel their personal information is kept confidential, they are more likely to seek necessary supports from the educational program without the fear of being stigmatized. Similarly, teachers must follow ethical guidelines to protect the privacy of their colleagues. Any knowledge about a colleague's personal information must be kept confidential so as to establish positive, professional relationships founded on mutual trust. Doing so facilitates productive collaboration among colleagues to benefit student success in learning.

Interactions with Students and Others in the School Community

The daily interactions among students, teachers, staff, and administration largely determine the quality of the school environment. A positive, safe, and professional school community is one in which educators adhere to ethical guidelines regarding interactions with one another and students. Communication with colleagues must be respectful of one another's privacy and confidentiality. This includes avoiding gossip and ensuring that all discussions about colleagues are factual, neutral, and professional in nature. In addition, interactions with members of the school community must **avoid discrimination** of any sort. Similarly, all interactions with students must be inclusive, accepting, and respectful of differences. In addition, educators must maintain proper **boundaries** when communicating with students. This includes avoiding communication outside of the school setting except in authorized situations and ensuring that all interactions maintain professionalism. Any interactions with students must avoid compromising their **physical or mental health**, **safety**, or **ability to learn**. By adhering to these ethical guidelines, educators can ensure that all communication with students and members of the school community contribute to establishing and maintaining a safe, appropriate, and professional learning environment.

Teacher's Role as an Advocate

Advocating for Students

The teacher's role as an advocate is invaluable in ensuring students receive the necessary support to facilitate their achievement. As teachers spend most of the school day with students, they are equipped with an understanding of how to best meet the unique needs within their classrooms. Teachers will inevitably encounter situations in which advocacy for students is integral to providing equitable learning opportunities. Students with **physical**, **social**, **emotional**, or **learning disabilities** need teachers to advocate on their behalf to ensure special education services or accommodations are implemented. Teachers may also need to advocate for **underprivileged students** to ensure they have equitable access to the learning materials, resources, and technologies necessary for success. Additionally, students experiencing **bullying** may need teachers to ensure the appropriate measures are taken to resolve the issue and maintain a safe learning environment. Effective advocacy requires teachers to listen and communicate with students to determine their needs and seek the appropriate avenues for support. Teachers must also communicate with colleagues, administration, and families to collaborate in addressing students' needs. In some instances, teachers may need to contact the board of education or education advocacy organizations specific to students' needs to ensure they are provided with adequate support.

Advocating for the Educational Profession

Teachers offer valuable perspectives regarding ways to enhance the quality of the education profession. As such, it is important that teachers advocate for themselves in order to help ensure they have the **conditions**, **resources**, and **support systems** necessary to facilitate student success. This includes advocating for equitable allocation of funding, learning materials, technology resources, and professional development opportunities that would help teachers more effectively meet students' learning needs. Teachers can advocate for the profession in a variety of ways. **Communicating frequently** with students, families, and administration allows teachers to discuss their needs and ways to improve the education system. Attending **PTA meetings, public forums**, or **school board meetings** allows teachers to voice their concerns and offer potential solutions. Teachers can also contact **state legislators** to influence their decisions regarding education policies that would impact the quality of the profession. In addition, there are numerous **education advocacy organizations** that teachers can join to connect with one another and influence such decisions. Taking measures to advocate for the education profession is an important part of creating a positive, productive school climate focused on supporting student achievement.

Professional Development

Available Resources and Support Systems

Effective educators continuously seek professional development opportunities to refine their teaching practice. There are multiple resources and support systems that teachers can utilize to develop their professional knowledge and skills. Within the school building, mentors are available to offer ideas, advice, and support in developing teaching practices and strategies to implement in the classroom for effective teaching and learning. The school's **instructional leadership team** (ILT) is also a valuable resource for educating teachers regarding current instructional practices to enhance student engagement and learning. Teachers can continue their professional education by enrolling in university courses or participating in state-initiated programs to stay informed on relevant pedagogical theories and practices. Service centers are also available that offer workshops, training, and conferences on a variety of topics related to education to support teachers' professional development. In addition, numerous digital support resources are available that allow teachers to enroll in courses, participate in informational webinars, and collaborate with other educators in professional learning communities to build and enhance their teaching practice.

Example Opportunities That Can Enhance Teaching Practice

Professional development opportunities are available to address a variety of needs for refining one's practice and developing pedagogical knowledge. Professional development trainings can serve to educate teachers on how to utilize and incorporate current technologies into the classroom as well as teach strategies for implementing relevant and engaging instructional techniques, materials, and resources into the classroom. These opportunities can also be beneficial in teaching educators how to demonstrate cultural competency and skills for productive collaboration with colleagues to enhance student learning. Teachers can also seek professional development opportunities to learn best practices for addressing a variety of student needs, such as intellectual, physical, social, or emotional disabilities, or linguistic needs of ELLs. Actively seeking and participating in professional development trainings helps to ensure teachers stay current on pedagogical theories that can serve as a framework for their instructional practice.

Effectively Utilizing Resources and Support Systems

The field of education is multifaceted and continuously evolving. As such, it is important that teachers of all experience levels engage in the vast array of **available resources** and **support systems** to develop and refine their professional skills. Doing so enhances students' learning, as teachers who actively seek professional development are more current on pedagogical theories and practices as well as instructional strategies, resources, and technologies to incorporate in the classroom. This allows teachers to design and implement more effective instruction, as it provides them with an increased range of knowledge and tools to enhance student engagement and understanding. In addition, as students' individual needs are diverse, participating in resources and support systems allows teachers to educate themselves on how to properly accommodate them to enhance the learning experience. Utilizing resources and support systems also enables teachers to learn from and collaborate with other educators in professional learning communities to continuously develop new skills, ideas, and instructional methods that enhance student learning.

Teacher Appraisals

Characteristics, Goals, and Procedures

Teacher appraisals are a method of evaluation intended to provide teachers with continuous feedback regarding their **performance** and areas in which they can improve their professional skills to enhance student learning. Feedback is provided periodically throughout the school year and derives from classroom **observations** typically conducted by the principal or grade-level administrator. Observations can either be **formally** scheduled and last the duration of a lesson or can be in the form of shorter, informal **walk-through** evaluations. In both instances, the observer watches and collects information as the teacher delivers instruction, directs learning activities, and interacts with students. The teacher's performance is then measured against **criteria** across several domains pertaining to planning, preparing, and delivering instruction. This score is used to provide the teacher with detailed feedback in post-observation meetings regarding their strengths and specific areas in which they can improve their practice to more effectively meet students' learning needs. Feedback is used to support the teacher in developing specific **professional goals** and strategies for improving their teaching skills.

Benefits of Appraisal Results in Improving Professional Skills

The results of teacher appraisals are beneficial in providing educators with **specific feedback** regarding areas in which they can improve their professional skills. Effective teachers understand the value of continuously **refining their practice** to enhance student learning and actively seek opportunities to do so; however, it may prove difficult for teachers to objectively assess their own efficacy in the classroom. Appraisal results communicate feedback from the outside perspective of the observer for a comprehensive evaluation of their performance, thus providing teachers with clarity regarding their strengths and areas for growth. This allows educators to effectively develop **professional goals** to improve their skills in targeted areas and **strategies** to achieve these goals successfully.

Working with Supervisors, Mentors, and Colleagues

Enhancing Professional Knowledge and Skills

When teachers collaborate with supervisors, mentors, and other colleagues, it facilitates a productive **professional learning community** that supports the continuous development of knowledge and skills related to education. Doing so provides teachers with the opportunity to work with educational professionals of varying backgrounds, experiences, and expertise. This exposes teachers to a wide range of **perspectives**, **approaches**, and **philosophies** that they can learn from to build and enhance their practice. In such a setting, teachers can interact with other professionals within the school community to share ideas, support one another, and collaborate productively in developing strategies to improve their efficacy in the classroom. Additionally, actively engaging with supervisors, mentors, and colleagues facilitates the open communication necessary for productive collaboration in effectively addressing issues to enhance the school community.

Addressing Issues and Building Professional Skills

Productive collaboration with supervisors, mentors, and colleagues is essential to addressing issues related to the educational program and continuously developing professional practices. There are multiple opportunities for such collaboration within the school community that accommodate varying purposes. By participating in **professional learning communities**, members of the educational program can collaborate and support one another in addressing concerns and building professional skills. In subject-area **department** or **team meetings**, educators can work together to share ideas, strategies, and resources related to their content areas for more effective instruction. Working with supervisors and mentors in **post-observation conferences** provides teachers with valuable feedback regarding their strengths and areas for improvement. Such collaboration is beneficial in creating specific goals and strategies for professional growth. Additionally, engaging in collaborative **professional development opportunities**, including workshops, conferences, programs, and courses, is beneficial in allowing educators to build upon one another's experiences, backgrounds, and expertise to enhance professional practices.

Professional Development Resources

The various professional development resources available to teachers and staff are discussed below:

- **Mentors/support systems**: Mentors and other dedicated support resources within the school system are intended to provide teachers with guidance to enhance their professional knowledge, skills, and expertise. These individuals are typically highly experienced and work with teachers to develop effective instructional strategies, classroom management techniques, and learning materials to improve their teaching skills.
- **Conferences**: Education conferences are multifaceted events in which teachers can learn about current developments in their field to improve their professional knowledge, pedagogical skills, and technical expertise. Conference events are composed of numerous professional development opportunities, including presentations on current pedagogical theories and practices, collaborative workshops, and training sessions regarding the implementation of new instructional strategies and technology resources. At these events, teachers can also network with one another to connect and share resources, ideas, and strategies that enhance their teaching practice.
- **Professional associations**: Education associations provide teachers with access to numerous professional development opportunities for improving knowledge, pedagogical skills, and technical expertise. These associations can be related to general education or be content specific, and they offer information regarding education conferences, workshops, training opportunities, and courses to enhance teaching practices. Professional education associations also allow teachers the opportunity to network with one another to build professional knowledge by sharing ideas, resources, and strategies to implement in the classroom.
- **Online resources**: Numerous online resources, including websites, blogs, webinar trainings, and discussion forums are available to support teachers in enhancing their professional knowledge, skills, and technical expertise on a variety of topics. Teachers can utilize these resources to learn current pedagogical theories and practices, instructional and classroom management strategies, and relevant technology resources to implement in the classroom for enhanced student learning. Online resources are also valuable for collaborating with other teachers in building professional knowledge and sharing ideas, learning materials, and resources that improve instructional practices.
- **Workshops**: Workshop training sessions provide teachers the opportunity to build professional knowledge, skills, and expertise by educating them on current instructional strategies, classroom management techniques, and digital resources in a hands-on setting. Workshops are typically dedicated to a specific pedagogical topic and allow teachers to collaborate with one another in learning how to implement it in their classroom.

- **Journals**: Education journals publish newly researched information regarding pedagogical theories and practices teachers can utilize to enhance their professional knowledge. These journals include scholarly articles and case studies regarding topics such as instructional strategies and practices, classroom management techniques, and the implementation of digital resources. Education journals allow teachers to stay current on pedagogical developments in order to continuously improve their teaching skills.
- **Coursework**: Engaging in coursework is beneficial in continuing formal professional education to enhance knowledge, pedagogical skills, and technical expertise. Doing so allows teachers to learn from other experienced educators regarding current educational theories, practices, instructional strategies, and technology resources. By participating in formal coursework, teachers can continuously build upon their teaching skills and stay current regarding developments in their field.

Reflection and Self-Assessment

Improving Teaching Performance and Achieving Professional Goals

Just as students are encouraged to reflect upon their academic performance, it is important that teachers **reflect** on and **self-assess** their own efficacy in the classroom. Doing so is integral for improving professional knowledge and skills to enhance student learning. Effective teachers continuously self-evaluate their performance to ensure they are providing engaging, relevant instruction that effectively meets students' learning needs for success. Frequently reflecting upon and assessing the effectiveness of their lesson plans, instructional strategies, assessments, and approaches to classroom management is beneficial in providing teachers with insight regarding their **professional strengths** as well as specific **areas for growth**. With this insight, teachers can identify the knowledge, skills, and strategies they need to improve upon to deliver more effective instruction. This ultimately allows teachers to set relevant professional goals to enhance their teaching practice and determine the steps they need to take in achieving them.

Methods

Continuous reflection and self-assessment through a variety of methods is beneficial in providing teachers with insight into the effectiveness of their teaching practice. **Reflecting on lessons** after they are finished allows teachers to self-assess their instruction by identifying specific elements that were successful as well as components that can be improved in the future to enhance student learning. By eliciting **student feedback**, teachers can evaluate whether their instructional strategies, lesson activities, and assessments promote student engagement and understanding. Working with **mentors** and **colleagues** to discuss the effectiveness of lessons, instructional approaches, and classroom management techniques is also valuable in facilitating self-evaluation of teaching practices to seek areas for improvement. In addition, teachers are typically provided the opportunity to **respond to post-observation feedback** prior to attending an appraisal conference. This provides teachers with the opportunity to reflect on their overall performance and prepare to collaborate with the observer in developing professional goals.

Participating in the Local Educational Community

Impact of Volunteering on Positive Educational Community

Participating in school activities, events, and projects positively impacts the nature of the school community and culture. When teachers and staff members volunteer their time to contribute in such a way, it strengthens **connections** to the school community that foster positive attitudes toward it. By actively engaging in activities, events, and projects, teachers and staff have the opportunity to collaborate in making **positive contributions** to the school community. This facilitates the development of relationships among colleagues that enhance their ability to work cooperatively in creating a positive learning atmosphere that benefits students and the educational program. Students are more supported in such an environment and develop positive attitudes toward learning and strong relationships with their teachers that enhance the overall school **climate**. In addition, as students are influenced by the behaviors, actions, and attitudes modeled by adults in the building, contributing positively to the school community encourages them to do the same.

Participation Opportunities

Participating in school activities, events, and projects is valuable in integrating oneself into the school community while making positive contributions. Such participation can occur through a variety of avenues, both within and outside of the school campus. Teachers can assist in school fundraisers, food and clothing drives, or field trips. They can also serve as tutors and lead school clubs or other extracurricular activities. By attending school sporting events, recitals, concerts, and plays, teachers can participate in the school community while supporting students. Events such as open-house nights, parent-teacher nights, and public forum meetings are also valuable opportunities to participate in the school community in a way that positively contributes to students' learning.

Enhancing the Educational Community

As teachers work closely with students, colleagues, and administration, their contributions to the school and district are integral in enhancing the school community. Teachers provide valuable insight regarding the needs of the educational program and ways to improve the school environment. As such, their participation in the school and district is beneficial in helping to ensure the needs of staff and students are adequately met to create a positive educational community. In addition, active participation in the school and district facilitates the collaboration necessary for establishing relationships among colleagues that contribute to a positive school culture and climate. Teachers can contribute to building such an educational community in a variety of ways. By participating in **school activities**, **events**, and **projects**, teachers can work cooperatively to create a positive learning atmosphere. Teachers can also attend **school meetings** and serve on focused **committees** to solve problems and influence decisions that improve the nature of the school environment. At the district level, teachers can communicate with members of the board of education and participate in **public forums** to express ideas, discuss concerns, and offer input regarding ways to enhance the educational community.

Family Involvement and Collaboration

Effectively Working and Communicating with Families

Utilizing multiple means of communication when working with students' families ensures information is **accessible** to and **inclusive** of all involved family members. As students' home lives are dynamic, conveying information through several avenues allows families in various situations to participate in their child's education. This is invaluable in establishing and maintaining the positive relationships necessary between students' families and schools for effective teaching and learning. General classroom information, including concepts being taught, important dates, assignments, or suggestions for activities to do at home that reinforce learning in the classroom, can be communicated both digitally and in written form. Newsletters, calendars, or handouts can be both printed and included on a class website to ensure accessibility for all families. Updates regarding individual students can be communicated electronically, through writing, or in person. Email, digital communication apps, and the telephone allow for frequent communication to address students' progress, express concerns, or offer praise. Teachers and families can also communicate through handwritten notes, progress reports, or students' daily agendas. In-person communication, such as during a scheduled conference, is beneficial for discussing individual students' progress and goals related to the education program in depth as well as ways to support their success in learning.

Building Positive Relationships That Enhance Overall Learning

Students are more supported and learn more effectively when the relationships between their teachers and families are founded on **mutual respect**, **understanding**, and **cooperation**. Establishing this positive rapport requires the teacher to work and communicate frequently with students' families. Doing so creates an inviting learning atmosphere in which family members feel welcomed and included as **equal contributors** to the educational program. This sentiment empowers and encourages family members to take an active role in their children's education, thus strengthening students' support systems and enhancing the overall learning experience. In addition, family members who feel a strong connection to their children's school are more likely to model positive attitudes toward education and reinforce learning at home. When teachers and family members communicate frequently, they develop a mutual sense of trust for one another. This allows for **productive collaboration** and the exchange of valuable insight regarding how to best support students' learning needs both within and outside of the classroom.

Appropriate Collaboration and Communication with Families

To effectively collaborate and communicate with students' families, the teacher must carefully consider appropriate methods for doing so. Communication and collaboration must always be **positive**, **respectful,** and **inclusive** to all families to ensure they feel welcomed as equal participants in their children's education. As such, the teacher must be mindful and responsive to the fact that students come from a variety of backgrounds, family dynamics, and living situations. This includes demonstrating **cultural competency** when interacting with families from different backgrounds, providing multiple and varied opportunities for family involvement, and communicating through a variety of means. Doing so ensures that families of varying situations have access to pertinent information and feel equally included in the educational program. The teacher must also be mindful of the nature and purpose of communication in order to ensure that sensitive details about individual students are shared only with appropriate family members. General classroom information, such as important dates, events, or assignments, may be shared publicly among the classroom community, whereas things like individual student progress or behavior records must be reserved for private communication with the appropriate family members.

INVOLVEMENT OF FAMILIES, PARENTS, GUARDIANS, AND LEGAL CAREGIVERS

STRATEGIES TO ENCOURAGE ENGAGEMENT

As students' family dynamics are diverse, it is important that the teacher implement a variety of methods to engage parents, guardians, and legal caregivers into the educational program. Doing so creates an inviting atmosphere in which family members of all situations feel encouraged to participate in their children's education. Efforts to engage families must always be **positive, inclusive**, and **accommodating** to a variety of needs, schedules, and situations. This includes ensuring that all opportunities for involvement are culturally sensitive, meaningful, and accepting of all families. Utilizing a variety of **communication methods**, such as weekly newsletters, calendars, phone calls, and electronic communication, ensures that opportunities to engage in the educational program are accessible to all families. Providing **multiple** and **varied** opportunities for involvement, such as family nights, field trips, award ceremonies, or inviting families to participate in classroom activities, further encourages family engagement in the educational program. This enables families in various situations to become involved in their children's education in the way that best suits their needs and abilities.

FORMS OF ACTIVE INVOLVEMENT

Active involvement in the educational program can take a variety of forms both within and outside of the classroom to accommodate differences in families' schedules, dynamics, and abilities. Providing multiple avenues for involvement engages families of various situations to actively participate in their children's education. Within the classroom, family members can **volunteer** their time to assist as teachers' aides, tutors, or chaperones. In addition, if a family member is skilled in an area related to instruction, the teacher can ask the family member to come in to speak or teach a lesson. Inviting family members to **visit the classroom** or participate in special class activities allows them to actively engage in the learning process and gain insight into the educational program. Outside of daily classroom activities, family members can be encouraged to participate by attending **family nights, school social events, fundraisers**, or **parent-teacher association meetings**. Active involvement in the educational program can also occur at home. By frequently communicating with teachers, assisting with projects or homework, and emphasizing the importance of learning at home, family members can be informed and actively involved in their children's education.

IMPORTANCE IN CHILDREN'S EDUCATION

As students spend a great deal of time between school and home, the degree to which their family is involved in the educational program significantly influences the quality of the learning experience. When teachers take measures to engage families in their children's education, they establish a welcoming tone that facilitates relationships founded on mutual respect, understanding, and acceptance. These positive relationships are necessary for encouraging and empowering families to actively participate in the learning process. Such involvement contributes to establishing a **positive learning community** in which teachers and families can collaborate productively to enhance students' learning. When students' families are actively involved in their education, it strengthens the **support system** in both influential areas of their lives, thus establishing a sense of security that allows them to confidently engage in learning. Families that participate in the educational program are more likely to emphasize its value at home by extending and reinforcing learning outside of the classroom. This is highly beneficial in promoting positive attitudes toward learning, academic achievement, and social and emotional development.

Influence on Student Learning and Development

The degree of family involvement in the educational program significantly influences the quality of students' learning and development. Learning is more effective when parents, guardians, or legal caregivers are actively engaged in their child's education, as this promotes positive relationships between students' school and home lives that strengthen their **support system** and encourage the extension of learning beyond the classroom. Families that participate in the educational program are likely to emphasize and model its importance at home, thus influencing students to adopt the same positive attitudes toward learning. This facilitates **academic achievement**, **decreased absences** from school, and **positive learning habits**. In addition, when families are actively involved in the educational process, they are more effectively able to support students with resources at home that reinforce concepts learned in the classroom to strengthen connections and understanding. Students develop healthy **social and emotional skills** as well when their families are actively involved in the educational program. This facilitates positive self-esteem and interpersonal skills that contribute to academic success and fewer behavioral issues in the classroom.

Benefits for Parents, Families, Guardians, and Legal Caregivers

Families, parents, guardians, and legal caregivers that are actively involved in the educational program gain greater **insight**, **understanding**, and **resources** that enable them to support their children's learning more effectively both within and outside of the classroom. Active engagement in the educational program fosters a positive rapport founded on mutual respect and support among family members, teachers, and the school. This provides family members with a sense of **confidence** in the merits of the educational program while contributing to the sense that they are **equal participants** in the learning process. These family members are more informed regarding what is being taught in the classroom and beneficial resources to reinforce learning at home. This leaves family members feeling more **empowered** and willing to reinforce their students' learning. In addition, participating in the learning process provides family members with a greater understanding of the characteristics and capabilities of their children's developmental level, thus equipping them with the knowledge to effectively support learning and growth.

Benefits for Effective Teaching

The involvement of families, parents, guardians, and legal caregivers in the educational program is highly beneficial for effective teaching. Family members that actively participate in the learning process are likely to develop a greater sense of **understanding** and **appreciation** of the teacher's role within it. Such involvement also facilitates positive and frequent communication with families that fosters relationships founded on mutual respect and increases the teacher's **morale** and effectiveness in the classroom. Active engagement from family members also allows the teacher to gain a better understanding of how to support individual students' needs. Family members provide valuable insight regarding students' cultures, values, beliefs, educational goals, and learning needs to allow for more effective teaching. In addition, family members that are involved in their children's education are more likely to reinforce and extend learning at home, thus allowing for more effective teaching in the classroom.

Positive Rapport

A positive rapport between teachers and families enhances the quality of the learning experience. Establishing these positive relationships requires that teachers frequently take measures to engage families in the educational program in ways that are **meaningful**, **relevant**, and **responsive** to varying situations, backgrounds, and needs. In doing so, teachers communicate the sentiment that all families are welcomed, valued, and considered equal participants in the learning process. This serves to create an open, inviting learning atmosphere in which family involvement is encouraged, thus fostering the **participation** and **communication** necessary for developing a mutual positive rapport. Working to build positive relationships strengthens the connection between schools and families that facilitates productive **collaboration** to best support and enhance students' learning.

Interacting with Families of Various Backgrounds

Diversities That May Be Encountered

Appropriate interaction when working and communicating with students' families requires teachers to recognize the wide range of diversities in characteristics, backgrounds, and needs that they will inevitably encounter. With **culturally diverse** families, the teacher will likely experience variances in language, values, traditions, and customs, including differences in beliefs regarding best practices for raising and educating children. **Socioeconomic** differences may influence the degree to which families have the ability and access to resources to support their children in learning. In some instances, socioeconomic differences may also impact the level of education that family members have attained and potentially the value they place on the importance of education. The teacher must also be mindful of the diversities that exist among **family dynamics**. Some families may have a single caregiver, whereas others may have many. Students may be only children, have several siblings, or come from a blended family. Differences in dynamics also include varying work schedules, lifestyle demands, and living situations that the teacher must consider when working and communicating with families. By acknowledging the diverse characteristics, backgrounds, and needs of students' families, the teacher can take measures to ensure appropriate and inclusive interactions that enhance the learning experience.

Appropriate and Productive Interactions

Recognizing the diverse nature of students' cultures, backgrounds, and experiences provides teachers with insight regarding how to interact with their families appropriately and productively. By self-educating to become **culturally competent** and building relationships with students, teachers develop an understanding of the unique characteristics, values, beliefs, and needs of each family. This enables teachers to tailor their communication with individual families in a way that is respectful, **culturally sensitive**, and responsive to their concerns and needs. Doing so ensures that all families feel welcomed and supported in the school environment, thus establishing positive relationships that encourage families to actively engage in the educational program and collaborate productively with teachers to enhance students' learning.

Possible Obstacles

As teachers work and interact with families of diverse backgrounds and experiences, they likely will encounter obstacles that must be addressed to facilitate effective communication. **Cultural differences** in values, beliefs, language, and nonverbal communication may cause misinterpretations between teachers and families that make it difficult to understand one another. It is, therefore, important that teachers educate themselves regarding students' backgrounds to learn how to communicate in a culturally sensitive manner. When language barriers are present, learning common words and phrases in the language or utilizing an interpreter is beneficial in facilitating communication. Family members may have experienced **negative interactions** with teachers in the past that affect their willingness to engage in communication. Taking measures to establish an inviting, accepting atmosphere that promotes open communication is beneficial in encouraging these families to become involved. **Lifestyle differences**, including varying work schedules, living situations, and family dynamics, may make it difficult to establish effective communication. In addition, **accessibility issues**, including lack of access to transportation, technology devices, or the internet, may hinder family members' abilities to maintain frequent communication. To address these issues, teachers must utilize several communication methods that accommodate families' varying needs and situations.

Considerations to Ensure Beneficial Interactions

The ultimate goal when working and communicating with families is to benefit students' learning and development. When teachers and families develop a positive rapport between one another, it fosters productive collaboration to support the students' educational and developmental goals. Doing so requires that teachers ensure all interactions with students' families are appropriate, respectful, and considerate. This includes demonstrating awareness of varying **backgrounds, characteristics**, and **needs** of each family and interacting in a way that is responsive and accepting of differences. Teachers must practice **cultural competency** when communicating with families, including recognizing differences in perspectives, values, beliefs, and nonverbal communication. Teachers must also consider families' unique situations, including differing **work schedules**, **living arrangements**, and **family dynamics** to ensure that all interactions are considerate of their time, accommodating to their needs, and supportive of their role in the educational program. When interacting with families, it is important that teachers practice active listening and respond appropriately, meaningfully, and constructively. This communicates to families that their opinions, goals, and concerns related to the educational program are respected, thus encouraging them to actively participate in supporting their children's progress and development.

Regular Communication with Families

Students' Progress and Important Classroom Information

Frequent communication regarding individual student progress and important classroom information is essential to actively engaging family members as equal contributors to the educational program. Doing so creates an inviting atmosphere focused on open and productive dialogue to enhance students' learning and development. Regular communication with families through a variety of methods establishes a strong connection between students' school and home lives that supports their achievement. When families are consistently updated and informed regarding their children's progress in the educational program, they can more effectively collaborate with the teacher to **proactively** address concerns and **implement necessary supports** for successful learning. Frequently communicating important classroom information, including curriculum, assignments, events, and opportunities for involvement, ensures that families are always informed regarding their children's educational program and ways in which they can actively participate. This equips family members with the knowledge and resources necessary to effectively support and reinforce learning both in the classroom and at home.

Review Video: Collaborating with Families
Visit mometrix.com/academy and enter code: 679996

Positive Rapport That Enhances Teaching and Learning

Regularly interacting and working with students' families facilitates the **continuous** and **open** line of communication necessary to establishing and sustaining a positive rapport. Building such positive relationships is integral to quality teaching and learning, as frequent communication allows families and teachers to develop a sense of mutual respect, trust, and understanding over time. By frequently communicating with families, teachers create a welcoming, inclusive learning environment in which family members feel encouraged and empowered to contribute as **equal participants** in their child's educational program. This facilitates productive collaboration between teachers and families that supports and enhances students' learning. Developing a positive rapport with family members is also valuable in providing teachers with insight regarding strategies to best support and accommodate students' learning styles, needs, and individual differences. When teachers and families have a positive relationship with one another, students feel more supported in their learning both within and outside of the classroom, thus promoting positive attitudes toward learning and academic achievement.

Listening and Responding to Families' Concerns

Actively **listening** and **responding** to students' families when interacting with them is an important part of building positive relationships that enhance teaching and learning. By listening attentively to families' concerns, ideas, and information regarding their child and the educational program, teachers gain a greater awareness of their unique backgrounds, characteristics, and experiences. With this understanding in mind, teachers can ensure that they respond to family members in a **sensitive**, **accepting**, and **empathetic** manner to promote the development of a mutual positive rapport. Doing so conveys the sentiment that family members are valued and respected as equal participants in the educational program, thus encouraging them to engage in positive communication to support their children's learning. Families can provide valuable insight regarding their children's learning styles, needs, and behaviors. When teachers listen and respond constructively to this information, they foster positive relationships with families by validating and including them in the learning process. In addition, listening and responding appropriately to students' families indicates acknowledgement and appreciation for their participation in the educational program that contributes to building positive relationships and encourages continued communication.

Conferences

Building Positive Relationships Between Schools and Families

Frequently conducting conferences with parents, guardians, and legal caregivers facilitates the consistent **in-person communication** necessary for building positive relationships founded on mutual understanding and respect. The conference setting provides a space in which teachers, school staff, and families can discuss the educational program and the student's individual progress as well as address concerns and collaborate in developing goals. By conducting conferences regularly, teachers, school staff, and families can maintain a continuous, **open dialogue** that provides insight regarding one another's perspectives, intentions, and roles in the educational program. This allows for increased understanding and appreciation for one another that contributes to building positive relationships. Families that attend conferences regularly feel more included in the educational program as equal contributors to their children's learning, thus encouraging them to establish positive strong connections with the school.

Support of Students' Success in Learning

Effective conferences between teachers and families are focused on open communication, productive collaboration, and strengthening the connection between students' home and school lives. When families and teachers work together in conferences to benefit the student, it strengthens their **support system** in both influential areas of their lives. This is beneficial in enhancing students' **academic achievement**, promoting **healthy development**, and encouraging **positive attitudes toward learning**. Conducting conferences frequently ensures that family members are consistently **informed** and **involved** as equal participants in their child's progress and the educational program. This equips families with the information, understanding, and resources to more effectively support their child's learning both within and outside of the classroom. In addition, effective conferences provide teachers with insight from families regarding students' learning needs, behaviors, and individual situations. With this knowledge in mind, teachers can work with families to develop a plan and implement strategies that best support students' learning and development.

Guidelines for Effectiveness

Family conferences are a valuable opportunity to discuss students' individual progress, collaborate to develop educational goals, and address concerns. To ensure conferences are productive, teachers must take measures to make families feel welcomed, respected, and included in the process. Conferences must be scheduled at a **convenient time** for all attending family members in order to accommodate varying needs and situations. It is also important that conferences take place in a comfortable, **inviting atmosphere**, as this establishes a positive tone and facilitates discussion. Teachers must arrive **on time** and **prepared** with specific information to discuss regarding the student, including positive remarks that highlight his or her strengths. This demonstrates that teachers know the student well and want him or her to succeed, thus making family members feel comfortable in discussing their child. Asking **open-ended questions**, encouraging families to talk, and practicing active listening is important in facilitating productive discussion as well as ensuring families feel heard and respected in their concerns. **Direct criticism** of the student must always be avoided; rather, teachers should focus on discussing ways that student can apply their strengths to improve in other areas.

Family Support Resources that Enhance Family Involvement

Families that are supported through school, community, and interagency resources are equipped to effectively support their child's learning and development. Often, families may be hesitant to become actively involved in their children's education because they lack the skills and understanding of how to do so. These support systems are beneficial in providing family members with the **tools, knowledge**, and **resources** that prepare them to effectively participate in the educational program and extend learning outside of the classroom. Such resources are valuable in educating families on the characteristics, needs, and abilities of their children's developmental level as well as strategies for developing and engaging in age-appropriate activities that support learning at home. This instills a sense of confidence within families regarding their ability to successfully support their children's learning that empowers and encourages them to become actively involved.

When families are supported through **school**, **community**, and **interagency** resources, they are able to more effectively become involved in the educational program. Numerous resources dedicated to educating families on ways they can support their children's learning are available to accommodate varying situations, needs, and abilities. Within the school, **teachers**, **guidance counselors**, and other **staff members** can provide valuable information regarding students' developmental characteristics, needs, and abilities as well as ways families can become involved to enhance learning within and outside of the classroom. **Support groups** hosted by the school enable families to share experiences and discuss ways to become involved in the learning process. Community support resources are often tailored to address the specific needs of families within the community. These resources offer **family education services**, such as classes, meetings, or programs, designed to provide families with the training, strategies, and knowledge necessary to become actively involved in their children's education. Several **national family support agencies** are also available to educate families on ways to become involved in their children's learning. Such agencies often have multiple locations as well as an array of digitally printed information, discussion forums, and training opportunities to enhance family involvement in learning.

Chapter Quiz

Ready to see how well you retained what you just read? Scan the QR code to go directly to the chapter quiz interface for this study guide. If you're using a computer, simply visit the online resources page at **mometrix.com/resources719/nesincgifted** and click the Chapter Quizzes link.

NES Practice Test

Want to take this practice test in an online interactive format?
Check out the online resources page, which includes interactive practice questions and much more: **mometrix.com/resources719/nesincgifted**

1. Which of the following descriptions of adolescent behavior is an example of how behaviorist learning theory explains human development?

a. A student sees struggling students getting more teacher attention and stops studying hard.
b. A student sees others getting higher grades and more praise and then begins studying hard.
c. A student receive a high grade and praise from the teacher and continues studying hard.
d. A student sees struggling students get less attention and decides to continue studying hard.

2. For most school districts, the written policy regarding student identification must: include provisions for continuing screening; include assessment procedures from a number of sources; ensure that all populations have assessment available; ensure final selections are made by at minimum three local educators with specialized training; and:

a. Include provisions about reassessment, exiting strategies, and readmission policies
b. Include provisions about furloughs, reassessment, exiting strategies, transferring students, and the district decision appeals process
c. None of the above; the district is not required to have a written policy
d. Include provisions about furloughs, reassessment, exiting strategies, transferring students, and parental involvement

3. What is true about instructing children in conflict resolution skills and processes?

a. Conflict resolution can be taught to children who are as young as eighteen months.
b. Children can only understand these concepts at school ages (six years and up).
c. Conflict resolution instruction has never been attempted with young children.
d. Children taught conflict mediation/resolution are unlikely to generalize these.

4. Both qualitative and quantitative assessments must be used when identifying elementary, middle, and high school students, with what exception (s)?

a. Teachers can choose to assess kindergarten students using only qualitative assessments
b. For students being assessed for exceptional leadership abilities, creativity, or artistic areas, teachers can chose to assess qualitatively only
c. Both a and b
d. Neither a nor b

5. What is the best way for a teacher to make sure that books in the classroom are at an appropriate reading level, neither too easy nor so difficult that beginning readers will become frustrated?

a. Administer a reading pretest to the class before selecting suitable books
b. Purchase books that are easy enough for even the newest of readers
c. Make sure that all the books are just slightly above students' reading level, so they will grow
d. Provide a wide variety of reading materials for children to choose from

6. Ten-year-old Ming has exceptional musical abilities. She can hear a piece of music once and immediately play it on a variety of instruments, and her singing range is phenomenal. She is new to the US, and speaks little English. She has learning disabilities and is dysgraphic. She is easily excited. Her classmates find her:

a. Delightful; her excitability coupled with her musical talents are entertaining
b. Odd; her lack of English, terrible handwriting, nervousness, and bizarre musical talents make her seem abnormal
c. Acceptable. Fifth graders typically don't exclude one another
d. Fascinating; her musical talent coupled with her excitability and lack of English make her an interesting distraction to their schoolwork

7. A differentiation strategy for students with high ability involves streamlining work to match ability, thereby creating a more challenging environment. This is called:

a. Curriculum packaging
b. Curriculum packing
c. Curriculum compacting
d. Curriculum packeting

8. A third-grade teacher is conducting a unit on patterns that occur and recur in nature in which students observe and record weather patterns for a month. Which of the following additional activities could this teacher incorporate to differentiate instruction for gifted and talented students?

a. Pairing these students with others that need additional assistance
b. Having these students investigate local weather patterns throughout history
c. Asking these students to record weather data for an additional month
d. Assigning these students to write an informational essay about their findings

9. A parent has approached his daughter's teacher and is frustrated because the child seems to be completely without motivation. The father has tried rewarding his daughter for exemplary work, punishing her for inadequate work, and reviewing her work before she turns it in to ascertain if it is complete, to no avail. The father knows the daughter is extremely capable intellectually and artistically. He feels both angry at what he sees as her laziness, and guilty for not being able to motivate her. The teacher tells him:

a. To modify his strategy. He should BOTH reward exemplary work and punish inadequate work at the same time
b. That until the child takes full responsibility for her actions, no one can motivate her. Withdrawing his involvement will likely result in the girl becoming more motivated
c. That gifted students value learning over performance. Her lack of motivation shouldn't be an occasion for blame. Instead of focusing on grades and performance, the father might consider exploring some learning opportunities in areas of the girl's interest. For example, a visit to an art museum followed by a trip to the library for books about a particular art movement might motivate the student
d. That he is doing all he can do; his methods are fine, and if he changes his course at this point it will do more harm than good

10. How should a teacher initially plan instruction to meet the needs of a highly diverse classroom?

a. On the first day of class, the teacher should ask each student to complete a survey to determine the students' cultural, ethnic, and racial background.
b. A good teacher should be intimately familiar with the major cultures within the local school district.
c. A teacher should plan lessons so that new material is introduced using a variety of different approaches.
d. Guest teachers from different ethnic backgrounds should occasionally be invited to teach so that all students will feel more comfortable.

11. When dealing with a class with widely varied levels of skill and knowledge, which of the following represents a harmful practice?

a. Giving extra attention to the lower performing students in class
b. Allowing the higher performing students to assist the lower performing students
c. Providing more individual tutoring time to higher performing students while letting lower performing students work independently
d. Providing specific feedback to lower performing students

12. A 4th grade teacher has three gifted students in his general classroom. One strategy for differentiating their learning is extending lessons throughout the curriculum by comparing common themes and issues, studying the associations within and between individual disciplines over the course of time and/or from more than one viewpoint. The teacher is adapting the __________ of his lessons in order to challenge his gifted students.

a. Complications
b. Complexity
c. Enhancement
d. Richness

13. Intelligence quotients (IQ) tests can help determine whether or not students have learning issues connected with intellectual ability. What could be a disadvantage of this kind of test?

a. These tests cannot identify gifted students.
b. These tests cannot reveal student strengths.
c. These tests cannot measure certain skills.
d. These tests cannot identify future success.

14. What kinds of teacher questions will get students actively involved in lesson content?

a. Only cognitively lower-level questions requiring students to remember and understand elicit student involvement.
b. Only higher-level questions requiring students to apply, analyze, evaluate, and synthesize elicit student involvement.
c. Cognitively lower-level and higher-level questions can elicit active student involvement.
d. Cognitively lower-level or higher-level questions will not get students actively involved.

15. Vertical alignment:

a. Refers to the curriculum-enhancing strategy of stacking lessons into complex groups in order to challenge gifted learners
b. Means working across the curriculum; various subjects are linked thematically and similar strategies are employed to make learning more relevant
c. Is seating students according to how well they are achieving academic goals
d. Refers to mapping the curriculum to build upon understanding and skills learned in the previous grade

Refer to the following for question 16:

A first-year science teacher has assigned her first group project of the year. She has divided the classroom into groups of four to conduct an experiment on the greenhouse effect by measuring the temperatures of two containers, with one having plastic wrap to simulate the greenhouse effect. The students must set up the project, conduct the experiment, and record their data. She wants all of the students to experience each part of the project and not divide into specialized roles.

16. How can the teacher ensure that all students are contributing equally during this cooperative learning exercise?

a. The teacher should circulate among the groups and observe how they are working together.
b. The teacher should assign one student in each group to monitor student participation.
c. The teacher should assign each student in each group a specific task to accomplish.
d. The teacher should avoid such exercises, since they inevitably end up with one or two students doing most of the work.

17. Piaget coined the term *schema* to describe:

a. Mental constructs for individual objects
b. Mental concepts of categories or classes
c. Mental programs only for motor actions
d. Mental ideas governing inborn reflexes

18. In the table below are several test scores for the same individual student, Mario.

Z-SCORE	STANDARD SCORE	SCALED SCORE	T-SCORE	PERCENTILE
3.70	155	20	87	99.99

Based on this table, which of the following is correct?

a. These must be scores Mario got on several different tests.
b. Mario scored much higher in some areas of a test than others.
c. If these are IQ scores, Mario must be a gifted student.
d. If these are IQ scores, Mario must have intellectual disabilities.

19. What is the difference between a raw score and a scale score?

a. Raw scores are used on specific tests to show how well a student did; this score is not necessarily consistent from test to test. A scale score translates raw scores onto a measurement common to all forms of testing for a particular assessment
b. There is no difference; both terms refer to the score a student receives
c. A raw score is shown as an error number while a scale score is indicated by a percentage. For example, if a student takes a test with 100 questions and misses 7, the raw score is -7 and the scale score is 93%.
d. Scale scores are used on specific tests to show how well a student did; this score is not necessarily consistent from test to test. A raw score translates scale scores onto a measurement common to all forms of testing for a particular assessment

20. Bruner, one of the central figures of the 'cognitive revolution,' later became critical of his earlier position and turned his attention to the matter of how _______ shapes thinking.

a. Creativity
b. Art
c. Science
d. Culture

21. According to Jean Piaget's four-stage theory of cognitive development, the distinction between people at the concrete operational stage (approximately 7–12 years of age) and the formal operational stage (approximately 12–16 years of age) of development is that:

a. Unlike those at the concrete operational stage, those at the formal operational stage can think logically in concrete terms.
b. Unlike those at the concrete operational stage, those at the formal operational stage are highly reliant on sensory and motor skills to learn.
c. Those in the concrete operational stage are capable of abstract thought, while those at the formal operational stage can think only in concrete terms.
d. Those in the concrete operational stage can think logically only with respect to concrete experiences, while those at the formal operational stage can reason in abstract and hypothetical terms.

22. According to the Javits Act, gifted and talented students are described as those who:

a. Have been assessed as having intelligence at least 30% above the national average, and are not receiving services or activities to develop those capabilities
b. Are in the top 5% of their age group in terms of intellectual, creative, artistic, or leadership areas, or in specific academic fields
c. Have achieved high accomplishment in intellectual, creative, artistic, or leadership areas or in specific academic fields, and who have not been recognized and honored in an appropriate manner
d. Have the capability for high accomplishment in intellectual, creative, artistic, or leadership areas or in specific academic fields, and who need services or activities not ordinarily provided by the school to develop those capabilities

23. Gifted students who receive a vertical score equal to or greater than the Met Standard at a grade level higher than their own have already met the standard at their grade level. Is this statement true or false?

a. True. This is one of the ways gifted students are identified
b. True, although a student might meet the standard at a higher grade level in one subject but not in all subjects
c. True. Additionally, gifted students whose vertical score in a particular subject is equal to or greater than the Met Standard at a higher grade level should be working at that higher level, either by taking those classes at that grade level or via differentiation
d. False

24. Why are open-ended responses of particular value to the teacher?

a. The encourage dialogue between teacher and student, or between student and peers
b. They give the teacher insight into how a particular student structures ideas, uses language, and demonstrates understanding
c. They are not of particular value because they cannot be measured and do not remain consistent through time
d. They support the gifted student's emotional and psychological development by demonstrating respect for the student's abilities

25. Strategies for establishing a logical-mathematical learning environment include all except which one of the following?

a. Conducting interviews
b. Venn diagrams
c. Thinking of probabilities
d. Discerning patterns

26. Johnny's IQ score places him in the 97th percentile rank of the population. This means that:

a. 3 percent of the population has an IQ score higher than Johnny's.
b. 97 percent of the population has an IQ score higher than Johnny's.
c. 96 percent of the population has an IQ score higher than Johnny's.
d. 3 percent of the population has an IQ score lower than Johnny's.

27. A strategy whereby the curriculum is modified in depth, complexity, and originality, and suggests the four concurrent directions of Core Curriculum, Curriculum of Connections, Curriculum of Practice, and Curriculum of Identity, is called:

a. Multiple Curriculums Modification
b. Parallel Curriculum Model
c. Creative Multiple Curriculums
d. Parallel Creative Curriculums

28. Which statement is true regarding principles of early childhood behavior management?

a. Punishing bad behaviors is more powerful.
b. Punishments and rewards work equally well.
c. Rewarding good behaviors is more powerful.
d. Rewarding good behaviors should be occasional.

29. Strategies for establishing a verbal-linguistic learning environment include all except which one of the following?

a. Classroom discussions
b. Stories told by the teacher
c. Task cards
d. Word walls

30. Of the four parenting styles identified by psychologists, which one is found most likely to result in children who have problems with authority figures, poor school performance, and poor self-regulation?

a. Authoritarian
b. Permissive
c. Authoritative
d. Uninvolved

31. Which of the following is *most* accurate about exceptional students who are gifted?

a. They typically have advanced social skills.
b. Their academic performance is superior.
c. Their IQ scores indicate their giftedness.
d. They typically have difficulty relating to peers.

32. Gifted and Talented underachievers can best be helped by parents and teacher who ______________ in an environment that___________.

a. Share consistent expectations / is flexible, respects the student's opinions, and does not demand absolute obedience
b. Demand excellence / is firm, unbending, clear, and consistent
c. Ask questions / is invigorating, inviting, inspiring, and flexible
d. Offer support / is loving, understanding, accepting, and respectful

33. Ms. Wing often groups her students by ability in order to provide them with efficient, challenging instruction that proceeds at a pace appropriate to their development. She has recently been under attack by some parents, who consider her methods elitist and potentially racist. The parents further point out that so-called 'gifted' students don't need the depth of support that failing students require. The position taken by the National Association of Gifted Children include(s) the following argument(s):

a. Athletically gifted individuals are regularly grouped by ability and have the best success in such groupings
b. All areas of professional or graduate study/ preparation involve grouping
c. Ability grouping is a means by which gifted ELLS, students with economic disadvantages, and those with learning disabilities can be challenged along with their true peers
d. All of the above

34. SAGES stands for:

a. Standard Assessment Games for English Students, and describes informal assessments based on cooperative games
b. Sagmore Adams Gates Educational Standards, and describes gifted standards for grades 1-3
c. Screening Assessment for Gifted Elementary Students, and describes a standardized assessment
d. Screening Assessment for Gifted Elementary Students, and describes an informal assessment

35. During Piaget's second stage of cognitive development, adults should realize that children's thinking is primarily:

a. Logical
b. Intuitive
c. Sensory
d. Motoric

36. Piaget's first stage of cognitive development involves:

a. Operations with concrete things
b. Sensory input and motor output
c. Operations with abstract things
d. Intuition and animism, not logic

37. Who is responsible for identifying gifted and talented students?

a. Each county establishes its own guidelines based upon State Board of Education criteria, which apply to all schools in the county
b. The State Board of Education is responsible for designing a systematic plan which includes assessment, evaluation, curriculum, and planning. Each district must abide by this overreaching plan, all owing slight modifications when necessary and approved
c. Each building designs its own system for identifying and serving Gifted and Talented students. It must follow loose guidelines suggested by the district, which in turn, follows loose guidelines suggested by the State
d. Each district develops and implements a program that is based upon criteria determined by the State Board of Education, which includes identifying and serving gifted and talented students

38. The first step in having a student considered for a gifted program is nomination via a Student Observation Form submitted by whom?

a. Teachers or parents
b. Other community members
c. School administrators and other personnel
d. Any of the above

39. Fifth-grade Esmeralda, a gifted writer, told the school counselor that it really isn't her fault that much of her school work never makes it to the teacher's hand. She perceives herself as fairly vulnerable in a difficult world. Her little brother goes through her book bag and tears up her papers. Her handwriting isn't very good no matter how hard she tries and she can't read her own notes. Her mother forces her to stay inside on nice days to do homework that is boring. Sometimes other kids on the bus take her homework and throw it away. Esmeralda is also convinced that when she does manage to turn in the work, the teacher herself misplaces it. She appears to believe her excuses, and doesn't see any way to overcome them. What's going on?

a. She has a high external locus of control
b. She has a low external locus of control
c. She has a low internal locus of control
d. She has a high internal locus of control

40. Which one of the following statements about objectives is *not* true?

a. Objectives are a communications tool aimed specifically at the students, not other audiences.
b. Objectives provide a way to evaluate student learning.
c. Objectives help focus and motivate students.
d. Objectives provide a way for teachers to measure their own effectiveness.

41. Gifted and talented teachers are required to have 30 hours of specialized training within the first semester of their teaching, followed by 6 additional hours of training per year. Who determines the material to be covered in this training?

a. The school board
b. It is legislated by the state
c. It is a district decision
d. It is federally mandated

42. Every Friday, a teacher works with her gifted classroom on creative problem solving. She has begun bringing in ordinary household objects and asking students to work in groups to come up with different ways they could use the items if they were shipwrecked on an island. What is the likely purpose of this activity?

a. To help students learn to think outside the box
b. To teach students how to organize their ideas
c. To help students learn how to work well in groups in the classroom
d. To activate the students' imagination

43. Which teacher characteristic will best help facilitate student cooperation in the classroom?

a. Rigid military-style discipline
b. Consistency in how rules are enforced
c. A playful, loving approach, even when rules are broken
d. Ignoring misbehavior so that the students will see that they can't get to you

Refer to the following for question 44:

Exhibit 1

Class Description

Ms. Jewel has been teaching third grade for several years and has a great deal of experience working with students of varying learning styles and needs. Until recently, the demographics of her school primarily included one culture, but this year has seen an increased population of ethnically diverse students. To create an inclusive learning atmosphere, the school administration has been encouraging teachers to emphasize the importance of celebrating diversity and appreciating one another's differences.

Ms. Jewel has been implementing several strategies to teach her students the value of diverse backgrounds, cultures, and experiences. To decorate her classroom, she has asked each student to bring in an item that represents their heritage to hang on the class bulletin board. In addition, Ms. Jewel has been working with the other third-grade teachers to plan a cultural celebration day in which students' families will be invited to participate.

At the beginning of the school year, Ms. Jewel reviewed her students' education records to gain insight into their backgrounds, abilities, and needs in order to plan instruction accordingly. She learned that, of her 28 students, four are from socioeconomically disadvantaged households. Two of these students are native Spanish speakers and possess beginner-level English proficiency skills according to their most recent NYSESLAT scores. Another student, Brian, has been identified as homeless. Brian is frequently absent from school and often arrives to class without necessary learning materials. Ms. Jewel has noticed that he is becoming increasingly withdrawn and struggles to make friends.

Carla has been medically diagnosed with ADHD that impedes her ability to focus in class and complete assignments. She has an individualized education program (IEP) to outline her accommodations, as well as her academic and behavioral goals. In addition, her literacy skills are below grade-level according to her score on last year's New York ELA assessment, for which she is receiving Tier 2 Response to Intervention (RTI) services. Ms. Jewel also works closely with the school reading resource teacher to develop strategies that support Carla's literacy development. Carla's parents are divorced, and her father lives in a different state, which sometimes makes it difficult for him to actively participate in her education. To remedy this, Ms. Jewel always ensures that he is included in communications related to Carla's academic progress, upcoming assignments, and important school events.

Ms. Jewel is preparing a unit on identifying character traits using details from a text. She has intentionally chosen a short story that includes several characters from diverse backgrounds, cultures, and experiences. After each lesson, Ms. Jewel uses a journal to reflect upon her instructional effectiveness as well as her students' level of engagement.

EXHIBIT 2

EXCERPT FROM MS. JEWEL'S LESSON PLAN

Topic: Character traits

Standard:

- **3R3**: In literary texts, describe character traits, motivations, or feelings, drawing on specific details from the text.
- **3RF4a**: Read grade-level text across genres orally with accuracy, appropriate rate, and expression on successive readings.

Essential Question:

- How do character traits influence one's feelings and motivations?
- What can we learn about a character from details in the text?
- How can we identify character traits?

Lesson Objectives:

- Students will be able to identify character traits using details from a text.
- Students will be able to explain how character traits influence one's actions and motivations.

Grouping: Students will work with teacher-assigned partners for a portion of the lesson.

Lesson Component	**Activity**
Introduction	Students will begin with a fill-in-the-blank activity in which they use adjectives to describe themselves. Students will be called upon to read their responses. The teacher will explain that character traits are used to describe people. The teacher will show a slideshow presentation to introduce the idea of character traits and explain how they affect one's motivations and feelings. The slideshow will include three brief passages. Students will be called upon to read the passages aloud and identify the characters' traits. Students will be given a handout that lists several character traits to reference later in the lesson.
Partner Activity	Students will work with a partner to read brief three- to five-sentence passages about various characters. Students will be asked to determine if each passage depicts positive or negative character traits. Students will then choose three characters from the passages and use in-text details to draw a picture that represents each description.
Whole-Class Activity	Students will take turns reading sections of a short story aloud to the class. Prior to reading aloud, students will have a few minutes to read the story silently to themselves. Students will independently answer a set of comprehension questions that correspond with the short story. The teacher will review answers with the whole class.
Individual Summative Activity	Students will be assigned to write a response in which they compare and contrast the character traits, feelings, and motivations of two characters from the short story.
Extension Activity	Selected students will be assigned to create original stories that include at least two characters with three different character traits each.
Accommodations	• Short stories will be scaffolded according to reading comprehension skills, and will include an English-Spanish glossary for complex terms. • Visual representations will be included in the presentation. • English-Spanish character trait vocabulary sheets will be provided. • Preferential seating/reduced distractions will be used. • Graphic organizers will be provided for the independent writing activity. • Extra time to write the response will be provided as necessary.

EXHIBIT 3

EXCERPTS FROM MS. JEWEL'S REFLECTION JOURNAL

DAY 1

Today, I introduced the topic of identifying character traits using details from a text. Overall, my students seemed engaged in the lesson, and especially enjoyed the fill-in-the-blank activity, in which they had the opportunity to describe themselves. Some students were eager to read their descriptions, while others, including my ELL students, did not raise their hand to volunteer. Carla struggled to focus during this activity, and I had to redirect her attention while other students read. She also seemed reluctant to read her description aloud when I called upon her.

DAY 2

Students worked with partners to sort positive and negative character traits. I strategically paired some students with others that could provide scaffolding, and although my ELL students were a bit uncertain of some vocabulary, this strategy seemed to help their overall understanding. Brian seemed especially quiet today and did not engage very much in the activity. He also appeared to let his partner do most of the work. Carla needed much less redirection during this lesson, as she seemed to enjoy participating in the hands-on activities.

DAY 3

Today, we focused on whole-class activities to introduce the short story. Students had a few minutes to read the story silently to themselves before being called upon to read aloud. When it was Carla's turn to read, she seemed to struggle with pronunciation and word recognition. She also struggled significantly with the comprehension questions. I am wondering if she needs more individualized support to further improve her literacy skills. I also called upon both of my ELL students to read aloud. While one seemed to have little difficulty reading aloud, the other read very quietly.

DAY 4

Students began working on their written responses, in which they compared and contrasted the traits, motivations, and feelings of two characters from the short story. Students were given graphic organizers to brainstorm ideas prior to beginning writing. While some students were engaged in this activity, many became distracted and needed redirection. Carla was particularly fidgety and was frequently out of her seat. Many students did not finish writing their responses, and I believe I will need to extend the unit an additional day so everyone can complete them. A few of my students finished early, and were assigned to create original stories in which they included characters that possessed various traits learned throughout the unit.

44. Which of the following best describes the purpose of including an extension activity in accommodating the learning needs of gifted students?

a. Enriching instruction to provide intellectually challenging learning opportunities
b. Rewarding students' efforts with a creative project
c. Providing student-led learning experiences
d. Allowing for flexibility in instruction to accommodate students' learning needs

45. Pfeiffer's Gifted Rating Scales is used to:

a. Weigh the pros and cons of entering a student into a gifted program
b. Determine what percentage of the budget should be allocated to gifted programs by considering what ratio such program(s) are scaled to
c. Measure gifted intelligence overall
d. Measure the degree of disability a gifted, learning-disabled student has

46. According to Bloom's taxonomy, knowledge, comprehension, application, analysis, synthesis, and evaluation belong to which domain?

a. Intellectual
b. Analytical
c. Cognitive
d. Mathematical

47. Which of the following would be the best strategy a teacher could implement to help students with issues forming social connections in late elementary school?

a. Role play asking questions about peers' interests.
b. Encourage students to approach any group they want to be friends with.
c. Assign students to work in groups based on who the teacher thinks would get along.
d. Encourage students to start playing sports.

48. Uneven social and intellectual development, being socially at variance with expectations of the classroom and of others at the same age, experiencing finely tuned emotions, and the resulting vulnerability is called:

a. Social inequality
b. Psychological ineptitude
c. Asynchrony
d. Serendipity

49. Effective teacher strategies for organizing and managing learning environments that result in high student engagement and low misbehavior include which of these?

a. Alerting student attention through a focus on the entire class
b. Concealing teacher awareness of student behavior from them
c. Designing and implementing activities without any overlapping
d. Having instruction proceed steadily without adding momentum

50. Kingore Observation Inventory (KOI) is used to:

a. The correct name is the Kingmore Ongoing Index; it is used as a continuous informal assessment
b. Evaluate students in the gifted program to determine if they should remain in the program
c. Assess the capabilities of English Language Learners with learning disabilities that might be considered for a Gifted and Talented program
d. Identify gifted and talented students, including those from culturally diverse backgrounds or those who live at or below the poverty level

51. Kaplan has determined that students with which set of beliefs achieve their goals at the highest level?

a. Belief in self; determination; strong work ethic; willingness to conform
b. Curiosity; adept at using multiple resources; willing to take risks; applies key words when asking questions
c. Single-mindedness; determination; belief in self; strong work ethic
d. Creativity; spontaneity; enthusiasm; joy

52. Self-efficacy, the belief in one's ability to succeed at a particular task, is influenced by past performance, observing the success of peers, verbal support and persuasion by others, and

a. A willingness to take risks
b. A creative approach to the task at hand
c. Strong self-esteem
d. Physiological cues that indicate nervousness, such as sweating hands; or cues that indicate confidence, such as a feeling of ease and control

53. According to Sternberg's triarchic model of intelligence, three central qualities comprise giftedness: componential intelligence (the ability to analyze), experiential intelligence (the ability to think creatively), and

a. Abstract intelligence
b. Analytic intelligence
c. Practical intelligence
d. Essential intelligence

Refer to the following for question 54:

EXHIBIT 1

CLASS DESCRIPTION

Mr. Hamlin is a new fourth-grade general education teacher to a class of 31 ethnically diverse students. The community in which he teaches is largely underserved, and many of his students are from socioeconomically disadvantaged backgrounds. One of his students, Lindsay, has begun displaying disruptive behavior in class, such as calling out, arguing with other students, and getting out of her seat during instruction. After speaking with the guidance office regarding her behavior, Mr. Hamlin learned that Lindsay has recently been placed into foster care.

To understand his students' needs, Mr. Hamlin has reviewed their state assessments from the previous year. The results indicate that eleven of his students have below grade-level literacy and math skills. Of these eleven students, three are intermediate-level English language learners (ELLs) and one has beginner-level English language proficiency skills.

In order to build positive relationships and learn more about the individual needs in his classroom, Mr. Hamlin wants to establish communication with his students' families, but often has a hard time getting a response when he reaches out. To encourage greater family involvement, Mr. Hamlin has created a class website in which he posts information about what the class is learning each week, pictures of student work, study tips, and important assignments.

Mr. Hamlin strives to emphasize respect and the celebration of differences in his class. However, while most of Mr. Hamlin's students get along with one another, they tend to associate primarily with classmates of their own ethnic group. To diversify his students' interactions, Mr. Hamlin leads a class meeting each morning in which students are free to share thoughts, discuss concerns, and ask questions.

Mr. Hamlin is preparing to teach a lesson on fraction equivalence. He has asked the school administration to visit his classroom to give him suggestions regarding strategies for more effectively connecting with and meeting the learning needs of diverse students. The school vice principal has decided to conduct an informal walkthrough evaluation of Mr. Hamlin's lesson and takes notes to give him feedback.

EXHIBIT 2

EXCERPT FROM MR. HAMLIN'S LESSON PLAN

Topic: Fraction equivalence	
Standard: (NY-4.NF) • Extend understanding of fraction equivalence and ordering.	
Essential Question: • How can two fractions with different numerators and different denominators be the same?	
Lesson Objectives: • Students will be able to compare two fractions with different numerators and different denominators. • Students will be able to explain why fraction a/b is equivalent to a(n)/b(n).	
Grouping: Students will be arranged in teacher-selected pairs for portions of the lesson.	
Lesson Component	**Activity**
Introduction	As a warm-up, students will be asked to identify familiar fractions based on pie-chart visual representations. The teacher will review the warm-up questions and show a slide presentation to review familiar fractions and relevant vocabulary. The teacher will then show several examples of equivalent fractions with different numerators and denominators, accompanied by visual models. Students will then see a short video clip to further explain fraction equivalence and ordering.
Whole-Group Activity	Students will be given a handout with several blank pie charts. The teacher will lead a whole-group activity in which students color in each chart to represent a given set of equivalent fractions.
Partner Activity 1	Students will work together in teacher-selected pairs to complete a set of task cards with varying practice questions and word problems related to comparing fractions.
Partner Activity 2	Students will work with their partner to demonstrate their understanding of fraction equivalence and ordering. Students will have the choice to create five relevant word problems, draw a series of charts to represent equivalent fractions, or complete an online quiz using the classroom computers.
Homework	Students will be assigned to log into an educational math website at home to complete and submit ten practice problems.
Accommodations	• Scaffolded texts for word problems • Extra time for processing as needed • Students paired with others who can provide scaffolding • Visual representations for ELL students

EXHIBIT 3

NOTES FROM INFORMAL OBSERVATION BY THE VICE PRINCIPAL

CLASSROOM ENVIRONMENT

Mr. Hamlin's classroom is brightly decorated with inspirational posters depicting individuals of varying backgrounds, displays of student work, and bulletin boards to reinforce topics learned in class. Various learning materials are available for student use, including notebook paper, pencils, rulers, and art supplies. Many of the items in his classroom are labeled, and he has created a word wall to emphasize high-frequency vocabulary related to the curriculum. Student desks were arranged in groups of three to five. Mr. Hamlin began with a class meeting in which he asked students how they were feeling and if they had any plans for the upcoming weekend.

LESSON ACTIVITIES

Students were learning about fraction equivalence and ordering. Mr. Hamlin began with a review to elicit students' prior knowledge and continued with a presentation with visual representations and a video clip on the new material. After the presentation, Mr. Hamlin asked students to indicate their level of understanding by showing a thumbs-up or thumbs-down hand gesture. Seven students indicated that they did not entirely understand the new concept, and Mr. Hamlin provided additional examples.

Students then transitioned to the lesson activities. Mr. Hamlin selected student pairs to complete a series of task cards and create a product that demonstrated their understanding of equivalent fractions. It appeared that Mr. Hamlin paired students that struggled to understand the presentation with others that could help. Most students worked well together, but some seemed uninterested in working with their partner. During the activities, Mr. Hamlin moved throughout the room to check for understanding and monitor students' progress.

Student Interactions and Engagement

Overall, students were respectful of one another during the class meeting, and seemed interested in listening to one another. Students did not seem to want to ask one another questions, but rather, to share about themselves. A few students were quiet during the discussion and chose not to share.

Most students worked well together during the partnered activities. However, a few seemed uninterested in working with their partners. One student tried to leave his partner and join another pair but was redirected by Mr. Hamlin. Students seemed most interested during the second activity, in which they got to choose how they demonstrated their understanding of equivalent fractions.

54. Which of the following could Mr. Hamlin have incorporated into his lesson to support students of varying needs and abilities more effectively?

a. Extension and enrichment opportunities for gifted and talented students
b. Individualized instruction for struggling students
c. Opportunities for frequent breaks throughout the lesson
d. The opportunity for students to select their own partners for the collaborative activities

55. Bloom's taxonomy describes the three types of learning as:

a. Cognitive, affective, and psychomotor
b. Intellectual, emotional, and social
c. Intellectual, creative, and psychological
d. Cognitive, creative, and psychomotor

56. How can including cooperative learning strategies in the classroom teach practical life skills to students?

a. Students learn to work independently, even when others are around.
b. Students learn interpersonal problem-solving skills that they will need later in life.
c. Students learn ways to score better on standardized tests.
d. Students learn the importance of physical exercise in their daily lives.

57. Mr. Santiago has grouped students with similar interest in architecture and very different learning styles. He has given them a complex project and suggested the initial step to designing the project involves a brief, intense period in which all group members suggest and consider any possible ideas without ranking or judging their value. He reminds them that a flexible mind is capable of taking in more information and making brilliant creative leaps. This creative approach to problem-solving is called:

a. Brainstorming
b. Brainraining
c. Multiple thought process
d. Creative braining

58. A middle school teacher has recommended a number of different approaches her students can take with a research project about their hometown. She has suggested students might like to study an aspect of community life (such as social clubs or church organizations) over a significant period of time; compare a variety of architectural styles that are currently found in homes in a certain area; or do a statistical analysis in an area of special interest. One of her students has particular interest in insects. The student has designed a project that tracks insect populations over a thirty-year period in order to understand how draining swampland, cutting trees, and other environmental changes affect such populations. Another student, a painter, is interested in a brief but important art movement that had its roots in the student's hometown. Two students whose parents have recently divorced are designing a project that examines changes the family unit over a century. What teaching strategy is the teacher using?

a. Continuum of learning experiences
b. Array of learning experiences
c. Simultaneous teaching within multiple disciplines
d. Intellectual freedom of choice

59. Of the following, which is a principle wherein Albert Bandura's theory *agrees with* behaviorist learning theory?

a. Consequences reinforce or punish behaviors.
b. Learning always results in a change in behavior.
c. Internal cognitive processes must be examined.
d. Social interactions are very important in learning.

60. Who, in addition to gifted and talented teachers, are required to take 6 additional hours of training annually?

a. Administrators and counselors who make programming or hiring decisions
b. Only the teachers are required to have annual training
c. Administrators who make programming or hiring decisions
d. All teachers, although only gifted and talented teachers are required to have the initial 30 hours of training

61. Qualitative measures:

a. Are standardized tests used to assess students
b. Are assessments that demonstrate to what degree a student's product (artistic or core) demonstrates a high degree of quality
c. Include all the documents, records, assessments, and products involving a student who is working solely independently, in quarantine
d. Are anecdotal records, observations, interviews, student products, checklists, and similar materials

62. What type of assessment is often used to identify gifted students in leadership, creativity, or artistic areas?

a. Qualitative
b. Quantitative
c. Both a and b
d. Formal and informal

63. What is the correct meaning of cognitive dissonance?

a. A cognitive processing disorder affecting understanding
b. A disruption of cognition caused by a sensory overload
c. A feeling of discomfort due to contradictory information
d. A lack of compatibility between instruction and learning

64. The Elementary and Secondary Education Act signed into law in 2002 is more commonly known as:

a. The Javits Act
b. I.D.E.A.
c. No Child Left Behind
d. Forward into the Future

65. In what areas do computers have the LEAST benefit for student learning?

a. Simple drills, such as teaching multiplication tables, because this frees up the teacher to work with the students on developing higher-level skills
b. Role-playing games that develop greater social awareness and that allow the students to participate more directly in the events they are learning about
c. Simulations of mechanical activities that help the students develop motor skills and reflexes
d. Exercises that teach higher-order thinking and professional skills

66. Mario is taking AP classes at his high school. This means:

a. Advanced Placement, in which all his high school coursework will also apply as college credits
b. Alternative Potential. These are small, experimental classes taught to students who have been identified as 'alternative learners'
c. Accountability Projects. These are independent studies in which an individual or small group works closely with a mentor, who may not be a teacher but someone with professional experience in the student(s) area of interest. Students are held accountable for their projects' designs, implementation, and successful conclusions
d. Advanced Placement, in which high schools offer coursework meeting criteria recognized by institutions of higher education. Often, college credit is earned when an AP exam in specific content areas is passed

67. Gifted children typically get similar results with different types of I.Q. tests, such as the Wechsler Preschool and Primary Scale of Intelligence (WPPSI), the Stanford-Binet Intelligence Scale (SB), and the Wechsler Intelligence Scale for Children (WISC).

a. Neither true nor false
b. False
c. True
d. These I.Q. tests are not given to gifted students

68. According to Erikson's theory of psychosocial development, which ability must be achieved during the period of adolescence?

a. Identity
b. Intimacy
c. Industry
d. Autonomy

69. Stephen has a very high IQ, but he must use a wheelchair and is almost completely immobilized except for limited use of one hand, with which he can only press buttons. His paralysis affects his vocal cords, so he cannot speak. Stephen excels in all academic subjects, most notably in the sciences and expressive and receptive language skills. His communication is limited by his disabilities. Which would be the most appropriate adaptive equipment for him in the classroom and elsewhere?

a. An adaptive pencil holder and paper holder, both attached to his wheelchair
b. A computer with a voice synthesizer that he can program to speak for him
c. An electrolarynx he can use for speech in place of his paralyzed vocal cords
d. A communication board with buttons he can press to select various words

70. Authentic assessment as it pertains to gifted students:

a. Assesses emotional development, using expressive models
b. Assesses learning using portfolios, performance, observations, and other assessments that model real-world representations
c. Assesses a student's sincerity or authenticity by using a lie-detector
d. There is no longer such an assessment; popular in the early 1970s, it was abandoned in 1992 because results lacked clarity or concise information

71. When presenting information, effective teacher communication is best achieved when the teacher uses which of the following types of phrases?

a. Because, for example
b. Not many, not very
c. Somewhere, somehow
d. Generally, usually

72. A student who participates in a Gifted and Talented program at her school has been invited to visit family members in China with her parents. She will attend school there, and also be tutored so that she doesn't fall behind. Her mother has asked how a two-month leave of absence will affect her participation in the Gifted and Talented program. Which of the following is most accurate?

a. If the student takes a leave of absence, she is out of the program
b. At any point, students will automatically receive furlough status of any length of time as long as the request is in writing six weeks prior to the furlough date
c. If the student takes a leave of absence, she is out of the program. She can enroll again if the district is willing, but must go through nomination and evaluation procedures
d. A student may be granted a leave of absence for specific reasons and for a pre-established length of time; the leave must be approved

73. A young child, angry at her father, momentarily wishes he would leave. Later, when her father moves out after a divorce, the child blames it on her earlier wish. Piaget called this:

a. Animism
b. Egocentrism
c. Magical thinking
d. Intuitive thinking

Refer to the following for question 74:

Exhibit 1

Class Description

Ms. Fenton has just begun teaching four sections of sixth-grade social studies in an ethnically and socioeconomically diverse community. Because she recently moved to the area, Ms. Fenton is unfamiliar with many of her students' cultures, backgrounds, and experiences. Although she wants to build interpersonal relationships with her students and their families, Ms. Fenton is often unsure of how to initiate and maintain positive communication. At the beginning of the year, Ms. Fenton attended back-to-school night, where she was able to meet some of her students' families. However, many family members could not attend due to demanding work schedules. In addition, many of Ms. Fenton's students come from immigrant backgrounds, and their families speak limited English.

Ms. Fenton has been working to create a learning environment that emphasizes the acceptance of and appreciation for diversity. Her classroom is decorated with several posters of prominent historical figures from various backgrounds to demonstrate the influence of diverse individuals throughout time. However, Ms. Fenton struggles to engage her students in learning and develop meaningful relationships with them. This year, the school administration has offered a monthly professional learning community (PLC) workshop focused on culturally responsive teaching practices and strategies. Ms. Fenton has been attending these meetings to learn how to meet the diverse needs of her students and build a positive sense of community in her classroom.

Ms. Fenton's students possess a range of learning styles, needs, abilities, and interests. In one of her classes, three students are identified as English language learners (ELLs) of varying proficiency levels. One of these students, Jaime, is an intermediate-level ELL who has been medically diagnosed with autism spectrum disorder, for which he has an individualized education program (IEP) to outline his accommodations. Jaime has difficulty interpreting social cues, and often struggles with speaking in front of groups of people. Despite relying on linguistic supports, Jaime continues to read below grade level. However, he is very interested in art, and prefers assignments that allow for creative expression. Another student, Julia, has recently joined Ms. Fenton's class. According to records from her previous school, she has been identified as a gifted and talented student.

After reviewing last year's New York State ELA assessments, Ms. Fenton learned that four of her students in this class possess below grade-level reading comprehension and writing skills. One of these students, Nicholas, has recently been diagnosed with an intellectual disability that impacts his literacy development, and the Committee on Special Education has asked Ms. Fenton to collaborate on the development of his IEP. Nicholas is a diligent student, and while he struggles with assignments that require intensive reading and writing, he excels during hands-on learning opportunities. Nicholas comes from a single-parent household, where he lives with his mother, who works two jobs and often has to leave Nicholas home alone. Nicholas does not have internet access at his house, which sometimes makes it difficult for him to complete homework assignments or study for upcoming assessments.

Ms. Fenton is preparing a lesson on the similarities and differences between early civilizations in the Eastern Hemisphere. The principal will be conducting an announced formal observation throughout the lesson.

EXHIBIT 2

EXCERPT FROM MS. FENTON'S LESSON PLAN

Topic: Early civilizations in the Eastern Hemisphere

Standard:

- **6.3a:** Humans living together in settlements develop shared customs, beliefs, ideas, and languages that give identity to the group.
- **6.3b:** Complex societies and civilizations share the common characteristics of religion, job specialization, cities, government, language/record keeping system, technology, and social hierarchy. People in Mesopotamia, the Yellow River valley, the Indus River valley, and the Nile River valley developed complex societies and civilizations.

Essential Question:

- What makes a society civilized? What are the characteristics of a civilized culture?
- How were early civilizations in the Eastern Hemisphere developed?
- How were early civilizations in the Eastern Hemisphere similar and different?

Lesson Objectives:

- Students will be able to explore Mesopotamia and the Yellow River valley by examining archaeological and historical evidence to compare and contrast characteristics of these complex societies and civilizations.
- Students will be able to identify the elements of a civilized culture and explain how these elements work together to create a functioning society.

Grouping: Students will work with teacher-assigned partners and groups for portions of the lesson.

Lesson Component	**Activity**
Introduction	Students will work individually to complete an anticipatory guide in which they agree or disagree with various statements regarding what constitutes a civilized society. The guide will also require students to look up definitions of content-specific vocabulary words related to the unit, as well as a brief written response on what they think makes a culture civilized. The teacher will lead a brief class discussion in which students are called upon to elaborate on their written responses.
Direct Instruction	Students will see a slideshow presentation on the development of civilized societies in Mesopotamia and the Yellow River valley. The presentation will include information about the geography of each region and characteristics of each society, as well as several images of artifacts from each culture. Students will fill out guided notes during the presentation.
Partner Activity 1	Each student will work with a teacher-assigned partner to complete station activities in which they explore Mesopotamia and the Yellow River valley. **Station 1:** Students will participate in an online scavenger hunt to locate specific information related to culture in Mesopotamia and the Yellow River valley, including language, art, religion, science, music, and daily life. Students will be asked to respond to corresponding questions as they work. **Station 2:** Students will participate in a virtual field trip to explore the geography and daily life of both regions and to view artifacts from each society. They will be asked to record their observations throughout the virtual field trip. **Station 3:** Students will be asked to imagine they are from either Mesopotamia or the Yellow River valley, and will write a diary entry to describe a day in their lives based on information learned thus far. **Station 4:** Students will be asked to create a drawing that reflects artistic styles found in either Mesopotamia or the Yellow River valley.
Partner Activity 2	Each student will work with his or her partner to create a Venn diagram in which they compare and contrast characteristics between the Mesopotamian and Yellow River valley civilizations and their own culture.
Summative Assessment	Students will work in teacher-assigned groups of three to five to create their own society using information learned about the development of civilization in Mesopotamia and the Yellow River valley. Students will be asked to include the following elements in their society: name/geographic location, language, architecture, agriculture, economy, religion, art. Students will create posters to represent their society and a written piece to describe the various elements of their civilization. Students will be given five class periods to complete the project, and will be given a rubric to outline evaluation criteria.
Accommodations	• Presentation will include visual representations. • English-Spanish glossaries for content-specific vocabulary will be provided. • Strategic student grouping will be used. • Extra time will be allotted as necessary, and students can work on the summative project at home, if needed. • Preferential seating/reduced distractions will be used. • Graphic organizers and a word bank will be provided for the summative portion.

Exhibit 3

Domain 1: Excerpt from Principal's Observation Notes

1a. Demonstrating Knowledge of Content and Pedagogy

- Ms. Fenton's lesson demonstrates an overall understanding of the content. Instructional activities are aligned with the developmental level of middle-school students.
- The summative project and portions of the station activities provided opportunities for flexibility and student choice.
- Ms. Fenton seems uncertain of how to engage diverse learners in instruction. During the introduction and slideshow presentation, many students were distracted and disengaged.

1b. Demonstrating Knowledge of Students

- Ms. Fenton demonstrates knowledge of individual learning needs, and integrates supports and accommodations accordingly, such as graphic organizers, word banks, preferential seating, and linguistic aids. She grouped students based on literacy abilities, and provided extra assistance to struggling students throughout the lesson.
- Instructional activities appealed to a variety of learning styles. The lesson included individual, collaborative, hands-on, and whole-class activities.
- There appeared to be an overall disconnect between Ms. Fenton and her students. At times, it seemed she was unsure of what to say to engage them in learning. Throughout the lesson, she had to continuously redirect students' focus to the task at hand.
- Ms. Fenton struggled to engage her students in the class discussion at the beginning of the lesson. Many seemed uninterested.
- Julia and her partner finished the online scavenger hunt and station activities quickly. They appeared bored and became off-task until the next segment of the lesson began.
- Ms. Fenton would likely benefit from keeping a journal to reflect upon her daily interactions with students.

1d. Demonstrating Knowledge of Resources

- Ms. Fenton used a variety of instructional resources, but seemed unsure of how to effectively utilize these resources to incorporate diversity into the unit.
- There was no evidence of resources for extension or enrichment of learning.

1e. Designing Coherent Instruction

- Ms. Fenton's lesson was well-structured and reflected conscientious planning. While her directions were clear, she often had to repeat herself, particularly when transitioning between activities, because students were off-task or distracted.
- Ms. Fenton's use of linguistic aids, such as visual representations and gestures, was beneficial in providing clarification for ELLs in the classroom.

Domain 2: Classroom Environment

2a. Creating an Environment of Respect and Rapport

- While Ms. Fenton exhibits a pleasant attitude in the classroom, there appears to be a lack of authentic interpersonal connections between her and the students. She seemed unsure of how to spark their interest in the topic.
- Students generally seem to get along with one another, but the atmosphere lacks a sense of positive and cohesive community.
- Ms. Fenton's lack of authentic connection with her students appears to be impacting the quality of her instruction.

2D. Managing Student Behavior

- Classroom expectations and consequences are posted in the classroom and visible to students.
- Students were generally respectful toward one another. In several instances throughout the lesson, however, they seemed to disregard Ms. Fenton's instruction. She frequently had to repeat directions or redirect students' focus to learning, which impacted her instructional time.

Domain 3: Instruction

3A. Communicating with Students

- Ms. Fenton was respectful and polite with students. Communication with students focused primarily on instruction.
- Ms. Fenton used a variety of approaches to teach content, using the rotation activity to appeal to multiple learning styles.

3B. Using Questioning and Discussion Techniques

- Ms. Fenton led a brief class discussion at the beginning of the unit, in which students shared their written responses. Some students seemed engaged, but others that were called upon seemed reluctant to share their responses. One student was unsure of what the discussion was about when called upon. When she asked Jaime to share, he spoke slowly and used a quiet tone of voice.
- At the end of the slideshow presentation, Ms. Fenton allowed time for students to ask clarifying questions.
- As students engaged in the station activities, Ms. Fenton moved throughout the room to ask students about their progress.

3C. Engaging Students in Learning

- Students were overall disengaged during the slideshow presentation, as it did not seem that they were able to make meaningful connections to learning.
- Overall, students enjoyed the rotation activities. Some, however, became off-task and did not complete all of the stations.
- Nicholas required significant individual assistance during the writing activity in the third station, but was particularly interested in the fourth station.
- Jaime also struggled during the third station activity and relied heavily on linguistic supports.
- Students were the most engaged when they began working on the summative project, in which they had the opportunity to develop their own civilizations.

3E. Demonstrating Flexibility and Responsiveness

- The summative project allowed for flexibility and student choice in demonstration of learning.
- Accommodations were implemented to provide instructional support. Students were allowed extra time as necessary and could work on their projects at home if needed.
- While the lesson was well-prepared, it was lacking in cultural responsiveness. Ms. Fenton's instruction focused primarily on the topic at hand, and did not seem to integrate students' backgrounds, cultures, or experiences.

74. Which of the following is the most likely reason Julia became off-task after finishing the online scavenger hunt and rotation activities?

a. The lesson lacked opportunities for extension and enrichment.
b. Julia was unaware of procedures for transitioning to the next activity.
c. Ms. Fenton was not enforcing classroom management expectations.
d. Julia has an undiagnosed learning disability that impacts her ability to focus.

75. Which method of lesson planning will help a teacher ensure that his lesson will take advantage of the multiple intelligences of different students?

a. Use a lesson-planning matrix to help devise learning activities that are organized according to different abilities.
b. Survey the students about what helps them to learn the most.
c. Design a seating plan so that the students who need the most help sit in the front.
d. Try to use more images and graphs in presentations.

76. Which strategy is key for managing in-class group work sessions?

a. Avoid spending too much time with any one group and neglecting others.
b. Make sure that none of the students in any group are good friends.
c. Avoid the temptation to walk around the room and interact with the groups.
d. Grade only the final result of the assignment, and not the students' individual participation.

77. A number of gifted high school students are in a Language Arts class. Is their AP teacher obliged to differentiate the program of study for the gifted students?

a. No; if the teacher is already running a student-centered classroom, allowing students choices in assignments, and using flexibility in student grouping, the teacher is already differentiating. No further modification is required
b. No. All students in Advanced Placement courses are, by definition, gifted. Therefore, differentiation is already taking place
c. No. The teacher can choose to differentiate the program, but by the time gifted and talented students have entered high school, they have internalized sufficient strategies to challenge themselves and independently promote their own education
d. Yes. If the teacher is already running a student-centered classroom, allowing choices in assignments, and using flexibility in student grouping, the teacher is already differentiating. The teacher has received additional training to allow him or her to continue to modify classroom assignments to more profoundly challenge the gifted students

78. The term 'depth' refers to a number of interconnected strategies employed when exploring an area of study in terms of content. Studying details, patterns, and cultural considerations; examining content from concrete to theoretical; moving from known and familiar to unknown and unfamiliar; and ___________ are among these strategies.

a. Weighing knowledge of the physical world and the spiritual world
b. Moving beyond theoretical concepts to real-world experience
c. Considering all previous knowledge and projecting future knowledge
d. Moving beyond fact to generalizations and principles

79. As described in a study by Dr. Siegle of the Neag Center for Gifted Education, self-efficacy is best defined as:

a. An individual's belief or feeling about his or her worth to the world or a specific part of it
b. An individual's belief or feeling about his or her ability regarding a specific undertaking
c. An individual's belief or feeling about his or her ability to accomplish a goal in an efficient manner
d. An individual's belief or feeling about how his or her worth will increase if he or she accomplishes a task efficiently and exceptionally well

80. In determining whether a gifted child is underachieving academically, what should be assessed?

a. The child's IQ
b. The child's academic ability
c. The child's academic performance
d. The child's psychological development

81. All but which of the following are critical values that are formed during the middle school years?

a. Respect for diversity
b. Commitment to continued schooling
c. Tolerance of those who are different
d. Higher-order thinking skills

82. When creating a Total Talent Portfolio, who is primarily responsible for deciding what to include, maintaining the portfolio, and establishing goals?

a. The student and the teacher working as partners
b. The teacher in the primary position, supported by the student
c. The student in the primary position, with the teacher to review and approve
d. The student is primarily responsible

83. To apply Bandura's theory, educators must realize that he emphasized ______ as the most important influence on learning.

a. nuclear conflicts
b. erogenous zones
c. cognitive abilities
d. social interactions

84. A class includes students with disabilities, gifted students, average students, and a variety of reading levels. To support reading, which type of instructional resources would afford the most benefits to the most students?

a. Printed materials
b. Pictorial materials
c. Multimedia materials
d. Manipulative materials

85. Binh is in fifth grade. He was identified as gifted in leadership in third grade and entered into a Gifted and Talented program. He has always been mercurial, energetic, and moody, but until now it was not apparent that his studies were affected. Because his classroom behavior has worsened and his grades have been affected, his fifth grade teacher wanted him evaluated for Attention Deficit Hyperactivity Disorder. Should he be diagnosed with ADHD, what will happen to his gifted and talented status?

a. Because this has been a documented, ongoing problem, the district will temporarily remove him from the Gifted and Talented program, concentrate on improving his issues with attention and hyperactivity, and then re-enroll him once those things are under control
b. He will remain in the program and it will be modified to become more appropriate for his learning needs. It is illegal to discriminate against students with learning or behavioral disorders
c. It will be discussed with the gifted teacher, his general classroom teacher, his parents, and Binh. If Binh promises to monitor his behavior and work to the best of his abilities, he will be permitted to stay
d. He will be removed from the Gifted and Talented program; his learning issues preclude advanced studies. If, at some future point, he wants to return to the program, he will have to be re-evaluated for it

86. Social and behavioral theories of learning stress the importance of:

a. Good behavior on the part of students
b. The social interactions of students that aid or inhibit learning
c. A reward system for good behavior or growth in skills
d. The direct connection between thoughts and speech

87. How does the theory of multiple intelligences address the learning needs of students?

a. It suggests quite simply that some students are smarter than others, and that teachers must accept that while a *C* is a bad grade for some students, that it is a very good grade for others.
b. It suggests that different people learn in different ways, and that teachers can give more students a better chance by using a variety of teaching methods in the classroom.
c. It suggests that every student has only two areas of talent in which he or she can excel, and that once these talents are identified, students should not be pushed in other areas.
d. It suggests that all students are equally intelligent and that they will learn if they are motivated enough.

88. The steps to curriculum compacting includes understanding learning objectives, identifying students who can master objectives most quickly, pretesting, streamlining instructional periods for students who understand objectives, and:

a. Recommending acceleration opportunities
b. Recommending students be advanced a grade
c. Reviewing assessments
d. Passing these students on to a Gifted and Talented teacher

Refer to the following for question 89:

Exhibit 1

Class Description

Ms. Hoffman has just begun a new school year teaching four sections of tenth-grade English to a culturally and socioeconomically diverse group of students. One of her sections is comprised of

31 students with a wide range of backgrounds, learning styles, and abilities. Ms. Hoffman has reviewed her students' previous education records, including assessment scores, to gain a deeper understanding of their individual needs. She has learned that nine of her students scored below grade level on last year's state assessments in English language arts. Of these nine students, three are English language learners (ELLs) with varying levels of proficiency, and another, Samantha, has recently moved to the area and enrolled in school. Samantha comes from a socioeconomically disadvantaged background, and has moved a great deal in the past, causing continuous interruptions in her formal education up to this point.

Another student, Luke, has been medically diagnosed with autism spectrum disorder and has an individualized education program (IEP). While Luke is typically a diligent student, he struggles with social cues and often has difficulty expressing himself clearly in writing.

Ms. Hoffman has begun working extensively with the school ELL teacher and special education department to find effective resources for supporting her students' learning needs.

While most of Ms. Hoffman's students appear to be getting along so far this year, she has noticed some growing racial tension between a few students in her class. To prevent escalation, Ms. Hoffman has been conscientiously making efforts to establish a positive classroom climate that emphasizes respect and appreciation for differences. Each week, she begins class with a brief meeting in which students can share experiences, discuss concerns, and ask questions. In addition, Ms. Hoffman included her students in the process of developing class norms and expectations. She plans to regularly implement team-building exercises to maintain a positive and inclusive learning environment.

Ms. Hoffman communicates with her students' families often. In addition to attending the school open-house night, she utilizes a variety of communication tools to ensure accessibility for all families, including sending text reminders, emails, and weekly progress reports, and frequently updating her class website. She has also invited families into the classroom to visit, observe, or volunteer as aides.

Ms. Hoffman is preparing a unit on writing arguments that will consist of a final project and a class debate. Students will be asked to consider whether personal technology devices should be allowed in school. The unit will last approximately one week, and will include both individual and collaborative portions. Throughout the unit, Ms. Hoffman will conduct formative assessments to reflect on her instructional effectiveness and student engagement. She has selected a group of three students to extend their project by drafting a proposal to present to the school administration.

EXHIBIT 2

Excerpt from Ms. Hoffman's Lesson Plan

Topic: Writing and presenting an argument on a specific topic

Standard:

- **WHST1:** Write arguments focused on discipline-specific content.
- **WHST1a:** Introduce precise claim(s), distinguish the claim(s) from alternate or opposing claims, and create an organization that establishes clear relationships among the claim(s), counterclaims, reasons, and evidence.
- **WHST1b:** Develop claim(s) and counterclaims objectively, supplying data and evidence for each while pointing out the strengths and limitations of both claim(s) and counterclaims in a discipline-appropriate form and in a manner that anticipates the audience's knowledge level and concerns.

Essential Question:

- What makes an argument credible and effective?
- What information and perspectives do I need to gather when crafting an argument?
- What is the significance of including counterclaims when presenting an argument?

Lesson Objectives:

- Students will be able to research and gather evidence to prepare an objective argument on a specific topic.
- Students will be able to analyze multiple perspectives to prepare an argument.
- Students will be able to support their claims with credible evidence from multiple perspectives.

Grouping: Students will work in teacher-assigned groups of three for a portion of the unit. Students will choose a side to participate in the debate portion of the unit.

Lesson Component	**Activity**
Introduction	Students will be shown a series of statements, and will be asked to move from one side of the classroom to the other to indicate whether they are for or against the argument presented in each statement. The last statement will be about using personal technology devices in school. The teacher will then lead a class discussion in which students are asked to elaborate on their stance regarding this topic, including potential pros and cons of utilizing personal technology devices in school. Students will see a short presentation that reviews the importance of supporting a claim with evidence, as well as the details of the upcoming unit.
Individual Activity	Students will be assigned to read two articles that present opposing viewpoints regarding the use of personal technology devices in school. Students will be asked to highlight key points of each article, including supporting evidence.
Small-Group Activity	Students will work together in groups of three to research and prepare an argument to support their stance regarding whether personal technology devices should be allowed in school. Student research will culminate in a final project of their choosing to present their argument.
Whole-Class Activity	Students will participate in a whole-class debate regarding whether personal technology devices should be allowed in school. Each side will choose a speaker, and will have five minutes at a time to present and defend their argument. Students will have a class period prior to the debate to practice presenting their arguments.
Formative Assessments	• After the presentation, students will be asked to indicate their level of understanding based on a scale of 1-5, with 1 indicating no understanding, and 5 indicating complete understanding. • During the individual activity, students will be given color-coded cards to indicate a need for assistance or clarification. • Students will complete an exit ticket at the end of each lesson to reflect on their understanding and progress. • The teacher will check frequently for understanding throughout all stages of the unit.
Accommodations	• Texts will be scaffolded during the individual activity. • Extra time will be allotted as needed for the individual and small-group activities. • Graphic organizers will be provided for the small-group activity. • The introductory presentation will be accompanied by visual representations.

Exhibit 3

Excerpts from Students' Exit Tickets

Question: Does your group believe that personal technology devices should be allowed in school? What part of the unit have you enjoyed the most so far? Which portion has been the most difficult?

Samantha

Our group is in favor of using personal technology devices in school because they can be useful for learning. So far, my favorite part of the unit has been working in a group because my classmates have been very helpful to me. I also think that the topic is interesting because we use technology in our everyday lives. The hardest parts of this unit for me so far have been understanding the articles and doing the research for our argument, but my group members have been doing most of it.

Luke

Our group is against allowing personal technology devices in school because they are distracting to students, and not everyone can afford their own device. So far, I liked reading the articles about the pros and cons of using personal devices in school because I got to work alone. The most difficult part for me has been working in a group because I don't know my classmates very well and don't know what to say to them. They are mainly working with each other while I watch, and I wish I could have done this project by myself. I also did not like the warm-up activity where we had to move around the room.

Isabel (ELL Student)

My group is in favor of using personal devices in school because technology is a big part of everyday life. So far, my favorite part of the unit has been working in a group because I like my group members and we are doing a good job at coming up with an argument. I also like that we get to pick our final project because I can be creative. I'm nervous about the debate part of the project though because I get nervous speaking in front of big groups of people.

89. Which of the following is the most likely reason Ms. Hoffman selected three students to extend their project by assigning them to draft a proposal for the school administration?

a. To demonstrate the real-world application of their learning
b. To support the learning needs of gifted students by challenging them academically
c. To ensure these students had an additional assignment in case they finished too early
d. To encourage collaboration among diverse groups of students

90. What is correct about the definition of independent study as an instructional strategy?

a. It involves only an individual student working alone.
b. It can include individuals, partners, or small groups.
c. It can involve paired students but not small groups.
d. It can involve small groups but not paired students.

91. The Total Talent model considers which of the following?

a. Student interest, learning styles, and extraordinary abilities
b. Student's abilities only
c. Student's interests and learning styles
d. A student's interests and learning styles and the student's cognitive ability are equally considered

92. Mrs. Cranston, a seventh grade science teacher, tries to provide her students with several options when assigning projects. This approach is useful because it fosters emotional development in which of the following areas?

a. Development of a variety of learning approaches
b. Development of self-concept
c. Developing a sense of autonomy
d. Developing identification with peer groups

93. Continuum of Learning Experiences refers to:

a. Challenging experiences and opportunities that resonate with the specific interests and abilities of high-level students
b. Unplanned learning experiences which are successful and therefore incorporated into the continuum
c. The correct term is Continuous Learning Events
d. Planned learning experiences that build upon a progressively stronger foundation from year to year

94. How many hours of annual training are required of gifted teachers to retain eligibility?

a. 15
b. 6
c. None
d. 3

95. "Gifted" students are federally defined as:

a. Those that score above 130 on a WISC test
b. There is no decisive federal definition; each state determines its own definition
c. Those who are academically 2 classes or more above peers
d. Those who exhibit extra-ordinary abilities in the areas of the arts, mathematics, science, business, or leadership

96. Parental permission to assess a student for a gifted program is:

a. Required
b. Not required, in order to avoid a hardship for students who meets the qualifications but do not have supportive parents
c. Not required; one of the premises of gifted education is developing a sense of independence and personal responsibility in students
d. Required only if a student requests parental involvement

97. Which of the following is a good example of appropriate content for an objective?

a. Compare and contrast science fiction and fantasy.
b. Complete Unit 6 in the vocabulary book.
c. Describe the similarities and differences of setting between the stories "Wilderness Adventure" and "PS 139."
d. Solve the arithmetic problems on p. 114 in your textbook.

98. Once a student has been nominated for a gifted and talented program via a Student Observation Form, he or she _______ be assessed.

a. Will
b. Might
c. Will not; nomination guarantees assessment
d. Must

99. Curriculum focusing on social awareness and adjustment, personal awareness and adjustment, a study of attitudes, values, and the individual's perceptions is:

a. Effective Curriculum
b. Sociological Curriculum
c. Affective Curriculum
d. Developmental Curriculum

Refer to the following for question 100:

EXHIBIT 1

CLASS DESCRIPTION

Mr. Morris has recently moved to a new city and begun teaching 8th-grade social studies. The school population is ethnically diverse, and Mr. Morris is unfamiliar with the backgrounds, customs, beliefs, and experiences of his students and their families. However, he is determined to build positive relationships and learn how to best meet the needs of his students and the community.

At the beginning of the school year, Mr. Morris reaches out to the administration regarding professional development opportunities that focus on methods for effectively teaching students of varying cultural backgrounds, and he self-educates regarding the priorities of his new community. He also attends the school's open-house night in order to meet his students' families and gain insight into their home lives and individual learning needs. In addition, Mr. Morris plans to involve himself in the school community by participating in such activities as PTA meetings and fundraisers and attending school sporting events. In the classroom, Mr. Morris focuses on creating a positive classroom community by conducting team-building exercises, icebreaker activities, and learning-style inventories to get to know his students. He creates a classroom newsletter and website to communicate important updates and intends to maintain frequent communication with families via conferences, phone calls, and emails.

Prior to beginning his first unit on the contributions and experiences of different immigrant groups throughout American history, Mr. Morris administers a diagnostic exam on the topic to assess his students' level of understanding. The results indicate a wide range of knowledge and abilities. Mr. Morris considers these results when planning lessons in an effort to proactively meet his students' needs by implementing the most effective instructional strategies and supports. He plans to deliver instruction through a variety of means, including presentations, class discussions, and hands-on activities, as well as opportunities for individual and small-group work in which struggling students are paired with others that can provide assistance. In addition, Mr. Morris carefully researches and seeks examples from the community that demonstrate positive contributions to today's society from varying immigrant groups. Throughout instruction, Mr. Morris conducts formative assessments to evaluate understanding and overall engagement in order to reflect upon and determine areas in which his instructional approaches may need adjustment to better support his students.

Exhibit 2

Excerpt from Mr. Morris's Lesson Plan

Topic: Immigration

Standard: Compare and contrast the experiences of different groups in the United States. Explain the contributions of specific groups to American society and culture (NYCCLS – 4.7a).

Essential Question:

- How have different immigrant groups contributed to shaping American society and culture throughout history?
- How do the experiences of early immigrants compare to those of recent immigrants?

Lesson Objectives:

- Students will be able to compare and contrast the experiences of early and recent immigrant groups in the United States.
- Students will be able to discuss ways in which early and recent immigrant groups have contributed to American society and culture.

Grouping: Students will be arranged in groups of three to five. The teacher will determine student groupings.

Lesson Component	Activity
Introduction	Students will be shown a political cartoon that refers to the United States as a melting pot. Students will be asked to discuss what they think that term means and how it applies to today's society. Students will then see a presentation on early immigrants to the United States, such as those from Ireland, Germany, and England, as well as recent immigrant groups from China, Vietnam, and Latin America. Throughout the presentation, the teacher will give examples of ways in which each group has influenced American society and culture, such as food, clothing, and music.
Individual Activity	Students will conduct independent online research regarding the contributions and experiences of a specific immigrant group that the teacher will assign. Some students will be assigned to research the same immigrant group for a later collaborative assignment.
Small-Group Activity	Students will work in groups of three to five with others that researched the same immigrant group. Working collaboratively, students will create a visual representation of their choosing (chart, comic strip, slideshow, skit, etc.) to depict their research findings. Members of each group will be assigned a specific role and present their visual representation to the class in a two- to three-minute presentation.
Whole-Group Activity	The teacher will lead a class discussion focused on comparing and contrasting the experiences and contributions of early versus recent immigrant groups in the United States. Throughout the discussion, the teacher will record key points on the chalkboard using a Venn diagram.
Extension/Enrichment	Gifted students will have the opportunity to extend their research on their assigned immigrant group by applying what they learned and imagining they are immigrating to the United States. These students will be asked to create a series of diary entries that detail their initial experiences based upon their research findings.

Exhibit 3

Notes from Mr. Morris's Formative Assessments

Diagnostic Exam

The diagnostic exam results indicate that most students possess basic knowledge of recent immigrant groups, but very limited understanding of the experiences and contributions of early immigrants. Extra focus on early immigrant populations may need to be included in the introductory presentation. While most students demonstrated appropriate grade-level reading comprehension skills, many were unfamiliar with key vocabulary related to the unit, and a few students indicated below grade-level reading comprehension skills. These students will need extra supports in the form of visual aids, graphic organizers, and selective grouping during instructional activities. Three students performed extremely well on the assessment. Extra learning opportunities for enrichment will be beneficial for these students.

Introduction

The presentation included slides, images, video clips, and opportunities for students to answer open-ended questions. During the presentation, I moved around the room to assess students' level of attentiveness. Students appeared to be the most interested in viewing the images and video clips, and most were highly engaged in the open-ended questioning segment of the lesson. A few students in the back of the classroom, who indicated low reading comprehension skills on the diagnostic exam, appeared bored throughout the presentation. I used proximity and maintained eye contact to redirect their focus. Students were asked periodically throughout the presentation to indicate their level of understanding by giving a "thumbs-up" or "thumbs-down" sign. If the majority of students showed a "thumbs-down" sign, I reviewed previous presentation slides and provided extra examples. Overall, students seemed to respond well and were most enthusiastic about the real-world examples of contributions from immigrant groups in everyday life.

Individual Activity

Each student was given a color-coded card to indicate their level of understanding as they conducted independent research. One side of the cards was green, and the other was red. Students were instructed to flip their cards to the red side when they needed assistance or clarification. During the activity, I moved throughout the room and stopped to help students that flipped their card to the red side. This method seemed to work well for students that do not typically ask for help.

Small-Group Activity

Throughout the small-group activity, I moved between groups to listen to student discussions, ask questions, address misconceptions, and ensure all students were on task. Assigning specific roles to group members appears to have helped maintain group focus. Struggling students seemed to be more engaged and productive when paired with others that could provide assistance.

Exit Ticket

Students were instructed to write down three new things they learned, two questions they had for further exploration, and one way in which their culture has positively contributed to shaping American society and culture as preparation for a long-term project. Most students appeared to have a firm understanding of the key points of the lesson. A few students, however, seemed to have struggled with differentiating the experiences between specific immigrant populations. This will be reviewed in the next lesson for clarification. Questions for further exploration were primarily focused on reasons why different groups of people immigrated to the United States, which will be addressed in a future lesson.

100. By incorporating opportunities for enrichment and extension, Mr. Morris does which of the following?

a. Prevents students that finish early from engaging in off-task or disruptive behavior
b. Strengthens students' understanding of diversity and its significance in shaping American society and culture
c. Provides gifted and talented students with extra work while they wait for their classmates to catch up
d. Acknowledges the learning needs of gifted and talented students by challenging them academically and intellectually

101. Of the following theories of cognitive development, which proposes discrete developmental changes?

a. Skinner's
b. Vygotsky's
c. Bandura's
d. Piaget's

102. Which of the following is a characteristic of indirect instruction?

a. It is delivered explicitly.
b. It has uniform lesson plans.
c. It is more structured by nature.
d. It involves exploratory activities.

103. A student who has tremendous leadership potential has been charged with a series of tasks. She will gather a variety of types of information that describe her areas of strength and continually update this information; she will categorize this material as pertaining to ability, learning styles, social skills, and special interest; she will create a time line to consider options and guide decisions in her differentiation; she will communicate with the teacher regarding these options and decisions; and she will use the information to communicate with mentors, parents, and others about her development. What is she doing?

a. Creating a Total Talent Portfolio
b. Developing a number of assessment tools
c. Developing a differentiation plan
d. Creating a Personal Growth file

104. To communicate high expectations to all students and avoid bias, what should teachers do?

a. Identify which students they expect less from as early as they can.
b. Avoid identifying student similarities that influence expectations.
c. Realize teacher expectations have more influence than behaviors.
d. Treat students differently according to what they expect of them.

Refer to the following for question 105:

Mr. Krick recently read an article about a new interactive computer game that is very effective at getting children interested in history. Although he has never seen the game himself, he is interested in the possibility of using it with his class.

105. Which of the following is generally true of using technology like this computer game in the classroom?

a. It causes students to become more immersed in the content they are learning.
b. Students can finish assignments faster so that more material can be taught.
c. It allows the lesson to become more accessible to students of varying abilities.
d. It helps the teacher use the materials in later years.

106. In regard to the process of writing a lesson plan, which of the following is true?

a. The steps of writing the plan may vary with the teaching model.
b. Experienced teachers won't need to write down as much as new teachers because some actions become automatic with time.
c. The lesson's opening, body, and closing should be written in order.
d. Only the parts of the lesson to be presented to the students need to be written down, not necessarily the pre-planning and editing tasks.

107. The National Research Center on the Gifted and Talented is:

a. A federally-funded center with the charter of developing effective methods of identification and testing of Gifted and Talented students, and programming for such students
b. A federally-funded center with the charter of developing effective methods of showcasing gifted students by funding venues for student performances and presentations
c. A privately-funded center with the charter of developing effective methods of showcasing gifted students by funding venues for student performances and presentations
d. A state-funded center with the charter of developing effective methods of identification and testing of Gifted and Talented students, and programming for such students

108. Students identified as gifted and talented can demonstrate a serious lack of motivation that hinders their performances, especially when they do not find a class interesting or useful. Two factors that contribute to underachievement are low self-efficacy and a lack of self-regulation skills. Which of the following is also a common reason for gifted and talented students to underachieve?

a. The student finds the work too challenging and gives up in frustration.
b. Gifted and talented students are sometimes ridiculed for their ability, which makes them less likely to want to perform at their best.
c. The student is commonly met with praise and special treatment at home and expects the same in the classroom.
d. The student finds the work too simple, so they dismiss or ignore it.

109. According to Piaget's theory of cognitive development, ______ and ______ are processes included in the overall process of ______.

a. assimilation; accommodation; adaptation
b. adaptation; assimilation; accommodation
c. accommodation; adaptation; assimilation
d. adaptation; accommodation; equilibrium

110. Each school district receives an annual allotment equal to that district's adjusted base allotment multiplied by 0.12 for each student per year. What percentage of students in average daily attendance can be considered for Gifted and Talented funding?

a. 2.5%
b. 5%
c. 10%
d. 8.3%

111. Differentiation is:

a. The practice of grouping students in terms of commonality; for example, grouping gifted students and average students separately
b. Modifying lessons for the unique needs of a particular student
c. Illegal in all 50 states, as it violates the 14th Amendment
d. The practice of grouping students in terms of their differences; for example, grouping gifted and regular students, or grouping native English speakers with non-native speakers

112. Providing opportunities for self-assessment is important primarily because:

a. It provides students with additional practice time on assignments
b. It allows teachers to collect more data for grading
c. It prepares students to evaluate their own work in the absence of an instructor
d. It provides a break from teacher-directed instruction

113. In the process of determining the rationale of an objective, the teacher should ask all of the following EXCEPT:

a. Does this objective have an important learning outcome?
b. Will this objective fit my planned activity?
c. Will my students be able to use this knowledge in the future?
d. Are the prior knowledge and skill levels of my students sufficient to achieve this objective?

114. Students who are gifted are required by federal law to have an Individualized Education Program (IEP).

a. True. Students in all 50 states receiving any form of special education must have such a plan
b. False. No such plan for children identified as Gifted and Talented has ever been federally mandated
c. Neither true nor false. IEPs are used exclusively for students with learning disabilities or mental insufficiencies
d. At one point this was true, but it has been overturned

115. The Total Talent Portfolio is a systematic method of gathering, analyzing, and classifying students' abilities in order to:

a. Protect gifted children with learning disabilities from falling through the cracks
b. Help the teacher determine how to enrich and accelerate students' learning based upon their individually unique profiles
c. Help older students with transition and placement into jobs at which they are likely to excel
d. Give teachers visual and logistical models whereby they can decide which cross-curriculum strategies are most likely to succeed for individual students

116. Dr. Acevedo has a gifted child in her fifth grade classroom. In order to keep the student engaged and motivated, which of these inclusion strategies should she permit the student?

a. Establish own learning goals; self-assess; move to an independent challenge activity when student understands the lesson; encourage student to work with peers close to his or her own intellectual level
b. Have student independently design his or her own curriculum based upon classroom assignments; self-assess and self-grade; help establish learning goals for the class
c. Help teacher design his or her own curriculum based upon classroom assignments; review student's assessments and grades with the teacher; suggest learning goals for the class
d. Help establish learning goals for the class; act as the teacher's assistant teacher; grade work of classmates for the teacher

117. What is most true about the relationship of teaching and classroom management?

a. Teacher management decisions are more complex when instruction is more demanding.
b. Encouraging student responsibility changes student behavior without affecting content.
c. When students solve novel problems and create products, teacher decisions are simpler.
d. Teachers focus on helping students meet academic demands instead of social demands.

118. In scaffolded instruction, what is the correct sequence (first to last) of these steps?

a. Teacher modeling, student think-alouds; student-teacher collaboration; student paired/small-group work, scaffolded as needed; independent student practice
b. Independent student practice; student-teacher collaboration; teacher modeling, student think-alouds; student paired/small-group work, scaffolded as needed
c. Student-teacher collaboration; student paired/small-group work, scaffolded as needed; independent student practice; teacher modeling, student think-alouds
d. Student paired/small-group work, scaffolded as needed; teacher modeling, student think-alouds; independent student practice; student-teacher collaboration

119. Which of these is NOT one of the major personality structures proposed by Sigmund Freud in his psychoanalytic theory of development?

a. Id
b. Ego
c. Libido
d. Superego

120. When considering behavior management with young children, which of these is most accurate?

a. Behaviors can be replaced regardless of their function.
b. To change a behavior, one must first know its function.
c. Behaviors need no change if one knows their functions.
d. The same consequences are applied for every function.

Answer Key and Explanations

1. C: Behaviorist learning theory states that receiving rewards for certain behaviors reinforces the behavior, or increases the chance the behavior will recur for more rewards. A student receiving positive reinforcement for studying hard will continue to do so. Social learning theory states people respond not only to direct rewards, but also to observing others receiving rewards, and will imitate rewarded behaviors. A student studying hard who observes struggling classmates getting more teacher attention may stop studying for comparable attention (A). A student observing classmates getting rewards for studying hard imitates that behavior (B). A student observing struggling classmates getting less attention will continue to study hard (D) to avoid losing the rewards. Choice C is an example of behaviorist learning theory, the others of social learning theory.

2. B: Include provisions about furloughs, reassessment, exiting strategies, transferring students, and the district decision appeals process. A district's written policy regarding student identification must include provisions for continuing screening; assessment procedures from a number of sources; insure that all populations have assessment available; insure final selections are made by at minimum three local educators with specialized training; and contain provisions regarding furloughs or leaves of absence, reassessment, exiting strategies, transferring students and the process by which appeals can be made.

3. A: It is true that conflict resolution steps have been taught successfully to children as young as eighteen months. For example, the HighScope EC curriculum, well known for its effectiveness, has sponsored the expert design of a conflict resolution approach for children aged eighteen months to six years. Conflict mediation and resolution have been taught in such settings as daycare centers, Head Start programs, preschools, nursery schools, and kindergartens. Therefore, choice C is not true. Instruction features the same steps used with adults, but adjusted commensurately with various EC developmental levels. Preschoolers are found to understand these concepts (B) when presented age appropriately. Teaching conflict mediation and resolution to young children is found to develop lifelong social skills and problem-solving skills; hence, children *do* generalize this learning (D).

4. C: Both A and B. Many teachers prefer to assess kindergarten students using only qualitative assessments. In areas of creativity, artistic and leadership abilities, teachers can chose to use only qualitative assessments.

5. D: Provide a wide variety of reading materials for children to choose from. Each classroom will have students who are just beginning to read and some that are reading fluently above grade level. Providing reading materials with an appealing variety of subject matter and broad distribution of reading levels will ensure that every child in the class can select an appropriate book to read.

6. B: Odd; her lack of English, terrible handwriting, nervousness, and bizarre musical talents make her seem abnormal. Many gifted children are highly sensitive and can be far more easily excited that their average peers. They may not know how to relate to other children, and as a result lack social skills. Ming's lack of English, terrible handwriting, nervousness and musical talents might make her seem abnormal to her classmates.

7. C: Curriculum compacting. Curriculum compacting is a differentiation strategy for students with high ability involves streamlining work to match ability, thereby creating a more challenging environment. The three steps to compacting are determining goals, identifying students, and offering acceleration and enrichment opportunities. Curriculum compacting eliminates repetition of lessons that have already been learned, and speeding up lessons to match the learner's pace.

8. B: Effectively differentiating science instruction includes incorporating activities that provide the appropriate level of challenge to align with the intellectual abilities of gifted and talented learners. Doing so sustains these students' engagement in scientific learning while promoting continuous development at a pace that corresponds with their individual needs. Differentiation for gifted and talented learners can be achieved through a variety of strategies, such as extending the scope of instruction, adding a layer of complexity to a summative assessment, or allowing for flexibility to explore personal interests. In this example, the teacher can accommodate gifted and talented students in the classroom by having them research local weather patterns throughout history. Such an activity would provide enrichment by allowing these students to explore the topic on a broader scale, identify long-term weather patterns, and ultimately gain a deeper understanding of occurring and recurring patterns in nature.

9. C: That gifted student's value learning over performance. Her lack of motivation shouldn't be an occasion for blame. Instead of focusing on grades and performance, the father might consider exploring some learning opportunities in areas of the girl's interest. For example, a visit to an art museum followed by a trip to the library for books about a particular art movement might motivate the student.

10. C: Introducing new material using several different strategies will help make it more accessible to a larger group of students, regardless of their specific backgrounds. While surveys and general knowledge about cultures may be useful, relying too much on generalized beliefs about cultures and what they value and find useful in instruction can be problematic.

11. C: In a highly diversified class, teachers often fall into the trap of allocating too much time to the higher performing students while neglecting the lower performing students. As a result, the lower performing students can become resentful and feel little incentive to work harder. The other options are generally recommended practices in classes with diverse levels of skill.

12. B: complexity. Complexity is one strategy for differentiating learning. Extending lessons throughout the curriculum by comparing common themes and issues, studying associations within and between individual disciplines over the course of time and/or from more than one viewpoint are ways a teacher can adapt lessons in order to challenge gifted students.

13. C: Although IQ tests can be beneficial for a number of reasons, they are limited in that they only measure certain subjects and skills. Because of this, they must be taken as part of a body of evidence that incorporates other tests and skills. Answer A is incorrect because IQ tests are one of the most popular ways to identify gifted students. Answer B is incorrect because these tests are designed to measure specific strengths and weaknesses. Answer D is incorrect because IQ tests often identify future student success in the areas tested.

14. C: Teachers can stimulate active student involvement in subject content by asking both cognitively lower-level questions requiring students to remember and understand information and cognitively higher-level questions requiring students to apply, analyze, evaluate, and/or synthesize information rather than only the former (A) or only the latter (B). Even simple factual questions engage students by requiring them to think about and respond to them; therefore, it is not true that questions will not promote active student involvement (D).

15. D: Refers to mapping the curriculum to build upon understanding and skills learned in the previous grade. Vertical curriculum allows teachers to efficiently assess learning from the previous year in order to effectively concentrate time on developing further understanding and skills rather than wasting time with lessons that are redundant in terms of what students already know.

16. A: It is the teacher's responsibility to observe and verify that students are following the instructions and participating equally. Answer B is likely to produce biased results. Answer C defeats the purpose of the exercise. The point is for the students to learn how to effectively work together on the group task. Answer D simply denies students the experience of learning this valuable lesson.

17. B: Schemata (plural of schema) are mental constructs or concepts of categories or classes of things, e.g., things I can suck on, things I can throw, furry four-legged animals, etc. They are not concepts of individual objects (A). They are not programs only for motor actions (C); they are ideas for categorizing different components of the environment. Inborn reflexes are not governed by ideas (D) but are automatic reactions.

18. C: If these are IQ scores, Mario scored in the 99.99th percentile. This means he scored higher than all but 0.01% of the population. With an IQ score at the very top of the population, Mario would be considered gifted. Therefore, option C is correct.

These scores all express the same measures in different terms. Z-score, T-score, and scaled score express the same values as standard score, but they are based on a different numbering system. Based on the table's headings, these are not scores from different tests. Therefore, option A is incorrect.

Nothing in the table indicates that these scores represent different parts of a test. The table names different types of scoring methods. Therefore, option B is incorrect.

If these are IQ scores, Mario's score is higher than most of the population's. In addition to adaptive skills measures, the definition of intellectual disabilities is largely based on IQ scores. The mildest (highest IQ) level of intellectual disabilities corresponds to a range of IQ scores between 70 and 55. Mario's score is 155. Therefore, option D is incorrect.

19. A: Raw scores are used on specific tests to show how well a student did; this score is not necessarily consistent from test to test. A scale score translates raw scores onto a measurement common to all forms of testing for a particular assessment.

20. D: Culture. Bruner's original position on education underwent a major shift by the mid 1990s. In The Culture of Education he expresses the position that it is impossible to think outside of culture; regardless of how interior or 'mental' the process, thinking requires the framework or grid of culture.

21. D: According to Piaget's theory, the distinction between people at the concrete operational stage (approximately 7–12 years of age) and the formal operational stage (approximately 12–16 years of age) of development is that those in the concrete operational stage can think logically only with respect to concrete experiences, while those at the formal operational stage can reason in abstract and hypothetical terms. Children at the sensorimotor stage (birth to 2 years old) rely on their sensory perception and motor skills to learn and understand the world around them, and children at the preoperational stage (approximately 3–7 years old) think in a literal, symbolic manner.

22. D: Have the capability for high accomplishment in intellectual, creative, artistic, or leadership areas or in specific academic fields, and who need services or activities not ordinarily provided by the school to develop those capabilities. The Jacob Javits Gifted and Talented Students Education Act (Javits) is a federal program that addresses the needs of gifted and talented children. The purpose of the Act is to coordinate programs of scientific research, projects, pioneering approaches, and the like to enhance schools' abilities to foster the educational needs of gifted and talented students.

23. D: False. Vertical scores at a particular grade level indicate the degree of mastery of that subject at that grade level. This number is unrelated to the Standards established at a higher grade level. Vertical scores are not the same as Standards.

24. B: They give the teacher insight into how a particular student structures ideas, uses language, and demonstrates understanding. Because open-ended questions are the beginning of dialogue, they also give the student the opportunity to express their ideas with creativity, and exhibit the degree of their abilities to abstract, find connections, analyze and assess ideas.

25. A: Conducting interviews is a strategy best used for verbal-linguistic students who use speaking, such as asking questions of another person, to learn. Students who are dominantly logical-mathematical learners will learn best in the areas of mathematics, science, and logic. Strategies in these areas include using Venn diagrams to logically illustrate relationships; thinking in probabilities, which emphasizes working with numbers; and discerning patterns, which is a mathematical thinking process.

26. A: Johnny's IQ score places him in the gifted range. His rank is in the 97th percentile. This means that only 3 percent (the remainder of 100 percent minus 97 percent) of the population has a higher score than Johnny's. Therefore choice A is correct.

Johnny's score is at or above the scores of 97 percent of the population, not above only 96 percent. Only 3 percent, not 97 percent, of the population scored higher than Johnny. Therefore, choices B and C are incorrect.

The percentage of the population with an IQ score lower than or equal to Johnny's is 97 percent, not 3 percent. 3 percent of the population has a score higher than Johnny's, not lower. Therefore choice D is incorrect.

27. B: Parallel Curriculum Model. This strategy modifies the curriculum in depth, complexity and originality and indicates four concurrent directions, Core Curriculum, Curriculum of Connections, Curriculum of Practice and Curriculum of Identity.

28. C: Behavioral principles have proven in many studies that it is more powerful to reward good behaviors than to punish bad behaviors (A); therefore, these are not equally effective (B). Good behaviors should be rewarded consistently, not occasionally (D). Positive reinforcement must be repeated consistently many times for young children to associate their behaviors with the rewards they receive as they will not instantly make this association.

29. C: Task cards are a strategy best used as a manipulative for tactile-kinesthetic learners. While a task card may have writing on it, the value to tactile learners is that a card is something that the students can touch, which makes the writing more real to them. Students who are dominantly verbal-linguistic learners will learn best when listening, speaking, reading, and writing. Consequently, activities such as classroom discussions, listening to a story read by the teacher, or reading the words listed on the classroom word wall are good strategies for reaching the verbal-linguistic learners in the class.

While learning styles do vary some from person to person, all people do need to learn from visual information, auditory information, and by hands-on learning. Different materials lend themselves to a different format, but where possible, the best practice when presenting information to others is to use a mixture of formats, including hands-on materials, visual, and auditory information to keep the materials engaging to all learners.

30. B: Permissive parents are nurturing, responsive, and communicative with their children; however, they avoid confronting and/or disciplining children and do not expect them to demonstrate much self-control or maturity. Consequently, their children tend to have problems with authority figures, poor school performance, and deficits in self-regulation. The children of unresponsive, overly strict, demanding, harshly punitive authoritarian parents tend to develop proficient technical and school performance and obedience, but they lack social skills, self-esteem, and happiness. The children of authoritative parents, who have the ideal parenting style, tend to develop competence, success, and happiness. Uninvolved parents, who are undemanding but also unresponsive, uncommunicative, detached, and maybe even neglectful, tend to produce children lacking competence, self-esteem, and self-control.

31. D: Some gifted students excel in all areas, including athletics and social skills (A), but not necessarily. Gifted children can have different abilities and interests than peers, making social interaction awkward. They may have difficulty relating to peers with more typical abilities and interests, resulting in peers who may not want to interact with them for being different. Some gifted children prefer academic/creative activities over social activities. Some gifted children show superior academic performance (B), while some do not. Some are bored by traditional curricula (including special education for the gifted) and lack motivation, while some use unconventional methods. As a child, Albert Einstein reportedly was failed in math by a teacher for achieving correct answers without following prescribed steps. Not all gifted children get high IQ scores (C) because giftedness also includes creativity or other forms not represented by IQ scores, not just intelligence. Some gifted children do not respond to standardized measures because they may think differently and/or be uninterested in test items.

32. A: Share consistent expectations / is flexible, respects the student's opinions, and does not demand absolute obedience. Gifted underachievers do best when teacher and parent expectations are consistent, and in learning and home environments are not overly rigid or demanding.

33. D: All the above. The National Association of Gifted Children (NAGC) has taken a strong position on grouping. NAGC argues that athletically gifted individuals, whether children or adults, are regularly grouped by ability and have the best success in such groupings. Furthermore, all areas of professional or graduate study/ preparation involve grouping. Yet another argument is that ability grouping is a means by which gifted ELLS, students with economic disadvantages and those with learning disabilities can be challenged along with their true peers.

34. C: Screening Assessment for Gifted Elementary Students, and describes a standardized assessment. Unlike many tools used to identify Gifted and Talented students, SAGES was designed expressly for that function. SAGES is also designed to reduce prejudice in gifted and talented testing.

35. B: During Piaget's second stage—the preoperational stage—toddlers' and preschoolers' thinking is primarily intuitive as opposed to logical (A); logic does not develop until later. Primarily, sensory (C) and motoric (D) bases of thought are more closely associated with Piaget's first stage—the sensorimotor stage—during infancy.

36. B: Piaget's first stage of cognitive development is called the sensorimotor stage. This is when infants respond to input they receive from the environment through their sensory organs by engaging in motor actions. When they realize how the environment then reacts to some of these actions, they respond again; this is called circular reactions. Operations with concrete things (A) occur during Piaget's third stage called concrete operations. Operations with abstract things (C) occur during Piaget's fourth and final stage called formal operations. Intuition and animism but not logic (D) occur during Piaget's second stage, which he called preoperational.

37. D: Each district develops and implements a program that is based upon criteria determined by the State Board of Education, which includes identifying and serving gifted and talented students.

38. D: Any of the above. To be considered for a gifted program, a student must be nominated. Anyone can make the nomination, including family members, teachers, school administrators and other school personnel, and community members who are familiar with the child's abilities.

39. A: She has a high external locus of control. Locus of control is the degree to which an individual believes she can control events or actions that impact them. The more in control an individual believes herself to be, the higher her internal locus of control. The less in control an individual believes herself to be, the higher her external locus of control. In this example, the student blames other students, her brother and her teacher for missing schoolwork, believing herself to have no control in these matters. Her locus of control is external, and the degree to which she feels out of control indicates it is also high.

40. A: The objective is like a public declaration for all to see – not only the students, but also other teachers, administrative staff, and parents who want to know what is going on that day and whether the objective has been clearly communicated to the students. One of the benefits of a clearly written, focused objective is that the teacher knows exactly what to evaluate – did the students learn the objective for the day? Another benefit is that the evaluation works in reverse also – providing a measure for the teacher to judge his/her own effectiveness. It is the primary purpose of an objective to focus the students on what they are to learn that day; in addition, a well-written objective might also motivate students to want to learn the day's lesson.

41. C: It is a district decision. Prior to assignment in the program, teachers who provide instruction and services for gifted students are required to have a minimum of 30 hours of staff development that includes nature and needs of gifted/talented students, assessing student needs, and curriculum and instruction for gifted students. However, how many hours to devote to each category is left up to the district to determine.

42. A: When teachers work on incorporating creative problem solving into a classroom by posing interesting questions or scenarios, they are helping students work on finding new solutions to problems when they arise. This helps students develop the way they think, which can help them in classes and in the outside world. This helps students learn practical skills that they can apply in the real world to help them overcome obstacles they may encounter in everyday situations. While this activity will likely activate the students' imagination, it is more likely that the teacher's main intention for this activity was to work on helping students develop their skills with creative problem solving.

43. B: When a teacher is consistent in how he or she runs her classroom, the students will more quickly understand the rules and will also recognize that the rules apply equally to everyone. Answer A can work in some classrooms, but some students will find this to be too intense. Answer C will lead to the students taking advantage of the teacher and misbehaving even more. Answer D will likely lead to chaos. While it is wise not to let the students "get a rise out of you," the teacher should always react so that it will be clear that misbehavior is not tolerated.

44. A: Accommodating the needs of gifted students requires that teachers include meaningful opportunities for extension and enrichment into instruction. This is necessary to provide these students with engaging and intellectually challenging learning experiences aligned with their unique abilities. By incorporating an extension activity in which selected students were assigned to create original stories, Ms. Jewel effectively acknowledges and implements learning activities that meet the needs of her gifted and talented students.

45. A: Weigh the pros and cons of entering a student into a gifted program. Pfeiffer's Scales is a time-efficient way to assess giftedness using six scales for students beyond kindergarten. It is administered by teachers and covers intellectual ability, academic ability, creativity, artistic talent, leadership ability, and motivation.

46. C: Cognitive. Bloom's taxonomy places knowledge, comprehension, application, analysis, synthesis and evaluation in the cognitive Domain.

47. A: Option A is correct because role play is an effective tool in having students practice certain social situations. Option B is incorrect because not all groups will welcome all children and encouraging students to try this could be damaging to their self-esteem. Option C is incorrect because it does not directly teach students how to initiate social connections. Option D is incorrect because not all students have a desire to play sports, so suggesting that all students should play might make students who do not like sports feel defeated.

48. C: Asynchrony. According to the Columbus Group (1991) "Giftedness is asynchronous development in which advanced cognitive abilities and heightened intensity combine to create inner experiences and awareness that are qualitatively different from the norm. This asynchrony increases with higher intellectual capacity. The uniqueness of the gifted renders them particularly vulnerable and requires modifications in parenting, teaching, and counseling in order for them to develop optimally."

49. A: According to research findings, teacher learning environment strategies that produce high student engagement and low student misbehavior include focusing on the whole class when alerting student attention (A); communicating teacher awareness of student behaviors to students (B); designing and implementing overlapping activities (C); and lesson planning and delivery that enable instructional momentum (D).

50. D: Identify gifted and talented students, including those from culturally diverse backgrounds or those who live at or below the poverty level. The Kingore Observation Inventory is an efficient assessment and differentiation process, identifies gifted and talented students via observing behaviors in seven categories.

51. B: Curiosity; adept at using multiple resources; willing to take risks; applies key words when asking questions. According to Kaplan, belief sets are a strong indicator of learning success. Students who are curious, can move comfortably between resources, are willing to take risks, and listens for key words in questions achieve their goals at the highest level.

52. D: Physiological cues that indicate nervousness, such as sweating hands; or cues that indicate confidence, such as a feeling of ease and control. Self-efficacy, the belief in one's ability to succeed at a particular task, is influenced by past performance, observing the success of peers, verbal support and persuasion by others, and physiological cues that indicate nervousness, such as sweating hands, or confidence, such as a feeling of ease and control.

53. C: Practical intelligence. According to Sternberg's Triarchic Theory of Intelligence, componential intelligence (the ability to analyze, think in abstract terms and efficiently process information), experiential intelligence (the ability to creatively combine unrelated information and to perceive patterns in material that, on the surface, appears to be unrelated) and practical intelligence (the ability to apply thinking skills to contextual situations by reassessing one's position in terms of strengths and weaknesses) are the three core qualities of giftedness.

54. A: Gifted and talented students have a unique set of abilities that are often overlooked in the classroom. These students must be challenged academically and intellectually in order to properly accommodate their learning needs to sustain engagement in learning. Incorporating opportunities for extension and enrichment would have helped create a more inclusive environment by allowing these students to build upon and strengthen their learning.

55. A: Cognitive, affective, and psychomotor. Bloom's taxonomy includes three types of learning. The cognitive has to do with mental skills and is concerned with knowledge. The affective involves feelings and emotions and is concerned with attitude. Psychomotor examines manual/physical facility and is concerned with skills.

56. B: Cooperative learning exercises (working in small groups) teach students how to solve problems in groups. These skills are essential to success in many jobs. Answer A is the opposite of cooperative learning. Answers C and D are unrelated to the topic of the question.

57. A: Brainstorming. Brainstorming is a highly-charged creative technique to approach problem-solving, in which group members spontaneously offer a wealth of associations, ideas and possible solutions. The group considers all possibilities without initial judgment, looking for creative possibilities that might otherwise be overlooked.

58. B: Array of learning experiences. An array of learning experiences is defined as a menu of challenging learning experiences or opportunities that fit the unique interests and abilities of advanced level students.

59. A: Whereas behaviorist learning theorists believe that learning always results in some change in behavior, Bandura disagrees, finding children could learn something new without necessarily producing new or different behaviors. Bandura agrees with the behaviorist concept that consequences (events immediately following behaviors) either reward them, reinforcing and increasing their probable recurrence, or punish them, decreasing their probable recurrence. Unlike behaviorists who insist only externally observable, measurable behaviors can be changed, Bandura emphasizes the importance of internal cognitive processes in learning and thus of examining their roles (C), as well as social interactions in learning (D).

60. A: Administrators and counselors who make programming or hiring decisions. All individuals who work with or for children identified as gifted or talented are required to complete 6 hours of training annually.

61. D: Are anecdotal records, observations, interviews, student products, checklists, and similar materials. In contrast, quantitative measures involve standardized testing.

62. A: Qualitative. While it is appropriate to use both quantitative and qualitative approaches to identify 1st-12th grade students in terms of general intellectual ability or specific academic subjects, a district may choose to apply qualitative assessments only in order to identify gifted students in areas of creativity, the arts and leadership.

63. C: Cognitive dissonance is a term coined by psychologist Leon Festinger to describe the discomfort we feel when considering contradictory information. We resolve this discomfort by rejecting certain information, or forming new schemata or changing existing ones to accommodate some information. This term is not related to a disorder (A), sensory overload (B), or incompatible instructional and learning (D) processes.

64. C: No Child Left Behind (NCLB). This legislation reauthorized the Elementary and Secondary Education Act, and allocated financial support for low-income student education, teacher recruitment, professional development, technology and the like. NCLB is aimed at increasing educational success and parental contribution, and charges districts with guaranteeing state proficiency standards in mathematics and reading are reached by 2014.

65. A: While useful in some contexts, computer-monitored drills do not represent the greatest use of computers. These drills can be accomplished without computers. Even if using computers for drilling exercises, the teacher should remain active with the students and would not be more "freed up" than if the drills were administered on paper. Role-playing games, simulations, and exercises that teach higher-order thinking represent uses of computers that provide benefits that are difficult to obtain without computers.

66. D: Advanced Placement, in which high schools offer coursework meeting criteria recognized by institutions of higher education. Often, college credit is earned when an AP exam in specific content areas is passed.

67. B: False. While average and developmentally delayed children typically get very similar scores in a variety of I.Q. tests, gifted children more often get radically differing scores from test to test.

68. A: Erikson identified a nuclear conflict to be resolved in each stage of psychosocial development. Babies confront basic trust versus mistrust, toddlers autonomy (D) versus shame and self-doubt, preschoolers initiative versus guilt, school-aged children industry (C) versus inferiority, adolescents identity (A) versus role confusion, young adults intimacy (B) versus isolation, middle adults generativity versus stagnation, and older adults integrity versus despair.

69. B: A computer with a built-in voice synthesizer would let Stephen program all the words in his vocabulary into it. He could express himself despite his paralyzed vocal cords. He has excellent expressive and receptive language skills and a high IQ, so this would be the best solution for him. Therefore, option B is correct.

Adaptive pencil and paper holders would not help Stephen, because he can only press buttons with one hand. He could not manipulate a writing implement due to his paralysis. Therefore, option A is incorrect.

An electrolarynx is used by some laryngectomy patients whose larynxes have been surgically removed because of laryngeal cancer. It is an alternative to learning esophageal speech. This device is handheld. Stephen could not hold it up to his throat as required. The device also requires the speech system's muscles to work. It emits a tone, and the user manipulates the tongue, lips, cheeks, and throat, as in normal speech, to modulate the tone into recognizable speech sounds. Stephen could not use this device due to his paralysis. Therefore, option C is incorrect.

A communication board with buttons would be a good option for a student who is younger or less intellectually gifted than Stephen. It would afford simpler communication of basic needs and feelings. With Stephen's high IQ and advanced academic skills, he can program a computer with more complex ideas and complete sentences. He would undoubtedly find the communication board limited and would be frustrated. Therefore, option D is incorrect.

70. B: Assesses learning using portfolios, performance, observations, and other assessments that model real-world representations. Authentic assessment tasks are not simply practice for the sake of practice; they are rehearsals for real-world experiences. They assess a wide array of literacy skills in the context of how that skill would be applied in the real world.

71. A: Words like "because" and "for example" have to be followed by a reasonably precise explanation that gives clarity to the communication. Clarity is critical to good communication. Vague or confusing language can reduce the effectiveness of presentations. Answer B gives examples of negated intensifiers—the use of words such as "many" and "very" that indicate something big, but that are qualified by a "not," which communicates a nebulous state. Answer C indicates an ambiguous designation or destination. How is the student supposed to figure out needed specific information, even how to find supplies in the closet, if the directions are so vague? Answer D has words with the problem of vague probability; the student doesn't know exactly how often or what percentage.

72. D: A student may be granted a leave of absence for specific reasons and for a pre-established length of time; the leave must be approved. The leave of absence must all be requested at minimum six weeks prior to the furlough date.

73. C: Piaget coined the term magical thinking to describe the illogical thought of young children when they believe their own internal thoughts or words cause external events to happen in the world. Animism (A) was what Piaget termed the belief of young children that inanimate objects have thoughts and feelings. Egocentrism (B) was what Piaget called the characteristic in young children of being unable to see things—literally and concretely, not just abstractly—from others' perspectives and believing that the world revolves around them. Intuitive thinking (D) is how Piaget generally described the thought of preoperational children who are not yet able to think using logic.

74. A: Gifted and talented students must be challenged intellectually and academically to reach their full potential and sustain their engagement in learning. As Julia has been identified as gifted and talented, it is likely she was able to quickly finish the lesson activities with greater ease than her classmates, and therefore would have benefited from learning opportunities that offered extension or enrichment. By incorporating such activities into the lesson, Ms. Fenton could have aligned instruction to Julia's unique learning needs, giving her an appropriate level of challenge to avoid off-task behavior.

75. A: A lesson-planning matrix makes it easier for teachers to plan their lessons around a variety of useful strategies. Answer B does not take into account how one will incorporate the students' various skills into lesson. Moreover, students are not always fully aware of their learning abilities. Answer C fails to address lesson planning at all, and it also might make the slower students feel that they are being unfairly singled out. Answer D is in fact one way to improve the comprehension of some students, but it is only one method, and will not especially help students who are not visually oriented.

76. A: The teacher should circulate around the room but should avoid spending too much time with any one group since this tends to distract the teacher's attention from what is going on in other groups. Answer B is not important, although the teacher should be sure that all students cooperate effectively on the project. Answer C is the opposite of what the teacher should be doing. By circulating among the groups and taking notes, the teacher can help with problems and verify that all students are actively participating. Answer D is incorrect, as it could lead to situations in which those who do not meaningfully participate receive good grades because other students work hard to finish the group work.

77. D: Yes. If the teacher is already running a student-centered classroom, allowing choices in assignments and using flexibility in student grouping, she is already differentiating. She has received additional training to allow her to continue to modify classroom assignments to more deeply challenge the gifted students.

78. D: Moving beyond fact to generalizations and principles. Depth involves exploring content within a discipline; analyzing from the concrete to the abstract, familiar to the unfamiliar, known to the unknown; exploring the discipline by going past facts and concepts into generalizations, principles, theories, laws; investigating the layers of experience within a discipline through details, patterns, trends, unanswered questions, ethical considerations.

79. B: An individual's belief or feeling about his or her ability regarding a specific undertaking. An unmotivated gifted student may have low self-efficacy, believing that a task, project or other undertaking is beyond his abilities.

80. B: The child's academic ability. Gifted children excel in one or more particular areas, but not many can be said to really excel across the board. Examining the gap between what a student is capable of and what that student is actually accomplishing is a good indicator of academic achievement.

81. D: Middle school is a critical time during which students develop a respect for diversity, make the decision to continue with school, and develop tolerance for those who are different. Middle school students also develop higher-order thinking skills, but this represents cognitive development rather than value development.

82. D: The student is primarily responsible. One of the purposes of the Total Talent Portfolio is to encourage student autonomy. In taking on responsibility in the selection of materials that will compose the TTP, updating the portfolio at regular intervals and establishing personal goals, the student assumes ownership and is therefore more committed. The teacher's role is that of a guide, primarily in the process of review.

83. D: Bandura's social learning theory places emphasis on social interactions as the most important context of, and influence on, learning. Bandura says children learn by observing and then imitating others' behaviors. Nuclear conflicts (A) were Erikson's term for the central crisis to be resolved in each of his psychosocial stages of development. Erogenous zones (B) were Freud's term for areas of the body where children's attention focused in each of his psychosexual stages of development. Cognitive abilities (C) were the focus of each of Piaget's stages of cognitive development.

84. C: The more modalities and media the learning materials include, the more they can address a larger number of varied student needs. There are two reasons for this: (1) if one modality or medium is not effective for certain students, then another one will be; (2) presenting the same information redundantly and through different modalities makes learning more effective for all students than presenting it through only one (A), (B), (D).

85. B: He will remain in the program and it will be modified to become more appropriate for his learning needs. It is illegal to discriminate against students with learning or behavioral disorders.

86. B: Social and behavioral theories of learning stress the importance of social interactions between students, as they can aid or inhibit learning. According to these theories, students do not just learn in isolation or in a one-on-one relationship with a teacher. They also learn attitudes toward education from their peers, sometimes positive and sometimes negative.

87. B: The theory suggests that some students learn better through verbal interaction, while others are more visual, physical, or artistic. By using a variety of teaching methods, rather than just lecturing or working problems on a chalkboard, a teacher will help ensure that more students will grasp a given topic. Any of these methods may be applied in the teaching of any subject.

88. A: Recommend acceleration opportunities. The steps to curriculum compacting include understanding learning objectives; identify students who can master objectives most quickly, pretest, streamline instructional period for students who understand objectives and recommending acceleration opportunities.

89. B: Gifted and talented students possess a unique set of abilities and learning needs that often go overlooked in a general education setting. Selecting, modifying, and implementing curriculum to challenge these students academically and intellectually is imperative to creating a supportive, inclusive, and engaging learning environment. By creating an opportunity for extension, Ms. Hoffman modifies instruction to provide enrichment for gifted students, thus accommodating their unique learning needs in a meaningful way.

90. B: The definition of independent study can encompass an individual working alone, two students working as partners, or small groups of students working together. Choices C and D are incorrect because they each exclude one of these formats, whereas choice B correctly includes all of them." In fact, teachers can even use independent study as an instructional strategy with the whole class. Regardless of the number of students, independent study is less teacher-centered/teacher-directed; the teacher functions as a facilitator and guide. Provided they have developed the required skills, students have more autonomy and choices with independent study.

91. D: A student's interests and learning styles and the student's cognitive ability are equally considered. Total Talent Portfolios include attention to student interests and learning styles in addition to cognitive abilities that have traditionally contributed to educational decisions.

92. C: Providing learning options is very useful in the middle grades because students are developing a sense of autonomy, and this allows them to exercise it. While the choices students make may reflect their self-concept or choice of peer group in some way, this is not the main area of development that such an exercise fosters. This exercise also reflects the fact that students have different learning styles, but this is not a developmental characteristic unique to middle school students.

93. D: Planned learning experiences that build upon a progressively stronger foundation from year to year. A Continuum of Learning Experiences is a multi-year construct that relies upon each previous year to provide the framework for further academic and artistic development.

94. B: 6. Teachers working with gifted students are required to complete 30 hours of professional development by the time they finish their first semester, followed by 6 additional hours annually.

95. B: There is no decisive federal definition; each state determines its own definition. This lack of cohesive classification can be problematic. For example, a child identified as gifted in one state may not be considered so in another. Should the child's family relocate, this could potentially cause a schism that is damaging to the student's equilibrium.

96. A: Required. Unless the student has been emancipated, a parent or guardian must give written permission before that student can participate in a Gifted and Talented program.

97. A: This objective is generic enough to emphasize knowledge and skills that would apply in a variety of situations – knowledge about science fiction and fantasy helps to evaluate a large number of reading selections. In this context, the content of an objective refers to the topic or subject matter students are expected to learn, stated broadly enough to apply across multiple texts or situations rather than tied to a specific assignment. The content of an objective should be specific enough that anyone reading it will understand the subject matter, yet broad enough to stand alone without requiring reference to particular materials. Consequently, choice B is not a good example of appropriate content because it refers to specific materials -- Unit 6 in the vocabulary book. In like manner, choice D refers to specific materials (p. 114 in the textbook). The content should also be generic enough that the emphasis is on knowledge and skills that are applicable in several contexts. Although choice C includes a clear skill, it is overly specific because it limits the objective to two particular stories. It would be improved by referring more generally to comparing settings between two stories or among short stories rather than naming specific titles.

98. B: Might. The decision of whether to assess a child is made by a committee and is partially based on observable academic strength according. If the G/T Committee decides a particular child should be assessed, parents must first give permission.

99. C: Affective curriculum. Gifted students often feel their differences; they can be more highly attuned to surroundings and nonverbal cues, and they may be reluctant to take risks that would propel them beyond their comfort zones. Affective curriculum allows them the opportunity to explore social and deeply personal aspects of their giftedness.

100. D: Providing gifted and talented students with meaningful opportunities to extend their learning allows them to progress at a pace that matches their abilities and learning needs. This helps to ensure that these students remain engaged in the classroom, deepens their understanding, and encourages them to continuously seek challenging learning experiences.

101. D: Piaget's theory posits four distinct stages of cognitive development, each with specific distinguishing characteristics and corresponding to approximate age ranges. Skinner's (A) theory of cognitive development is behavioral. It does not include stages but focuses on the premise that changes in behaviors over time represent learning and that this learning occurs through the antecedent and consequent events immediately before and after a behavior, which increase or decrease the probability of the individual's repeating the behavior. Vygotsky's (B) theory also has no stages and focuses on sociocultural influences as sources of learning. Bandura's (C) social learning theory has no stages either; it focuses on learning through observation, imitation of models, and vicarious learning.

102. D: Indirect instruction promotes student exploration, inquiry, discovery learning, problem solving, and learning abstract concepts and patterns. It is delivered implicitly, whereas direct instruction is delivered explicitly (A). Lesson plans vary, whereas direct instruction uses uniform lesson plans (B). It is less structured, whereas direct instruction is more structured (C). Direct instruction promotes piquing initial student interest; learning facts, rules, and sequences; and analyzing text/workbook material. Whereas indirect instruction is student-centered, direct instruction is teacher-centered.

103. A: Creating a Total Talent Portfolio. A TTP gathers a variety of types of information describing a student's areas of strength and interest and tracks it through time, updating as appropriate. This information is categorized (typically with a chart) and studied in order to set goals and determine differentiation. The gifted student is encouraged to develop autonomy by being primarily responsible for her TTP.

104. A: To communicate high expectations to all students, teachers should identify students they expect less from as soon as possible, because it is hard to accept or modify negative expectations already formed. Research finds student similarities influence teacher expectations, though teachers resist admitting this; therefore, experts advise teachers to identify similarities (B) for actively preventing biases from controlling their thoughts and/or behaviors. Since teacher behaviors have more influence than teacher expectations, not vice versa (C), teachers must identify their different behaviors toward low-expectancy students. They must also consciously treat high- and low-expectancy students the same, not differently (D).

105. C: Technology allows opportunity for lessons to become more accessible to students of differing abilities. Technology use in the classroom lets teachers more easily adapt lessons to meet the specific needs of students and allows students the ability to access help easier in lessons, as well as the opportunity to investigate and develop assignments more deeply than without technology. The other options can be benefits, but they are not usually inherently true of technology use in a lesson. While technology can lead to more engaging content, simply allowing students to use technology in class does not automatically lead to students becoming more immersed in what they are doing. Also, technology can help some students finish assignments faster, but this is not always the case, and technology may increase the amount of time needed to finish certain assignments. While technology can help the teacher by having ready materials for future use, this can often be a hindrance to best instructional practices as lesson planning should be tailored to the instructional needs of the class at hand and not treated as a simple template.

106. B: The lesson plans for an experienced teacher do not have to be as detailed as they should be for a new teacher because some actions become second nature to a teacher after a while. The steps to writing a good lesson plan do not vary with the teaching model but are the backbone of every lesson. The lesson opening, body, and closing do not need to be written in order; in fact, it is often best to write the body of the lesson first so that the teacher has had a chance to thoroughly think through the lesson before deciding on an appropriate opening. Since the lesson plan has a set pattern, all parts must be written, including pre-planning steps and editing tasks, not just the parts that will be presented to the students.

107. A: A federally-funded center with the charter of developing effective methods of identification and testing of gifted and talented students, and programming for such students. The National Research Center on the Gifted and Talented is one of three components of the Javits Act, a reauthorization of The Elementary and Secondary Education Act.

108. D: The student finds the work too simple, so they dismiss or ignore it. Gifted and talented students learn best when they are interested in the material, allowed to explore it independently and are challenged by it. They are not motivated by grades or products so much as by the learning process.

109. A: Assimilation is fitting a new experience into an existing schema. Accommodation is altering an existing schema or forming a new schema to accommodate a new experience. These two processes are part of the overall process of adaptation, i.e., adjusting one's thinking to the environment via interacting with it. This adaptation process helps the individual to maintain equilibrium, or balance.

110. B: 5%. School districts are given an annual allotment equal to a particular district's base allotment multiplied by 12 per student per year. No more than 5% of the total number of students can be considered for Gifted and Talented funding.

111. B: Differentiate for those students who understand the concept but arrive at incorrect answers. By reviewing their steps, the teacher can determine why answers are incorrect and can demonstrate the correct approach. Concept is more important than content. If the students truly understand the 'how', they have the tools they need to arrive at the 'what'. However, if a student demonstrates the same type of error repeatedly, she may not fully understand the concept. Concept is more important than content.

112. C: Incorporating self-assessment into the classroom is important because it prepares students for the future when they will need to evaluate their own work in the absence of an instructor. Option a is incorrect because additional practice time is not the purpose of self-assessment. Option b is incorrect because self-assessment should primarily support student learning, not data collection. Option d confuses the instructional goal of self-assessment.

113. B: Lesson objectives should have an important outcome, should be useful to the students in the future, and should be at a knowledge and skill level appropriate to the students; however, activities should be planned to fit the objective, not the other way around. Every lesson plan should be concerned with an important learning outcome. Trivial lessons are a waste of time and damage student interest; therefore, all lesson plans should include an important objective. The knowledge gained by a lesson should also be something students can use in the future; otherwise, the lesson has no point. The lesson should also be comprehensible to the students because teaching above their skill levels leaves them unsuccessful and frustrated; teaching below their skills levels leaves them bored.

114. B: False. No such plan for children identified as gifted and talented has ever been federally mandated. While gifted children do receive special education in terms of differentiation, federal law does not require they have IEPs as learning disabled children are.

115. B: Help the teacher determine how to enrich and accelerate students' learning based upon their individually unique profiles. The Total Talent Portfolio is a systematic method of gathering, analyzing and classifying students' abilities, given equal weight to interests and learning styles as to cognitive skills to aid the teacher in deciding how to enrich and accelerate students' individualized learning based upon their unique profiles.

116. A: Establish own learning goals; self-assess; move to an independent challenge activity when she understands the lesson; encourage her to work with peers close to her intellectual level. Research has proven these techniques more deeply engaged gifted students that traditional methods, and contribute to such students' degree of motivation.

117. A: When instruction is more demanding—e.g., when students are asked to solve novel problems and create products—teacher decisions are not simpler (C) but more complex. When teachers encourage student responsibility, both teachers and students approach and understand instructional content differently (B). Teachers must not only help students meet academic demands for comprehension and manipulation of subject content, but also help them meet social demands (D) for effective demonstration of their content knowledge in interactions with others.

118. A: In scaffolded instruction, first the teacher models performance of a new and/or difficult task and asks students to do think-alouds about it. The second step involves collaboration between students and teacher. The third step entails paired or small-group student work on the task, with teacher support as needed. In the fourth step, students practice the task independently.

119. C: The libido is part of the id according to Freud. It represents psychic energy as well as sex drive. Freud's three major personality structures are the id (A), which generates unconscious impulses; the ego (B), which realistically regulates acting on id impulses; and the superego (C), which pursues morality and perfection.

120. B: Behaviors occur for reasons, to meet needs. Thus, one must know what function or purpose they serve before one can change them. An undesirable behavior can be replaced with a more desirable one, but the replacement behavior must serve the same purpose as the undesirable one, so (A) is incorrect. While knowing a behavior's function is necessary, this does not eliminate the need to change it (C). Knowing a behavior's function informs not only the choice of a replacement behavior, but also which consequences to apply to the undesired behavior. The same consequences will not work for every function (D) a behavior can serve. For example, a tantrum behavior the function of which is to get attention will not respond to a certain consequence the same as when its function is to express frustration.

How to Overcome Test Anxiety

Just the thought of taking a test is enough to make most people a little nervous. A test is an important event that can have a long-term impact on your future, so it's important to take it seriously and it's natural to feel anxious about performing well. But just because anxiety is normal, that doesn't mean that it's helpful in test taking, or that you should simply accept it as part of your life. Anxiety can have a variety of effects. These effects can be mild, like making you feel slightly nervous, or severe, like blocking your ability to focus or remember even a simple detail.

If you experience test anxiety—whether severe or mild—it's important to know how to beat it. To discover this, first you need to understand what causes test anxiety.

Causes of Test Anxiety

While we often think of anxiety as an uncontrollable emotional state, it can actually be caused by simple, practical things. One of the most common causes of test anxiety is that a person does not feel adequately prepared for their test. This feeling can be the result of many different issues such as poor study habits or lack of organization, but the most common culprit is time management. Starting to study too late, failing to organize your study time to cover all of the material, or being distracted while you study will mean that you're not well prepared for the test. This may lead to cramming the night before, which will cause you to be physically and mentally exhausted for the test. Poor time management also contributes to feelings of stress, fear, and hopelessness as you realize you are not well prepared but don't know what to do about it.

Other times, test anxiety is not related to your preparation for the test but comes from unresolved fear. This may be a past failure on a test, or poor performance on tests in general. It may come from comparing yourself to others who seem to be performing better or from the stress of living up to expectations. Anxiety may be driven by fears of the future—how failure on this test would affect your educational and career goals. These fears are often completely irrational, but they can still negatively impact your test performance.

Elements of Test Anxiety

As mentioned earlier, test anxiety is considered to be an emotional state, but it has physical and mental components as well. Sometimes you may not even realize that you are suffering from test anxiety until you notice the physical symptoms. These can include trembling hands, rapid heartbeat, sweating, nausea, and tense muscles. Extreme anxiety may lead to fainting or vomiting. Obviously, any of these symptoms can have a negative impact on testing. It is important to recognize them as soon as they begin to occur so that you can address the problem before it damages your performance.

The mental components of test anxiety include trouble focusing and inability to remember learned information. During a test, your mind is on high alert, which can help you recall information and stay focused for an extended period of time. However, anxiety interferes with your mind's natural processes, causing you to blank out, even on the questions you know well. The strain of testing during anxiety makes it difficult to stay focused, especially on a test that may take several hours. Extreme anxiety can take a huge mental toll, making it difficult not only to recall test information but even to understand the test questions or pull your thoughts together.

Effects of Test Anxiety

Test anxiety is like a disease—if left untreated, it will get progressively worse. Anxiety leads to poor performance, and this reinforces the feelings of fear and failure, which in turn lead to poor performances on subsequent tests. It can grow from a mild nervousness to a crippling condition. If allowed to progress, test anxiety can have a big impact on your schooling, and consequently on your future.

Test anxiety can spread to other parts of your life. Anxiety on tests can become anxiety in any stressful situation, and blanking on a test can turn into panicking in a job situation. But fortunately, you don't have to let anxiety rule your testing and determine your grades. There are a number of relatively simple steps you can take to move past anxiety and function normally on a test and in the rest of life.

Physical Steps for Beating Test Anxiety

While test anxiety is a serious problem, the good news is that it can be overcome. It doesn't have to control your ability to think and remember information. While it may take time, you can begin taking steps today to beat anxiety.

Just as your first hint that you may be struggling with anxiety comes from the physical symptoms, the first step to treating it is also physical. Rest is crucial for having a clear, strong mind. If you are tired, it is much easier to give in to anxiety. But if you establish good sleep habits, your body and mind will be ready to perform optimally, without the strain of exhaustion. Additionally, sleeping well helps you to retain information better, so you're more likely to recall the answers when you see the test questions.

Getting good sleep means more than going to bed on time. It's important to allow your brain time to relax. Take study breaks from time to time so it doesn't get overworked, and don't study right before bed. Take time to rest your mind before trying to rest your body, or you may find it difficult to fall asleep.

Along with sleep, other aspects of physical health are important in preparing for a test. Good nutrition is vital for good brain function. Sugary foods and drinks may give a burst of energy but this burst is followed by a crash, both physically and emotionally. Instead, fuel your body with protein and vitamin-rich foods.

Also, drink plenty of water. Dehydration can lead to headaches and exhaustion, especially if your brain is already under stress from the rigors of the test. Particularly if your test is a long one, drink water during the breaks. And if possible, take an energy-boosting snack to eat between sections.

Along with sleep and diet, a third important part of physical health is exercise. Maintaining a steady workout schedule is helpful, but even taking 5-minute study breaks to walk can help get your blood pumping faster and clear your head. Exercise also releases endorphins, which contribute to a positive feeling and can help combat test anxiety.

When you nurture your physical health, you are also contributing to your mental health. If your body is healthy, your mind is much more likely to be healthy as well. So take time to rest, nourish your body with healthy food and water, and get moving as much as possible. Taking these physical steps will make you stronger and more able to take the mental steps necessary to overcome test anxiety.

Mental Steps for Beating Test Anxiety

Working on the mental side of test anxiety can be more challenging, but as with the physical side, there are clear steps you can take to overcome it. As mentioned earlier, test anxiety often stems from lack of preparation, so the obvious solution is to prepare for the test. Effective studying may be the most important weapon you have for beating test anxiety, but you can and should employ several other mental tools to combat fear.

First, boost your confidence by reminding yourself of past success—tests or projects that you aced. If you're putting as much effort into preparing for this test as you did for those, there's no reason you should expect to fail here. Work hard to prepare; then trust your preparation.

Second, surround yourself with encouraging people. It can be helpful to find a study group, but be sure that the people you're around will encourage a positive attitude. If you spend time with others who are anxious or cynical, this will only contribute to your own anxiety. Look for others who are motivated to study hard from a desire to succeed, not from a fear of failure.

Third, reward yourself. A test is physically and mentally tiring, even without anxiety, and it can be helpful to have something to look forward to. Plan an activity following the test, regardless of the outcome, such as going to a movie or getting ice cream.

When you are taking the test, if you find yourself beginning to feel anxious, remind yourself that you know the material. Visualize successfully completing the test. Then take a few deep, relaxing breaths and return to it. Work through the questions carefully but with confidence, knowing that you are capable of succeeding.

Developing a healthy mental approach to test taking will also aid in other areas of life. Test anxiety affects more than just the actual test—it can be damaging to your mental health and even contribute to depression. It's important to beat test anxiety before it becomes a problem for more than testing.

Study Strategy

Being prepared for the test is necessary to combat anxiety, but what does being prepared look like? You may study for hours on end and still not feel prepared. What you need is a strategy for test prep. The next few pages outline our recommended steps to help you plan out and conquer the challenge of preparation.

Step 1: Scope Out the Test

Learn everything you can about the format (multiple choice, essay, etc.) and what will be on the test. Gather any study materials, course outlines, or sample exams that may be available. Not only will this help you to prepare, but knowing what to expect can help to alleviate test anxiety.

Step 2: Map Out the Material

Look through the textbook or study guide and make note of how many chapters or sections it has. Then divide these over the time you have. For example, if a book has 15 chapters and you have five days to study, you need to cover three chapters each day. Even better, if you have the time, leave an extra day at the end for overall review after you have gone through the material in depth.

If time is limited, you may need to prioritize the material. Look through it and make note of which sections you think you already have a good grasp on, and which need review. While you are studying, skim quickly through the familiar sections and take more time on the challenging parts.

Write out your plan so you don't get lost as you go. Having a written plan also helps you feel more in control of the study, so anxiety is less likely to arise from feeling overwhelmed at the amount to cover.

Step 3: Gather Your Tools

Decide what study method works best for you. Do you prefer to highlight in the book as you study and then go back over the highlighted portions? Or do you type out notes of the important information? Or is it helpful to make flashcards that you can carry with you? Assemble the pens, index cards, highlighters, post-it notes, and any other materials you may need so you won't be distracted by getting up to find things while you study.

If you're having a hard time retaining the information or organizing your notes, experiment with different methods. For example, try color-coding by subject with colored pens, highlighters, or post-it notes. If you learn better by hearing, try recording yourself reading your notes so you can listen while in the car, working out, or simply sitting at your desk. Ask a friend to quiz you from your flashcards, or try teaching someone the material to solidify it in your mind.

Step 4: Create Your Environment

It's important to avoid distractions while you study. This includes both the obvious distractions like visitors and the subtle distractions like an uncomfortable chair (or a too-comfortable couch that makes you want to fall asleep). Set up the best study environment possible: good lighting and a comfortable work area. If background music helps you focus, you may want to turn it on, but otherwise keep the room quiet. If you are using a computer to take notes, be sure you don't have any other windows open, especially applications like social media, games, or anything else that could distract you. Silence your phone and turn off notifications. Be sure to keep water close by so you stay hydrated while you study (but avoid unhealthy drinks and snacks).

Also, take into account the best time of day to study. Are you freshest first thing in the morning? Try to set aside some time then to work through the material. Is your mind clearer in the afternoon or evening? Schedule your study session then. Another method is to study at the same time of day that you will take the test, so that your brain gets used to working on the material at that time and will be ready to focus at test time.

Step 5: Study!

Once you have done all the study preparation, it's time to settle into the actual studying. Sit down, take a few moments to settle your mind so you can focus, and begin to follow your study plan. Don't give in to distractions or let yourself procrastinate. This is your time to prepare so you'll be ready to fearlessly approach the test. Make the most of the time and stay focused.

Of course, you don't want to burn out. If you study too long you may find that you're not retaining the information very well. Take regular study breaks. For example, taking five minutes out of every hour to walk briskly, breathing deeply and swinging your arms, can help your mind stay fresh.

As you get to the end of each chapter or section, it's a good idea to do a quick review. Remind yourself of what you learned and work on any difficult parts. When you feel that you've mastered the material, move on to the next part. At the end of your study session, briefly skim through your notes again.

But while review is helpful, cramming last minute is NOT. If at all possible, work ahead so that you won't need to fit all your study into the last day. Cramming overloads your brain with more information than it can process and retain, and your tired mind may struggle to recall even previously learned information when it is overwhelmed with last-minute study. Also, the urgent nature of cramming and the stress placed on your brain contribute to anxiety. You'll be more likely to go to the test feeling unprepared and having trouble thinking clearly.

So don't cram, and don't stay up late before the test, even just to review your notes at a leisurely pace. Your brain needs rest more than it needs to go over the information again. In fact, plan to finish your studies by noon or early afternoon the day before the test. Give your brain the rest of the day to relax or focus on other things, and get a good night's sleep. Then you will be fresh for the test and better able to recall what you've studied.

Step 6: Take a Practice Test

Many courses offer sample tests, either online or in the study materials. This is an excellent resource to check whether you have mastered the material, as well as to prepare for the test format and environment.

Check the test format ahead of time: the number of questions, the type (multiple choice, free response, etc.), and the time limit. Then create a plan for working through them. For example, if you have 30 minutes to take a 60-question test, your limit is 30 seconds per question. Spend less time on the questions you know well so that you can take more time on the difficult ones.

If you have time to take several practice tests, take the first one open book, with no time limit. Work through the questions at your own pace and make sure you fully understand them. Gradually work up to taking a test under test conditions: sit at a desk with all study materials put away and set a timer. Pace yourself to make sure you finish the test with time to spare and go back to check your answers if you have time.

After each test, check your answers. On the questions you missed, be sure you understand why you missed them. Did you misread the question (tests can use tricky wording)? Did you forget the information? Or was it something you hadn't learned? Go back and study any shaky areas that the practice tests reveal.

Taking these tests not only helps with your grade, but also aids in combating test anxiety. If you're already used to the test conditions, you're less likely to worry about it, and working through tests until you're scoring well gives you a confidence boost. Go through the practice tests until you feel comfortable, and then you can go into the test knowing that you're ready for it.

Test Tips

On test day, you should be confident, knowing that you've prepared well and are ready to answer the questions. But aside from preparation, there are several test day strategies you can employ to maximize your performance.

First, as stated before, get a good night's sleep the night before the test (and for several nights before that, if possible). Go into the test with a fresh, alert mind rather than staying up late to study.

Try not to change too much about your normal routine on the day of the test. It's important to eat a nutritious breakfast, but if you normally don't eat breakfast at all, consider eating just a protein bar. If you're a coffee drinker, go ahead and have your normal coffee. Just make sure you time it so that the caffeine doesn't wear off right in the middle of your test. Avoid sugary beverages, and drink enough water to stay hydrated but not so much that you need a restroom break 10 minutes into the test. If your test isn't first thing in the morning, consider going for a walk or doing a light workout before the test to get your blood flowing.

Allow yourself enough time to get ready, and leave for the test with plenty of time to spare so you won't have the anxiety of scrambling to arrive in time. Another reason to be early is to select a good seat. It's helpful to sit away from doors and windows, which can be distracting. Find a good seat, get out your supplies, and settle your mind before the test begins.

When the test begins, start by going over the instructions carefully, even if you already know what to expect. Make sure you avoid any careless mistakes by following the directions.

Then begin working through the questions, pacing yourself as you've practiced. If you're not sure on an answer, don't spend too much time on it, and don't let it shake your confidence. Either skip it and come back later, or eliminate as many wrong answers as possible and guess among the remaining ones. Don't dwell on these questions as you continue—put them out of your mind and focus on what lies ahead.

Be sure to read all of the answer choices, even if you're sure the first one is the right answer. Sometimes you'll find a better one if you keep reading. But don't second-guess yourself if you do immediately know the answer. Your gut instinct is usually right. Don't let test anxiety rob you of the information you know.

If you have time at the end of the test (and if the test format allows), go back and review your answers. Be cautious about changing any, since your first instinct tends to be correct, but make sure you didn't misread any of the questions or accidentally mark the wrong answer choice. Look over any you skipped and make an educated guess.

At the end, leave the test feeling confident. You've done your best, so don't waste time worrying about your performance or wishing you could change anything. Instead, celebrate the successful completion of this test. And finally, use this test to learn how to deal with anxiety even better next time.

Review Video: Test Anxiety
Visit mometrix.com/academy and enter code: 100340

Important Qualification

Not all anxiety is created equal. If your test anxiety is causing major issues in your life beyond the classroom or testing center, or if you are experiencing troubling physical symptoms related to your anxiety, it may be a sign of a serious physiological or psychological condition. If this sounds like your situation, we strongly encourage you to seek professional help.

Online Resources

Due to our efforts to try to keep this book to a manageable length, we've created a link that will give you access to all of your online resources:

mometrix.com/resources719/nesincgifted

It's Your Moment, Let's Celebrate It!

Share your story @mometrixtestpreparation